The Logic of China's New School Reforms

Brill's Series on Chinese Education

Series Editor

Gerard A. Postiglione (*The University of Hong Kong*)

VOLUME 05

The titles published in this series are listed at *brill.com/bsce*

The Logic of China's New School Reforms

Selected Essays on Education by Zhong Qiquan

By

Zhong Qiquan

Translated by

Wan Hua

BRILL

LEIDEN | BOSTON

 This book is the result of the translation licensing agreement between Higher Education Press (Beijing) and Koninklijke Brill NV. This book is translated into English from the original «学校变革的逻辑» by 钟启泉 with financial support from **the Chinese Fund for the Humanities and Social Sciences (中华社会科学基金)**.

Library of Congress Cataloging-in-Publication Data

Names: Zhong, Qiquan, author.
Title: The logic of China's new curriculum reforms : selected essays on
  education by Zhong Qiquan / by Zhong Qiquan ; translated by Wan Hua.
Description: Boston ; Leiden : Brill, [2022] | Series: Brill's Series on
  Chinese Education, 2212-7437 ; volume 04
Identifiers: LCCN 2021032815 (print) | LCCN 2021032816 (ebook) | ISBN
  9789004470118 (Hardback : acid-free paper) | ISBN 9789004473300 (eBook)
Subjects: LCSH: Educational change–China. | Education–China–History. |
  Education and state–China–History.
Classification: LCC LA1131.82 .Z4586 2022 (print) | LCC LA1131.82 (ebook)
  | DDC 370.951–dc23
LC record available at https://lccn.loc.gov/2021032815
LC ebook record available at https://lccn.loc.gov/2021032816

Typeface for the Latin, Greek, and Cyrillic scripts: "Brill". See and download: brill.com/brill-typeface.

ISSN 2212-7437
ISBN 978-90-04-47011-8 (hardback)
ISBN 978-90-04-47330-0 (e-book)

Copyright 2022 by Koninklijke Brill NV, Leiden, The Netherlands.
Koninklijke Brill NV incorporates the imprints Brill, Brill Nijhoff, Brill Hotei, Brill Schöningh, Brill Fink, Brill mentis, Vandenhoeck & Ruprecht, Böhlau Verlag and V&R Unipress.
All rights reserved. No part of this publication may be reproduced, translated, stored in a retrieval system, or transmitted in any form or by any means, electronic, mechanical, photocopying, recording or otherwise, without prior written permission from the publisher. Requests for re-use and/or translations must be addressed to Koninklijke Brill NV via brill.com or copyright.com.

This book is printed on acid-free paper and produced in a sustainable manner.

Contents

Preface: Seeking Logic for School Reforms in the New Era   IX

1   The Transformation of Value in the New Curriculum Reform   1
  1   Holistic Student Development   1
      1.1   *The Whole Person Fragmented by Contemporary Education*   1
      1.2   *The Meaning of the Whole Person*   2
  2   Back to Students' Life World   4
      2.1   *The Loss of Meaning of Life World*   4
      2.2   *Back-to-Life Curriculum*   5
  3   Knowledge Construction for Individual Understanding   7
      3.1   *The Absence of Personal Knowledge*   7
      3.2   *Knowledge Construction with Personal Meaning*   8
  4   Creating School Culture with Characteristics   9
      4.1   *The Ignorance of Characteristic School Culture*   10
      4.2   *Reconstruction of School Culture*   10

2   Conceptual Reconstructions and Curriculum Innovation in China   14
  1   Reconstructing the Concept of Knowledge and Curriculum Innovation   15
  2   Reconstruction of the Concept of Learning and Curriculum Innovation   22
  3   Reconstruction of Classroom Culture and Curriculum Innovation   29

3   The KAP Theory   38
  1   Definition and Significance of KAP   38
      1.1   *Defining KAP*   38
      1.2   *Significance of Defining KAP*   40
  2   Knowledge Philosophy of KAP   42
      2.1   *KAP Manifests the Appeal for Human Science*   42
      2.2   *KAP Is Based on the New Philosophy of Knowledge*   43
  3   KAP Manifests the Law of Mental Development   44
  4   Framework and Task of KAP Chain Teaching Design   45
      4.1   *Teaching Goals as Hypotheses*   45
      4.2   *Framework of the KAP Chain Teaching Design*   46
      4.3   *Core Tasks in Advancing KAP Chain Teaching Design*   48

4 On Integrated Practice Activity Course (IPAC): Contents, Characteristics, Values and Potential Misconceptions   51

   1   Defining IPAC: A Model for Curriculum Development   51

      1.1   *IPAC and the Traditional Subject-Separation System are Motivated by Two Different Theories of Curriculum Development*   52

      1.2   *Two Models of Curriculum Development Based on Two Different Views of Learning*   53

   2   Value of IPAC: Integration of Wisdom and Integration of Knowledge   55

      2.1   *As a Brand New Model in Curriculum Development, IPAC Is Geared to a Contemporary Model of Knowledge Production*   55

      2.2   *IPAC: "Not Just a Formal Structural Change in Curriculum Development, but a Profound Substantial Innovation of Curriculum Values"*   58

      2.3   *Systematic Research on the Modern Knowledge Production Model Provides the Theoretical Basis for the Simultaneous Development of the Separation and Integration of Subjects*   61

   3   Implementation of IPAC: Strengths and Misconceptions   62

5 Dialogues and Texts: The Transformation of Teaching Norms   67

   1   Teaching: Activities of Communication and Cooperation   67

   2   Dialogues and Texts: Conceptual Reconstruction of Teaching and Teaching Materials   70

   3   Transformation of the Teaching Paradigm   77

6 Towards a Humanistic Curriculum Evaluation   82

   1   Curriculum Evaluation: Redefining the Concepts   82

      1.1   *Defining Curriculum Evaluation*   82

      1.2   *Focus of Curriculum Evaluation and Its Innovation*   84

   2   Humanistic Curriculum Evaluation: Blueprint of the Reform   84

      2.1   *Transformation from Cumulative Learning to Constructive Learning*   84

      2.2   *Transformation from Evaluation for Score Purpose into Evaluation for Learner Purpose*   87

   3   Transformation of Curriculum Evaluation from Utilitarian Consideration into Humanistic Consideration   89

   4   Humanistic Curriculum Evaluation: A Qualitative Description   91

   5   Humanistic Curriculum Evaluation: A Cultural Renovation   94

      5.1   *Transformation from Credential Society into Learning Society*   94

CONTENTS   VII

5.2 *Transformation from Unilateral Lopsided Development into Holistic Development* 95

5.3 *Transformation from Black-Box Evaluation into Evaluating Evaluation* 97

7 **Innovation in the Teachers' Education System in China** 99
1 Historical Development of Teacher Education 99
2 Curriculum Standards of Teacher Education: Key to System Innovation 105
   2.1 *Diagnosis of the Current Situation of Teacher Education in China* 105
   2.2 *Discussion on the Framework and Core Contents of Curriculum Standards of Teacher Education* 110
   2.3 *Curriculum Reform of Basic Education Calls for a Professional Image of Teachers* 116
3 Re-Conceptualization: The Precondition of System Innovation of Teacher Education 119
   3.1 *Learning Profession and Professional Learning* 119
   3.2 *Reconceptualization and System Innovation* 122

8 **Teaching Practices: Analytical Modes and Philosophies—Comments on the Assumption of Teaching Particularism** 126
1 Development of Teaching Practice Mode: From Behaviorism to Constructivism 126
   1.1 *Behaviorist Mode of Teaching Practice: Making Class No Difference to Amphitheater* 127
   1.2 *Teaching Practice Mode of Social Constructivism: Classroom for Social Interaction* 130
2 Teacher's Practice Thinking in Social Constructivism: Significance, Features and Research Issues 132
   2.1 *Significance of Promoting Teacher's Practice Thinking* 133
   2.2 *Features of Teacher's Practice Thinking* 134
   2.3 *Cultivation of Teacher's Practice Thinking* 136

9 **New Challenges in Teachers' Training** 140
1 Opportunities and Predicaments of Teacher-Training 140
   1.1 *Opportunities: Ideological Motivation and Knowledge Resources from New Curriculum Reform* 140
   1.2 *Predicament: Struggle between Exam-Oriented Education and Quality-Oriented Education* 143
2 Prevention of the Regeneration Chain of Exam-Oriented Education 145

VIII   CONTENTS

3   Seeking Self-Discipline and Innovative Teacher-Training   150
     3.1   *Methodology of Teacher-Training from the Perspective of Teachers' Knowledge*   150
     3.2   *Teachers Training Supported by Government Policy, Theoretical Basis and Practical Experience*   152

10   **The Development of Future Educators**   155
     1   Educator Development and TEC Innovation   155
     2   Laying Foundations for China's TEC Innovation   158
          2.1   *Study of Children*   158
          2.2   *Study on Teachers*   161
          2.3   *Study on Teaching Materials*   167

11   **Critical Comments on Kairov's Pedagogy**   172
     1   Part I   173
          1.1   *Ideological Basis of Soviet School Construction and Aberration of "Deschooling"*   174
          1.2   *School Policies in 1931 and Vicissitudes of Kairov's Pedagogy*   181
     2   Part II   189
          2.1   *Criticism of Pedagogy "Overlooking Children" and Significance of "Argument about Development"*   190
          2.2   *The Confrontation between Zankov's New Teaching System and Kairov's Teaching Principles*   194
          2.3   *Divergence between "Development-education Theory" of Cultural-historical School and Kairov's Pedagogy*   198

12   **A Review of the Paedological Research of the Vygotskian School**   207
     1   Vygotsky's Development-Education Theory   209
          1.1   *Methodological Basis and the Developmental Culture-History Theory*   209
          1.2   *Two Hypotheses of Vygotsky's Developmental Theory*   212
          1.3   *Education-based Theory of Children's Development*   215
          1.4   *Internally Unified Development Process of Life Concept and Scientific Concept*   217
          1.5   *Inner Language Theory and Personality Theory*   219
     2   Development of Paedological Research of Vygotskian School   221
          2.1   *Theoretical Hypothesis of Development-Mastery Theory*   221
          2.2   *Theoretical Hypothesis of Self-Development Theory*   228
          2.3   *Rivalry between Development-Mastery Theory and Self-Development Theory*   232
     3   Modern Significance of Paedological Research of Vygotskian School   234

Preface

Seeking Logic for School Reforms in the New Era

Marking the end of the Kairov Era pedagogy, China's New Curriculum Reform revitalizes China's education sector and emphasizes the development of each student. In contrast, Kairov's pedagogy has no concept of curriculum, no position for children and no appeal for educational democracy. It was the product of cultural despotism and was abandoned long ago by the former Soviet Union in 1950s. However, in China there are still a considerable number of faithful followers in the circle of education theory, who are determined to safeguard it. This is representation of fogyism and self-importance of some bigots, and a necessary result of isolation and blindness deep rooted in the minds of some educators in China. As the world is developing, so schools should develop along with it. Curriculum development is always regarded as a central issue in any educational system. As curricula and teaching materials specifically manifest educational requirements, so specifications of teacher training, setup of teaching facilities and even strategies of administrative management should center on how to implement the curriculum. Therefore, it stands to reason to start from curriculum reform and seek its logic in the new era.

We firmly believe that any curriculum development should work in line with the following three principles: (1) Inheriting and developing the cultural heritage of mankind. (2) Responding to social reality. (3) Satisfying the needs of children's development. Educational contents should be the specifications of educational goals. Therefore, the "curriculum development" can be regarded as a task that reflects the selection and arrangement of educational contents. Intentionally or not, it manifests the developer's view on education, knowledge, learning and children. However, the school curriculum is not simply a preset "runway", but the process of running along the "runway". That is to say, it is not just a static conventional framework and schools' educational plan, but also a dynamically generated process in which teachers and students can carry out cultural exploration in certain educational situations. What deserves our attention is that it has already become a common practice in curriculum reforms all over the world to reconstruct the concept of "elementary learning abilities" and teach student to "learn how to care about others".[1] The traditional emphasis of elementary learning abilities on reading, writing and arithmetic has taken on new meanings. What's more, the focus of elementary learning abilities

---

1   Nel Noddings, *The Challenge to Care in Schools: An Alternative Approach to Education*, trans. Yu Tianlong 于天龙. Beijing: Educational Science Publishing House, 2003, 221.

has been shifted from 3R (reading, writing and arithmetic) to 3C (caring, concern and connectedness). Schools in the new century's elementary education strive to create an environment filled with care instead of cruel competition. They attach great importance to students' personality cultivation and pluralistic development, because every student exists as an independent individual with multiple intelligences. If the traditional skills of reading, writing and calculating were pursued in international elementary education courses since the 19th century, then the present-day elementary learning skills stressed in the courses based on "caring ethics" highlight the concept of "learning to care". To enable students to be familiar with "integrated knowledge" via "curriculum integration" is another major appeal of today's curriculum reform. "Curriculum integration", both deconstructive and constructive, is a curriculum strategy and curriculum awareness as well. It follows no fixed patterns and its essence is to excel. Schools are not the places that simply supply knowledge. Their top priority is to develop students whose knowledge is not given by teachers but commanded by themselves. Courses that promote learners' development are designed to explore the truth, rather than just teach existing knowledge.

Without reforms in classroom teaching, there will be no real implementation of the new curriculum. Classroom teaching is always related with some kind of culture that students are trying to adapt themselves to. Therefore, the question is what kind of "classroom culture" that teachers should create. The traditional teaching mode is a "memorizing type of teaching culture", in which teachers' role is to convey information to students whose role, in turn, is to receive and restore the information and act accordingly. Teachers' instruction has completely taken the place of students' learning. Teachers are dominating and manipulating the students. Such kind of classroom teaching is no better than a lifeless "slaughterhouse of minds". Where there is no dialogue, there is no communication and where there is no communication, there is no real education.[2] Classroom teaching itself is a practice of vigorous dialogues which guide the students to communicate with the objective world, with others and with themselves. Through dialogues, an active, cooperative and reflective mode of learning is being created in the trinity or "three in one" process of cognitive practice, social practice and ethical practice. Classroom teaching as a practice of dialogues has transcended dualism by stressing the integration of subjectivity and objectivity, knowledge receiving and discovering, knowledge deconstruction and construction, knowledge abstraction and specification, as well as knowledge explicitness and implicitness. We need to seek for a revolutionary transformation of classroom teaching, namely, transformation of teaching from "lecture-centered model" to "dialogue-centered model", and

---

2 Paul Freire, *Pedagogy of the Oppressed*, trans. Gu Jianxin 顾建新, Zhao Youhua 赵友华, & He Shurong 何曙荣. Shanghai: East China Normal University Press, 2001, 4.

PREFACE

transformation of classroom culture from "memorizing model" to "thinking model". In this way, the relation between teacher and learner is deconstructed, to make room for a shared space and time for knowledge construction and creative activities. And so the teaching paradigm has also undergone an innovative transformation, which, ultimately, is a revolution and innovation that transforms the input-oriented teaching into an intake-oriented learning.

The development of school curriculum in the new era requires the transformation of teacher education—from "teaching-book-smith training" to "reflective educator cultivation", so as to realize the "incorporation of practice into theories and theories into practice". Meanwhile, we should encourage "research methodology for practical purposes", a notion of learning based on the knowledge-construction and teacher-cooperation. In the past, the technological image of a teacher was his ability to master scientific expertise. However, the connotation of teaching is sophisticated and constantly changing, and scientific theories and technologies that support practice are uncertain. Hence, the point is, we should not simply strive to put the narrowly confined theories and technologies in one academic field into practice, but try to overcome challenging problems by using insights from experience and cognition of "reflecting in actions and acting in reflections" in complex situations. A good teacher is not one who is free from flaws and imperfections, but one who dares to challenge. As rich experience alone does not make a real practitioner of education, so empty theoretical eloquence alone does not make a true practitioner of education either. A good practitioner of education is not made by fighting alone, designing goals and making top-down teaching plans. A good teacher must grow out of a bottom-up grass-root reform. The Ministry of Education of P. R. China issued *Professional Standards for Teachers* and *Curriculum Standards for Teacher Education* at the beginning of the 21st century. The aim of these two standards is to shake off the fetters of traditional normal college education system to help teachers develop from "skilled artisans" to "reflective practitioners". In the practice of teacher education reform, the pedagogy of international teacher education advocates "three laws of teachers' development" sheds important light on this issue: the more it is anchored in the demand of teachers' reform, it is more effective; the more it is anchored in the realistic life of grass-root teachers, it is more effective; the more it is anchored in the teachers' practical reflection, it is more effective.[3]

The developmental view of the New Curriculum can be summarized as "Children First". Its starting point and destination are: respecting children, understanding children and developing children. Respecting children means

---

3   Fred Korthagen, *The Practice of Realistic Teacher Education*, Taketa Shinko trans. Tokyo: Gakubunsha, 2010, 65.

to understand that childhood is a unique period in the life span with unique characteristics and values. Understanding children means that children are human beings with multiple intelligence in their "development" and "relationships". They are not "young adults" and their education should not follow the model of "adults". Developing children requires us to believe that children are independent constructers of knowledge and the responsibilities of schools and teachers lie in ensuring their "learning rights". The implementation of New Curriculum supported by this developmental view of "Children First" curriculum stands in sharp contrast with Kairov's pedagogy, the dominant theory of education ever since the founding of P. R. China. Kairov's pedagogy takes Stalin's ideology as its yardstick and abandons the thought of Dewey and others simply because they are regarded as baneful thoughts from the bourgeoisie. The fatal defect of this theory is its denial of children and the research on children. At the beginning of new China when everything awaited to be reconstructed, learning from Kairov's pedagogy was the first "ideological emancipation" in China's education. And now after 30 years of reform and opening up to the outside world, China's education needs a second emancipation of educational ideology. Kairov's pedagogy is the result of Stalin's cultural autocracy in the 1930s. Its educational ideology is also the result of the political hype after it underwent criticism of the 1930s over the "pedology" and "de-schooling" of the 1920s. Therefore, it had only been active for 8 years before it faded completely, doomed to fail for its doctrine of "anti-children" and "anti-education". It considers teaching as a major concept but treats curriculum as a minor one. The consequence of "emphasizing teaching while neglecting curriculum" is serious in that for many years China's education administration regarded curriculum reform simply as an improvement of teaching materials and methods or updating of textbooks on the one hand, and low degree of awareness of curriculum and inability of curriculum development on the other hand, with the result of "test-orientation" in primary and secondary education. The concept of curriculum has been narrowed down into school subjects, school subjects down into teaching materials, teaching materials down into knowledge points, and finally teaching down into stuffing knowledge points into the minds of learners. Kairov's pedagogy is an errant "fortress" of test-oriented education. If this fortress is not pulled down, there will be no fundamental change of educational ideology and system, not to mention constructing a system of quality-oriented education.

If the New Curriculum reform in the last decade laid its emphasis on the top-down design and mobilization of new ideology, the next decade will witness a change of focus on the bottom-up teaching innovation from grass-root teachers. The transformation and innovation will be accompanied by collisions between new and old ideas, and thus initiate a symphony of different voices.

It can bring more benefit than harm because the collision and symphony can bring vitality to the curriculum development and teaching practice in elementary education in China. The central part of school reform is its curriculum, and the core of curriculum reform is classroom activities. The primary concern of classroom reform is the professional development of teachers. Based on a series of theories and practices that have emerged in the New Curriculum reform over the last 10 years, this book discusses issues related to "curriculum reform", "classroom transformation", "teacher training", "reflection on theories", etc. The reform is still going on and our discussion here is but a beginning. However, in these academic discussions, we can hope to shake off the restrictions from the past, summarize all kinds of experiences, come up with new perceptions and discover new hopes. Projects for further exploration will be infinite.

References

Fred Korthagen. *The Practice of Realistic Teacher Education*, trans. Taketa Shinko. Tokyo: Gakubunsha, 2010.

Nel Noddings. *The Challenge to Care in Schools: An Alternative Approach to Education*, trans. Yu Tianlong 于天龙. Beijing: Educational Science Publishing House, 2003.

Paul Freire, *Pedagogy of the Oppressed*, trans. Gu Jianxin 顾建新, Zhao Youhua 赵友华, & He Shurong 何曙荣. Shanghai: East China Normal University Press, 2001.

CHAPTER 1

The Transformation of Value in the New Curriculum Reform

In June 2001, China's Ministry of Education launched the eighth round of the National Curriculum Reform (NCR) and published the *Compendium of Curriculum Reform for Basic Education (Experimental)* (referred to henceforth as the Compendium). The sound development of each student is seen as the most important task of education. This reform suggests an ongoing fundamental value transformation in basic education. It aims at transforming the domination of traditional knowledge/skills and exam-orientated curriculum with its single target, rigid content, and inflexible structure, to a contemporary education system that targets nurturing students' healthy characteristics and whole personality. Specifically, four aspects of the transformations are presented: (1) turning curriculum targets for knowledge transmission into goals that develop the whole person; (2) turning the subject knowledge-centered curriculum into content that connects students' lives and experiences; (3) turning the learner from being a knowledge slave to being a learner that builds his/her own personal knowledge; (4) turning the lack of school culture into a rich school culture.

1 Holistic Student Development

A human exists as a whole with a twofold meaning: the wholeness of a person and wholeness of life. Firstly, the holistic development of a person should involve physical, emotional and spiritual development. Secondly, the development of a person is situated within a life, which includes one's interaction with the world as constituted by human beings themselves, the natural world, and society.

1.1 *The Whole Person Fragmented by Contemporary Education*
For the wholeness of human beings, a school curriculum is supposed to provide appropriate content, time and space. However, the wholeness of the child has been seriously neglected in the traditional curriculum. On the one hand, the meaning of life has been taken out of the strict academic disciplinary curriculum that led to students' unilateral development. For a long time, school

© KONINKLIJKE BRILL NV, LEIDEN, 2022 | DOI: 10.1163/9789004473300_002

curriculums have worshiped rational knowledge, while non-academic knowledge, such as children's surroundings, background and experience, has been marginalized. Thus, cultural or spiritual meaning has been covered over and the curriculum has become a product of abstract knowledge. Meanwhile, spiritual loss in school culture is exacerbated by mechanical and one-way indoctrination. This has denied students' critical thinking, ignored their understanding, imagination and creativity, and meant that the only thing that matters is following the rules of a given textbook and rigid syllabus. Under these circumstances, the meaning of life has been overlooked and the curriculum has become a powerful limit on students' spiritual development. As a consequence of the disconnect between learning and the spiritual, students who merely talk insincerely or live a prescribed life, such as mental illness scientists, are no longer seen as whole people.

On the other hand, the disconnected and disintegrated wholeness of children's lives is an inevitable consequence of a curriculum identified via academic disciplines as they themselves had been institutionalized and bureaucratized, and a result of dualism and utilitarianism as they consider nature and social others as operating and controlling objects.[1] Essentially, the self and the world are united, but when the world is objectified by humans, the self is also objectified. Therefore, a person is not a whole but rather an alienated self. This resonates with what Herbert Marcuse called a single dimensional man, a person eager to control, enslave and use everything, but lost in external conception, authority, fame and fortune.

How to develop a whole person through education? The wholeness of an individual is not an accumulation of different types of subject knowledge. It can be reached in two ways: one enriching students' life meanings through experience and individual innovative performance, and the other through discourse and communication with the natural world, society and the real self.

1.2 *The Meaning of the Whole Person*

Firstly, the whole person means the balanced development of one's intelligence and personality. Karl Theodor Jaspers said that, "Education is about the nurture of human souls, not the accumulation of irrational knowledge".[2] The NCR changed its emphasis from simple knowledge transmission to a focus on integrating knowledge and spiritual development into students' learning. To

---

1   Pinar William, Reynolds William, Slattery Patrick, & Taubman Peter, *Understanding Curriculum: An Introduction to the Study of Historical and Contemporary Curriculum Discourses.* New York: Peter Lang Publishing, Inc., 1995, 484.
2   Karl Jaspers, *What Is Education*, trans. Zou Jin 邹进. Beijing: Joint Publishing Company, 1991, 4.

THE TRANSFORMATION OF VALUE IN THE NEW CURRICULUM REFORM 3

reach this goal, new curriculum standards have been created as substitutes for the long traditional teaching syllabus, and this has had two implications. It has required students to master specific subject knowledge and skills, setting high common standards, which has led to students' rotated learning. While new curriculum standards were the minimum requirement for learning, no specific curriculum content was prescribed. In other words, the new curriculum began to take students' experience into account, recognizing that the whole person would develop only when his/her knowledge was co-constructed along with his/her experience. On the other hand, the new curriculum standards concern process and methods as equally important to knowledge, skills, affection, attitude and value, together comprising three-dimensional targets. The process contains instrumental and objective values. For example, a student may confront problems, confusion, setbacks and failure in the process of inquiry, but this process is an inevitable ingredient of learning and growth. Knowledge is assimilated into one's whole experience through the process and then converted into spiritual strength and life wisdom.

Secondly, the whole person means an individual's harmonious development with nature and society. John Dewey told us a fully integrated personality exists only when successive experiences are integrated with one another. It can be built up only through a world of related objects.[3] The curriculum target for the development of the whole person should integrate nature, society and self. The new curriculum, on the one hand, has adopted a holistic perspective to elaborate on three relational goals, namely the relationship between student and self (e.g., develop good physical and psychological conditions, healthy aesthetic interests and lifestyles), the relationship between student and others as well as society (e.g., develop social responsibilities, work hard to serve the people), and thirdly the relationship between students and nature (e.g., develop a spirit of innovation, practical ability, scientific and humanistic quality, environmental awareness). These three relationships contribute to a person's natural, social and self development, eventually benefiting his/her overall personality. On the other hand, the new curriculum replaced the existing subject-based curriculum, and emphasized the child's life and experience, natural, social and self, serving as resources for curriculum development. For example, the integrated practice activity course (IPAC) is a new kind of curriculum, and its content selection and organization are based on these three relationships. IPAC advocates the ethics principles of activity. Through IPAC, a person develops care toward nature, and becomes the revealer and protector in the process of

---

3   Lin Xiangda, 林向达, Zuowei meijie guocheng de kecheng yanjiu 作为媒介过程的课程研究 [*Curriculum Studies as a Medium Process*]. Japan: Rin@na. rim.or.jp, 2002.

exploring nature; a person improves his understanding, tolerance and sympathy, and enhances the capability to criticize and serve society in experiencing and participating in democratic society; a person fosters the virtue of cherishing life, and pursues his personality in identifying the self and realizing the human value and dignity. The meaning of the curriculum was apparent when the nature, the society and the self were incorporated into students' experience, as Dewey said that, "the point of school curriculum is not to succeed in making us specialists in the academic disciplines...The point of school curriculum is to goad us into caring for ourselves and our fellow human beings, to help us think and act with intelligence, sensitivity, and courage in both the public sphere—as citizens aspiring to establish a democratic society—and in the private sphere, as individuals committed to their individuals."[4]

2   Back to Students' Life World

Edmund Husserl introduced the concept of life world that "the world is our world, valid for our consciousness as existing precisely through this 'living together.' We, living in a wakeful world-consciousness, are constantly active on the basis of our passive possession of the world...the world pre-given in this together, belongs, the world as world for all, pre-given with this ontic meaning."[5] The idea of life world has multiple implications for education, the activity in a real world that takes place in teachers' interactions with students. Life world is where education happens, and it is an important resource to construct students' experience. Curriculum is students' curriculum which should be constructed on students' dialogues and understandings with teachers.

2.1   *The Loss of Meaning of Life World*

Throughout the 20th century, how to deal with the relationship between the scientific world and the life world is a fundamental issue of educational reform.[6] Then, curriculum content was mainly selected by the scientific world, and reform was mainly adapted to the changing scientific world. Scientism was the dominant value of curriculum reform, which in turn became the

---

4 John Dewey, *How Do We Think: Experience and Education*, trans. Jiang Wenmin 姜文闵. Beijing: People's Education Press, 1991, 268.

5 Husserl Edmund, *The Crisis of European Sciences and Transcendental Phenomenology*, trans. Zhang Qingxiong 张庆熊. Shanghai: Shanghai Translation Publishing House, 1988, 98.

6 Zhang Hua 张华, Kecheng yu jiaoxuelun 课程与教学论 [Theory on Curriculum and Instruction]. Shanghai: Shanghai Educational Publishing House, 2000, 422.

THE TRANSFORMATION OF VALUE IN THE NEW CURRICULUM REFORM 5

medium that promoted scientism. The scientist curriculum deprived us of a life world, and education thus lost its meaning. In reality, the primary and secondary school curriculum swang between rational knowledge and children's experience, failing to deal with the relationship between scientific and life worlds. Although students' experience was considered, it was suppressed and ignored in the classroom. When students' life and experience were removed, the monotonic and tedious curriculum and form of instruction resulted in a lack of joy and passion in students' learning experience. When life world was lost, students were colonized as actors acquiring knowledge, rather than living persons in a real social world.

For a long time, the measurement of curriculum was dominated by scientific, rational and positive rules. Therefore, curriculum design was based on logical sequences such as from concrete to abstract, and the curriculum system aimed to build a pure reason-based knowledge system. The current curriculum structure overemphasizes disciplinary rules, trapped in its high standards and deep and extensive pitfalls, causing it to deviate from students' lived reality. In this curriculum system, the teacher is the tyrant who sets standards, controls the procedure, and dominates what is right knowledge, norms and disciplines for students. However, most teachers are unable to develop their own characteristics and can only impart the standard knowledge required by way of examinations. In a normalized and unified system, the individual became a processed product. As a result of worship of theoretical knowledge, dominance of scientific world and ignorance of students' lives, they were immersed in redundant logical calculations and became passive knowledge receivers; the curriculum overlooked students' life worlds, and humanity was thus hidden in the curriculum. The instrumental rationality of contemporary curriculum eventually resulted in the marginalization of what was human. Conversely, marginalization aroused student consciousness of I-as-myself, motivating him/her to explore the real experience of his/her heart.

2.2   Back-to-Life Curriculum

"Although objective scientific logic transcends the concrete subjective life world, it can only be true when it goes back to the life world and is proved by life world."[7] Nowadays, the scientific world retains its dominant influence on the curriculum and its content, resulting in the dehumanization of schooling. The separation between contemporary curriculum and life world has been consistently criticized and the connection needs to be reconstructed.

---

7   Ni Liangkang 倪梁康, Xianxiangxue jiqi xiaoying 现象学及其效应 [*Phenomenology and Its Influences*]. Beijing: SDX Joint Publishing Company, 1996, 131.

Curriculum reform should go back to the life world, and refocus on the development of the human.

Since the 1970s, a paradigm shift has emerged in the field of curriculum studies. The Tyler Rationale that represents traditional curriculum development has been criticized and re-conceptualized. Re-conceptualists have argued that curriculum is not just about required ranges, sequence guides, or rigid textbooks, but also about lived experience and life itself. As William Pinar said, "Curriculum incorporates those literal and institutional meanings, but is by no means limited to them...... Curriculum becomes the site on which generations struggle to define themselves and the world."[8] Curriculum should emphasize students' experience and their immediate feelings, not just focus on the accumulation of previous knowledge. Furthermore, postmodernists such as William Doll Jr., have shifted their focus from dogmatic learning materials to a focus reintegration of teachers with learners, with Doll proposing the "4R" principles of curriculum: rich, recursive, relational, rigorous.

This round of NCR mentioned at the beginning of this chapter implies the idea of the back-to-life world. The compendium described the curriculum goals as "refreshing hard, complicated, biased, and outdated curriculum content, changing the overemphasis on discipline-centered knowledge, and strengthening the relevance of curricula to students' lives, society, and the development of science and technology, focus on students' learning interests and experience, select generic knowledge and skills for lifelong learning."[9] The new curriculum content identifies the connection between reform and students' life, concern for students' interests and experience, value for students' development of personality, seeing students as subjects of learning instead of objects of learning material. In addition, the new curriculum laid equal stress on scientific and life worlds. Life world is an important resource and context for curriculum content. The back-to-life curriculum has broken the shackles of the simple scientific world, integrating human experience, the real world and culture.

The compendium pointed out the systematic design of the nine-year curriculum for compulsory education. Specifically, primary education (grade 1–6)

8　Pinar William, Reynolds William, Slattery Patrick, & Taubman Peter, *Understanding Curriculum: An Introduction to the Study of Historical and Contemporary Curriculum Discourses.* New York: Peter Lang Publishing, Inc., 1995, 848.

9　Zhong Qiquan 钟启泉, Cui Yunhuo 崔允漷, & Zhang Hua 张华, eds., Weile Zhonghua minzu de fuxing, weile meiwei xuesheng de fazhan——Jichu jiaoyu kecheng gaige gangyao (shixing) jiedu 为了中华民族的复兴，为了每位学生的发展——基础教育课程改革纲要（试行）解读 [*For the rejuvenation of the Chinese nation, for the development of each student-Interpretation of the basic education curriculum reform outline (Experimental)*]. Shanghai: East China Normal University Press, 2001, 3.

has adopted an integrated curriculum, secondary education (grade 7–9) has combined subject curriculum with integrated curriculum, and high school education (grade 10–12) has employed mainly subject curriculum. This fundamental restructuring of the curriculum highlights integration, flexibility and balance, and has put great effort into weakening boundaries between subjects, and facilitating knowledge flow between them. For each phase, the new curriculum has reasonably planned and organized learning opportunities for students, reinforced subject selection based on personality, and ensured the comprehensive, balanced and harmonious development of each student. In short, the new curriculum has advocated back-to-life world education.

3 Knowledge Construction for Individual Understanding

Knowledge is the core of educational content and the foundation for achieving educational goals. Knowledge profoundly influences curriculum ideology, instruction and learning styles. To understand the concept of knowledge is a precondition for constructing new meaning around teaching and learning.

3.1 *The Absence of Personal Knowledge*

Traditional curriculums worshiped an objectivist epistemology, and from this perspective, knowledge is seen as general, external and managed truth. Influenced by the epistemology and the Cartesian separation of subject and object, the curriculum is just a pile of facts, theories and methods turned into a medium of knowledge transfer. Individual life and experience is removed from such an objectified curriculum, and a person's emotions and personality are eliminated from the process. Education thus abandons and rejects personal understanding. As Bertrand Russell put it, the community knows both more and less than the individual: it knows, in its collective capacity, all the contents of the encyclopedia and all the contributions to the proceedings of academic organizations, but it does not know the warm and intimate things that make up the color and texture of an individual life.[10] The pursuit of scientific and objectified knowledge pays the price of abandoning personal knowledge.

Personal knowledge, something not fully expressed but defined by Michael Polanyi as tacit knowledge, has deeply affected human cognitive competence.[11] It dominates all principles of knowledge because "we can know more than we

---

10   Bertrand Russell, *Human Knowledge*, trans. Zhang Jinyan 张金言. Beijing: Commercial Press, 1987, 9.

11   Michael Polanyi, *The Tacit Dimension*. London: Routledge & Kegan Paul, 1996, 4.

can tell."[12] Knowledge that can be expressed in words and numbers only represents the tip of the iceberg of the entire system of possible knowledge. A significant amount of tacit knowledge is hidden and supports explicit knowledge.

As some knowledge is tacit, personal knowledge can only be obtained through the learner's experience and practice. However, influenced by the traditional concept of knowledge, teaching is one-way knowledge impartation, and students are only knowledge containers and their innovative and creative abilities are constrained. The absence of personal knowledge in the curriculum has a large number of negative effects: teachers and students are enslaved by knowledge from textbooks, losing the ability, confidence and courage to appreciate and criticize, which more importantly destabilizes the foundations of one's knowledge innovation, democratic construction and social development. As Foucault asked, "the passion for knowledge, if it is a 'given' (as opposed to a constructed) element in perception, what exactly is the meaning (of the knowledge)?"[13] The curriculum system for basic education in the 21st century must restore the legitimacy of personal knowledge.

3.2 *Knowledge Construction with Personal Meaning*

Knowledge obtained through direct experience of daily life may be transformed into personal knowledge. The curriculum must bridge the connection of knowledge and human life, and make sense for individual development.

The new curriculum firstly establishes the new concept of knowledge. One of the curriculum goals is to emphasize students' active learning and ability to inquire, and cultivate students' generic problem-solving and creative thinking skills. It indicates that knowledge should be viewed as inquiry actions or creative processes, rather than objectives that are certain and separated (from the learner). The individual is internalized in the process, coming together with other individuals in a knowledge community. Here, individuals and knowledge are integrated. As learners participate in the community, the knowledge gained is related to individuals' interests, emotions and beliefs. Curriculum content is no longer a matter of simple rules and conclusive arguments, but rather consists of students' lives, personal knowledge and experience. Curriculums become resources of teachers' and students' meaning creation, earn each the right to speak for themselves, instead of being enslaved by knowledge.

---

12   Xiao Guangling 肖广岭, Yinxing zhishi, yinxing renshi he kexue yanjiu 隐性知识、隐性认识和科学研究 [Tacit knowledge, tacit cognition and scientific research]. *Studies in Dialectics of Nature*, 1999, (8), 8.

13   David Ray Griffin, *The Reenchantment of Science: Postmodern Proposals*, trans. Ma Jifang 马季方. Beijing: Central compilation & Translation Press, 1998, 9.

Secondly, the new curriculum adopts a new approach to teaching and learning, stressing individual students' learning styles and personality, to restructure the concept of teaching, learning and the teacher-student relationship. For example, inquiry-based learning is required in all subjects, and the IPAC provides opportunities for independent learning. A self-regulated, cooperative, inquiry-based learning approach calls for teachers and students' participation and knowledge creation. Teachers no longer simply teach textbooks, but also explore everything that students are experiencing. Learning, on the one hand, is the process by which students continuously explore, query, and express their opinions; on the other hand, it is a collective action that transcends the individual level and develops teamwork and group consciousness. Authentic dialogues are built between teachers and students, which narrow the gap between those who consider themselves knowledgeable and those whom they consider to know nothing. Authority awareness is gradually eliminated during this exploration, leading students to pursue their ambitions, seeking to change the spiritual state. In a broader sense, the new curriculum attempts to build the tendencies and belief of continuous innovation, the pursuit of progress, and ultimately achieve the great rejuvenation of the Chinese nation.

Thirdly, the new curriculum establishes assessment with personal meaning, to guarantee individual knowledge construction. The compendium is geared to promoting educational functions of assessment and enhancing students' development. This concerns assessment as the meaning construction of evaluators and those evaluated, and focuses on student's reflective ability and responsibility for their learning through active participation. The assessment values for pluralism and individual difference is fully respected. In addition, qualitative assessments such as portfolio assessment, Socratic seminars, and performance exhibitions, are used to complement deficiencies in traditional assessments of students' achievement. The assessment content focuses on describing students' responses and characteristics, to improve the developmental value of assessment.

4   Creating School Culture with Characteristics

School culture refers to shared norms, values and assumptions by teachers and students shaped within specific social structure, physical environment and social relationships in a specific school which distinguishes the members of one school from another. Curriculum reform not only involves renewal, improvement and balance of content, but also aims at the creation of an ideal school culture. The change of school culture is the deepest level of curriculum and instruction reform, and how to build characteristic school culture is the core issue for reform.

4.1 The Ignorance of Characteristic School Culture

In reality, education becomes an act of depositing,[14] in which students are the depositories and teachers are the depositors. Instead of communicating, the teacher issues communiques and makes deposits which the students patiently receive, memorize, and repeat. The banking concept of education leads to an anti-dialogical,[15] teacher-student relationship. Various factors contribute to the anti-dialogical relation, such as the traditional mandated teaching syllabus, the rigidity of the education institution, the isolation between school and community, and the uniform requirements of the examination system (especially *gaokao*). Two aspects are apparent: firstly, school culture is dominated by institutionalized anti-dialogical culture. For example, collaborative culture and dialogical culture existing in the apprenticeship and teaching and research group (TRG) was supposed to be an effective way to enhance teachers' development, and now is distorted by examinations, focusing only on students' achievements. Secondly, the school is isolated from the community and the construction of school culture overlooks students' needs. All these factors lead to a poverty in school culture, and a lack of school characteristics.

The lack of school characteristics will result in two problems. At the macro level, institutionalized anti-dialogical structure controls curriculum and makes the school curriculum uniform and rigid. School autonomy is limited, and thus students' innovative and practical abilities are constrained. At the micro level, the hard, complicated, biased, and outdated curriculum system generates poor student performance, and sees students' personality development suppressed. Moreover, teachers' professional development is restricted, as they can only teach the given materials and have difficulty practicing their teaching specialties. Therefore, school culture is hard to improve by way of the teachers and students in such a curriculum system. The aim of curriculum reform is to reexamine the connotations of culture and to create unique school culture with rich characteristics.

4.2 Reconstruction of School Culture

Reconstruction of school culture is the ultimate goal of curriculum reform. School is not a bureaucratic institution, or barrack, or company, or prison, but

---

14   Paul Freire, *Pedagogy of the Oppressed*, trans. Gu Jianxin 顾建新, Zhao Youhua 赵友华, & He Shurong 何曙荣. Shanghai: East China Normal University Press, 2001, 25.

15   Ibid, 40.

a learning organization. Rebuilding school culture is a process that develops new values, beliefs and norms, changing from didactic teaching to dialogic teaching, from tyrannical dictatorship to equal partnership, and from resources monopolization to resource sharing. The compendium offers opportunities to build new and characteristic school culture and three aspects are highlighted: democratic management culture, collaborative teacher culture, rich environmental culture.

Since the 1980s, international trends have focused on the democratic and open aspects of curriculum development. The polarization of curriculum management, namely complete centralization and decentralization, is fiercely criticized. The compendium seeks to build democratic and balanced curriculum management culture through a three-dimensional system. It points that the replacement of a centralized curriculum management by a three-dimensional system of national, local and school curriculum management so as to render the curriculum adaptive to local areas, schools, and students. The multi-dimensional curriculum management system learns from international experience, and more importantly, is a response to China's reform reality. It breaks the traditional centralization of the curriculum and reconsiders the needs and local context of schools and thus promotes the democratic management of the curriculum. School-based curriculum (SBC) captures much of the reform spotlight. It refers to school-owned curriculum autonomy in terms of curriculum rights, teachers becoming agents in developing the curriculum, and the school being the site at which the curriculum is developed.

The democratic decentralization of curriculum management indicates that curriculum reform is a process involving all members. The idea of multi-dimensional curriculum management empowers teachers to participate in curriculum development and makes teachers into agents of curriculum development at school level. When teachers gain autonomy, they can actively communicate with others, and gradually develop a partnership culture among staff, thereby enhancing their professional development. Under this circumstance, teachers develop practical thinking based on practical knowledge, and improvisational thinking in the implementation of their courses, thus becoming more active, emotional, and deliberate in carrying out teaching. They can reflect on complexity from multiple perspectives and continuously construct and reconstruct a teaching framework in complex contexts. In addition, integration curriculum is required in the new curriculum, and collaboration among teachers is necessary in conducting IPAC. The collaboration will facilitate teachers' sense of teamwork, promote teachers' professional autonomy, compensate for individual teachers' knowledge and skill deficiencies, and break down isolated teaching culture.

School culture consists of not only these explicit aspects of culture such as educational goals or curriculum forms, but also implicit cultural forms such as trust relationships among teachers and students, and the climate in the school and classrooms. The implicit culture affects students tremendously, just as Phillip Jackson described as the influence of the hidden curriculum. Jackson conducted intensive observations of elementary school classrooms and noted that the non-academic experience of schooling seemed to be a powerful mechanism for transmitting values and beliefs to children. It is necessary for us to view school surroundings from the perspective of the hidden curriculum. The culture surrounding the school does not refer to visible curriculum resources, but rather to invisible things that exercise a subtle and lasting influence on students. The new curriculum realizes the importance of the hidden curriculum, so it focuses on the explicit curriculum, as well as students' daily life and experience. For teachers, democratic management culture and collaborative teacher culture is nurtured by empowering them. The aim is to create a rich school culture in keeping with its surroundings, to achieve the goal of students' comprehensive and harmonious development.

References

John Dewey. *How Do We Think: Experience and Education*, trans. Jiang Wenmin 姜文闵. Beijing: People's Education Press, 1991.

Husserl Edmund. *The Crisis of European Sciences and Transcendental Phenomenology*, trans. Zhang Qingxiong 张庆熊. Shanghai: Shanghai Translation Publishing House, 1988.

Paul Freire. *Pedagogy of the Oppressed*, trans. Gu Jianxin 顾建新, Zhao Youhua 赵友华, & He Shurong 何曙荣. Shanghai: East China Normal University Press, 2001.

David Ray Griffin. *The Reenchantment of Science: Postmodern Proposals*, trans. Ma Jifang 马季方. Beijing: Central compilation & Translation Press, 1998.

Karl Jaspers. *What Is Education*, trans. Zou Jin 邹进. Beijing: Joint Publishing Company, 1991.

Lin Xiangda 林向达. Zuowei meijie guocheng de kecheng yanjiu 作为媒介过程的课程研究 [*Curriculum Studies as a Medium Process*]. Japan: Rin@na. rim.or.jp, 2002.

Ni Liangkang 倪梁康. Xianxiangxue jiqi xiaoying 现象学及其效应 [*Phenomenology and Its Influences*]. Beijing: SDX Joint Publishing Company, 1996.

Michael Polanyi. *The Tacit Dimension*. London: Routledge & Kegan Paul, 1996, 4.

Bertrand Russell. *Human Knowledge*, trans. Zhang Jinyan 张金言. Beijing: Commercial Press, 1987.

Pinar William, Reynolds William, Slattery Patrick, & Taubman Peter. *Understanding Curriculum: An Introduction to the Study of Historical and Contemporary Curriculum Discourses.* New York: Peter Lang Publishing, Inc., 1995.

Xiao Guangling 肖广岭. Yinxing zhishi, yinxing zhishi he kexue yanjiu 隐性知识、隐性认识和科学研究 [Tacit knowledge, tacit cognition and scientific research]. *Studies in Dialectics of Nature*, 1999, (8), 18–21.

Zhang Hua 张华. Kecheng yu jiaoxuelun 课程与教学论 [*Theory on Curriculum and Instruction*]. Shanghai: Shanghai Educational Publishing House, 2000, 422.

Zhong Qiquan 钟启泉, Cui Yunhuo 崔允漷, & Zhang Hua 张华, eds. Weile Zhonghua minzu de fuxing, weile meiwei xuesheng de fazhan—Jichu jiaoyu kecheng gaige gangyao (shixing) jiedu 为了中华民族的复兴，为了每位学生的发展—基础教育课程改革纲要（试行）解读 [*For the rejuvenation of the Chinese nation, for the development of each student-Interpretation of the basic education curriculum reform outline (Experimental)*]. Shanghai: East China Normal University Press, 2001.

CHAPTER 2

Conceptual Reconstructions and Curriculum Innovation in China

Wang Cesan published an article entitled, "Treating the Educational Tendency of Despising Knowledge Seriously—Revisiting a Discussion about the Proposal on the Transition from Exam-oriented Education to Quality Education."[1] In this article, he criticizes curriculum innovation in China for reflecting a tendency to "despise knowledge." He further illustrates the kind of education that, as he claims, values knowledge. He makes statements such as, "The essence of curriculum is knowledge," "Knowledge is like a treasure box that has numerous treasures inside," "The main obligation of instruction is to open the door to knowledge for students, so that the knowledge may be internalized and finally externalized on the students' part," "Primary and secondary schools should mainly adopt a teacher instruction-centered pedagogical mode," "Preexisting knowledge should be imparted by teachers to students," "Teachers impart knowledge, and students receive knowledge," "We cannot say it is generally wrong to 'teach for exams, and learn for exams," and "Exam-oriented education is not wrong. Conditioned on the special history of China, it reflects a specific form of comprehensive education development in China, and all-round development of individual students."[1] In this chapter, we take great pleasure in airing some of these viewpoints for discussion.

It is true that knowledge is an important constituent element of personality. The primary function of curriculum and instruction is letting students acquire knowledge, and these process tends to take place in schools. The problem is that, for students, all-round development of individual students means finding out what real knowledge is, and what valuable learning is, as well as what education is. Next, we will focus on the concepts of knowledge, learning, and classroom culture, and elaborate on the basis of concept reconstruction regarding curriculum innovation.

---

1 These are all cited from Wang's article, and below. See Wang Cesan 王策三， Renzhen duidai "ingshi zhishi" jiaoyu sicao—zai ping you "ingshi jiaoyu"xiang suzhi jiaoyu zhuangui tifa de taolun 认真对待"轻视知识"的教育思潮—再评由"应试教育"向素质教育转轨提法的讨论 [Treating the educational tendency of despising knowledge seriously—A revisit to the discussion about the proposal on the transition from exam-oriented education to quality Education]. *Peking University Education Review*, 2004, (3), 48–57.

© KONINKLIJKE BRILL NV, LEIDEN, 2022 | DOI:10.1163/9789004473300_003

CONCEPTUAL RECONSTRUCTIONS

1 Reconstructing the Concept of Knowledge and Curriculum Innovation

In some sense, the history of human intellect is the history through which human beings explored the nature of the world and the knowledge. This exploration has never stopped. To date, although different understanding of knowledge coexists, a consensus has been reached that knowledge is neither purely objective nor separated from learners' subjective understanding, and that the learning process is not as simple and mechanical as opening a treasure chest of knowledge and then transplanting information into students. Instead, the process of learning is a process through which students construct their own understanding of objects. That is, knowledge is constructed subjectively by learners. If students are not actively involved in their own expression of knowledge, learning cannot take place.

From the perspective of the sociology of knowledge, it is the interaction of subjects' cognition and the outside world, namely, the interaction of individual learners and the social and cultural value systems, that gives rise to knowledge. Particularly when it comes to the construction of school knowledge (i.e., knowledge acquisition), learning is the process and product of interaction between teachers and students in the classroom context. Teachers' knowledge cannot be indoctrinated abruptly to students. Rather, students rely on their own knowledge construction. In other words, knowledge acquisition features both subjectivity and objectivity. In particular, non-verbal feelings, as the subjective component of knowledge, are a key contributing factor in the significance of knowledge. Knowledge will not have any significance in shortage of these subjective components.

This dynamic force aiming at active formation or integration of experiences was termed tacit knowledge by M. Polanyi (1966).[2] He believes that tacit knowledge is an indispensable force for the formation of knowledge, and thus incredibly valuable. Tacit knowledge differs from explicit knowledge. The former can neither be expressed verbally nor coded and characterized objectively. However, it follows individual learners like a shadow, and constitutes the foundation of individuals' knowledge construction. It should be particularly noted that constructivists, especially social constructivists, emphasizes the constructive opportunity of learning activities in their view of knowledge. However, this does not mean that they are contemptuous of or reject reflective opportunity.[3]

---

2   Michael Polanyi, *The Tacit Dimension*. London: The University of Chicago Press, 1966.
3   Tanaka Konji, *Theory and Method of New Education Evaluation*. Tokyo: Japan Standard Corporation, 2002, 22.

In fact, even J. Piaget, a key figure in constructivism, viewed the process of knowledge acquisition as a dialectical development process of constructive opportunity (or assimilation) and reflective opportunity (or adjustment). Therefore, it can be said that constructivism does not merely emphasize constructive opportunity. Instead it maintains the idea of constructive opportunity through an emphasis on reflective opportunity. In this way it spells out the dialect of the two types of opportunities.

Nevertheless, some old traditional curricula took the knowledge view of objectivism, regarding knowledge as universal, external to human beings, and as a truth for humans to discover and absorb. In this sense, curricula based on the separation of the subjective and the objective become the sole natural carrier of knowledge. This is the connotation of Wang's claim that the essence of curriculum is knowledge. This type of knowledge floats away from real life. Each and every student, as a representative of authoritative and absolute knowledge, worships it. Therefore, the process of classroom teaching involves totally removing the individual constituents of humanity from the scope of knowledge. Pursuit of this objective knowledge is at the expense of individual knowledge elements. Furthermore, it is against the dialectics outlining the two types of opportunities for knowledge construction, namely, constructive opportunity and reflective opportunity.

A retrospective look at historical development suggests that research on the acquisition of knowledge in psychological science has undergone three stages globally, or three milestones. These stages are marked by research on behavioral psychology, information processing and situated cognition respectively. The first milestone is behaviorism. In behaviorism, knowledge acts as a unit of behavior, as the collection of systematic sets of stimulus-response. Therefore, knowledge acquisition is the connection of stimulus-response based on the formation of stimulus-response out of experience. From the perspective of behavioral psychology, the essence of curriculum development is how to strengthen and adjust specific stimulus-response connections and consolidate knowledge that students have learned by means of extrinsic motivation in the form of rewards and punishments. Thus, in behavioral psychology, teachers are administrators who control students' behavior through rewards and punishments, and students are passive learners who accept rewards and punishments. Teachers transfer knowledge in one way, and students only receive ready-made knowledge.

The second milestone is cognitivism. In cognitive psychology, research on information processing shows that knowledge acquisition generally refers to development of the ability to understand concepts, and master approaches of logical reasoning and problem solving. Semantic structural networks that constitute information are formed during this process. The semantic structural networks of information, called schemas, consist of mental images and mental processing based on the proposition. Thus, cognitivists advocate curricula that aim to develop students' ability to understand concepts, logical reasoning and problem-solving during information processing. Cognitivism further stresses that students' intrinsic motivation such as intellectual curiosity and interest contributes to the formation of semantic structural networks of knowledge. In information processing, teachers assume the role of transmitting information, but it is necessary for them to pay attention to information presentation skills, in order to arouse students' curiosity. In this sense, teachers are the guides of information processing, and students are proactive transactors of the information and consequently, knowledge builders. For students, it is of significance to reason and solve problems with partners. However, the role of these partners may not be that important.

The third milestone is constructivism. In situated cognitive psychological research, knowledge is gained through individuals' interaction with the world around them. Therefore, knowledge acquisition is a process of participatory communication and cultural practice, and also a process during which individuals develop the ability to interact with the world around them. On the one hand, constructivism stresses that individuals' knowledge is constructed through personal experience in the external world, and knowledge is just individuals' understanding of their own experiences and the significance they confer to the experiences. On the other hand, constructivism stresses that social culture is the main driving force of human beings' intellectual development and construction. It also emphasizes the importance of internalization of social culture and the impact of linguistic signs on the ability to construct.

Knowledge is constructed gradually upon interaction between individuals and society. Meanwhile, individuals go through adaptations and development. For students, the school environment has a unique role to play in the expansion of the body of knowledge. That being said, situated cognition research stresses the necessity for school education to develop curricula that facilitate students' involvement in practice-based communication. Under this concept of knowledge acquisition, students learn by means of individual involvement in communication practice. It can be said that students immerse themselves in activities through communication. According to situated cognition theory, teachers are guides and participants of communication practice, while students are also participants of communication practice as well as active knowledge builders. In addition, in situated cognition, the role of partners is rather important. Partners are important co-builders of knowledge during the process of knowledge acquisition.

The three milestones show that we understand what knowledge is through a cognitive developmental process. Step by step we are getting closer to the truth of knowledge for human beings. Curriculum innovation is faced with the issue of reconstructing the knowledge concept. In the developmental process, the abundant output of research in the field of contemporary cognitive science deserves our attention.

In the field of cognitive science, research on knowledge acquisition shows how knowledge is constructed among individuals. Most cognitive scientists believe that learners must interact with problems to be solved in a context of learning. They believe that it is only in this way that they can have a clear understanding of the issues concerned. Learners must construct meaning actively, and interact with others through dialogue and the thinking process so as to understand activities taking place in the context of learning and discover solutions to their problems. Cognitive science and research on learning in this field include cases that show repeated mechanical memorization is perhaps effective in the short term to cope with such routine tasks and tests. However, it is not efficient for in-depth understanding and memorization of complex information or the solving of complicated problems. Therefore, students may have some knowledge that they have no idea how to use, inert knowledge, which has no use in their development.

Under the exam-oriented education system, mastery of this kind of inert knowledge becomes a means to ensure success in exams. Students focus on accumulating inert knowledge at school. The inert knowledge accumulated is used to pursue success in exams, as if it were an exchange of commercial goods. This is truly commercialization of school knowledge. On the backdrop of commercialization of school knowledge, no matter how outdated the knowledge schools provide is and how far away it is from reality, nobody needs to interfere. It is unquestionable as long as this type of knowledge contributes to successes in exams. In addition, the process of accumulation of this type of commercialized knowledge and the tasks to be undertaken, after all, rely on individual learners to undergo the entire process alone. In the exam-oriented education system that is conditioned on selection and classification, learners are always in fierce competition with others like rivals during the process of knowledge accumulation and learning tasks fulfillment.[4] Moreover, the variety of teaching methods adopted in the exam-oriented education system cannot enable students to engage in active learning. In fact, the trend of intensified indoctrination in exam-oriented education has severely damaged the physical

---

4   Zhong Qiquan 钟启泉. Xiandai kechenglun 现代课程论 [*The Study of Modern Curriculum*]. Shanghai: Shanghai Educational Publishing House, 1989, 452, 535.

and mental development of students. Faced with this harsh reality, how can we remain indifferent? Provided that the exam-oriented education system has been denounced throughout the country, it is incredible for one to openly raise the banner to promote the concept of teaching for exams and learning for exams. It is even so for one to advocate that examination-oriented education is a specific form of comprehensive development of education. In this sense, it is also a specific form of all-round development of individual students. Wang's own words work here, "This is really against the facts, reason, and logic, hence ridiculous."

What then features as knowledge acquisition of curriculum innovation based on the new view of knowledge?

First, the emphasis is on the experience basis of knowledge. The subject of knowledge is the significance of knowledge constituted by experiences, rather than the accumulation of meaningless representations. A concept must be established regarding concrete experiences, otherwise being meaningless. For example, the concept of animal is composed of many specific experiences of animals. The experience forms its meaning categories, so that the concept of animal will not remain as an assembly of abstract representations of animals. If one only remembers representations such as cow, sheep, or horse, and name them animals, the meaning of animal cannot be formed.

Immanuel Kant speculates that human beings' experiences can be distinguished as innate and acquired experiences. The acquired experiences here are also known as empirical knowledge, referring to knowledge directly built on humans' sensory experiences. These kinds of empirical knowledge form all sorts of knowledge through continuous classification, induction and aggregation. Consequently, scientific knowledge of a range of disciplines came into being, characterized by their external features. This knowledge is an indicator of human civilization and an important asset of mankind.

Similarly, students' knowledge acquisition is ultimately dependent on their own lifestyle and sensory experience, which is called their empirical view of knowledge. Knowledge acquisition is affected by preexisting knowledge of learners. To be more specific, knowledge acquisition is not only subject to constraints of internal and external factors, but also influenced by knowledge that has been constructed by individual learners. Prior knowledge or schema that students have obtained is often associated with the acquisition of new knowledge. That is to say, it is easier to acquire new knowledge given the schema is associated. In this way, new knowledge emerges into preexisting knowledge and constructs a richer schema of the knowledge.

Second, the process of knowledge construction is emphasized. Although experiences contribute to the formation of knowledge, the latter is not equal to the accumulation of experiences. Constructivism covers both empiricism and rationalism. The former emphasizes knowledge and regards experiences as material that forms knowledge, while the latter emphasizes the role of innate rationality. Only through use of reason can experiences be turned into knowledge. Therefore, such use of reason is in the activities through which knowledge is constructed. Therefore, reason and experience are not mutually exclusive, but rather complementary. Neither can be overlooked.

In the view of constructivism, knowledge constructed is not instilled into the mind of a person from outside intact. Rather it is derived from individuals' continuous effort to organize their experiences. Students thus actively construct knowledge. In other words, students' subjective knowledge acquisition does not happen through storing the intact form of knowledge that should be acquired. Students need to associate knowledge that should be acquired with existing knowledge that they have acquired, and integrate the old and new. Therefore, to make knowledge acquisition possible, knowledge should not be taught and learned separately. New groups of knowledge should be combined with preexisting knowledge. To make this happen, teachers have to arrange learning activities in such a way that students will engage willingly and dynamically. Meanwhile, students have to learn in the context in which they have to make use of knowledge that they have acquired before, and associate the existing knowledge with what they are going to learn.

Third, the synergic nature of knowledge is emphasized. Human knowledge is neither absolutely objective nor absolutely subjective, but rather is a synergy of knowledge. Here, synergy refers to ongoing and multiple channeled communications between individuals. Human knowledge is constructed through the mutual cooperation of human beings generation after generation. The development of individual knowledge is facilitated through the contribution and collaboration of many. The development of individuals' knowledge and knowledge of human beings must rely on the "conversation of mankind."[5] This conversation happens via the media of linguistic signs created by people, and passed on generation to generation.

Students' knowledge acquisition is constrained by internal and external factors. Internal restrictions refer to inherent constraints. For example, it is well known that inherent constraints work in the learning of both language and mathematics. External constraints, on the other hand, are generally the result of other people or their behaviors, and are generally referred to as constraints to social and cultural knowledge acquisition. According to situated cognition

---

5   Kenneth A. Bruffee. Collaborative Learning and the conversation of mankind. *College English*, 1984, November, 635–652.

theory, knowledge is always embedded in a certain physical or cultural context. If we say that information processing theory regards knowledge as the operation of signs in an individual's mind, then situated cognition theory is concerned with the association of knowledge as existing in an individual's mind in the context in which the knowledge was acquired or used. What was acquired is knowledge embedded implicitly in a physical and cultural context, therefore knowledge acquisition involves a situated culture.

A question closely related to how knowledge can be acquired is what real knowledge is. The objective knowledge of academic disciplines is not equal to students' subjective knowledge. There must be a process through which objective knowledge of academic disciplines can be turned into students' intrinsic knowledge. Students do not really acquire knowledge when they are asked to open the treasure box and acquire ready-made knowledge. This is because ready-made knowledge cannot automatically merge into students' existing knowledge system, even when specific and concrete knowledge had been provided.

In classroom teaching, mutual communication happens between and among teachers and students with textbooks and life experiences as a medium. Only via this medium can students acquire all sorts of knowledge. Students are not purely knowledge recipients. Instead, they are dynamic explorers, and builders of significance and knowledge. As E.Cassirer points out, "It is impossible to instill truth into one's soul, just as it is impossible to offer vision to one born blind. It is impossible to obtain truth if it is not through non-stop collaboration in which some people raise questions and some others answer the questions."[6] Knowledge can hardly be acquired merely through lecturing by the teacher.

Characteristics of knowledge acquisition, as disclosed above, have laid a theoretical foundation for the curriculum innovation we have proposed. This theoretical foundation stresses three layers of connotations of knowledge acquisition. (1) Knowledge acquisition is the process through which learners' own experiences become rational and practically useful. It is not about memorizing facts; (2) Knowledge (significance) acquisition is not passive indoctrination, but a learn-initiated construction; (3) Knowledge acquisition is meant to reach a consensus through learners' interaction and negotiation with others.

S. J. Jang compares the differences between traditional and constructivist pedagogy, and points out that traditional teaching methods adopt three basic principles that objectivism abides by. These three basic principles stand in

---

6 Ernst Cassirer, An Essay on Human.trans Gan Yang 甘阳. *Beijing: Xiyuan Publishing House,* *2003,* 10.

opposition to constructivism.[7] Firstly, students are viewed as a piece of empty paper so that teaching and learning can happen in a way that centers on teachers' instruction, whilst students absorb knowledge passively. For this reason, students need to be indoctrinated by teachers. However, teaching should be aimed at guiding students to actively construct knowledge rather than instilling existing knowledge in them, because teachers' and students' experiences differ after all. Teachers' cognition is not similar to that of students'. Secondly, traditional pedagogy regards knowledge as existing objectively, taking knowledge presented in textbooks is absolute truth that will never change, and the purpose of learning therefore as to memorize these truths. However, knowledge is not a truth that exists objectively, but a series of subjective experiences constructed in individuals' minds. Thirdly, traditional pedagogy maintains that the significance of knowledge exists objectively in textbooks and teachers' words. Students only need to listen quietly in order to receive ready-made knowledge through teachers' indoctrination. However, the text and the words themselves are just tangible but not of quality. The symbols, whose meanings are conferred by speakers and listeners, are themselves meaningless. Knowledge is a social construct that develops through interaction and consultation between learners and others. The above two propositions reveal the watershed of the two types of concepts of knowledge. If one sets off only from the old traditional view of knowledge, it will result in the return of traditional teachers. This does not comply with the objective rules and requirements of social development.

2 Reconstruction of the Concept of Learning and Curriculum Innovation

In his book *Emile*, J. J. Rousseau conveys the idea that human beings begin to learn from the moment of birth. This general definition of learning indicates the process by which people master new forms of behaviors through interaction with the environment. However, learning based solely on life experiences has two problems. First, it is hard to grasp knowledge and skills that are needed in future social life only from limited life experiences. Second, knowledge and views obtained from life experiences are not right all the time, and may sometimes be wrong. Therefore, people should examine and amend their knowledge and views. Schools are institutionalized learning sites at which these problems

---

7 Zhang Shizhong 张世忠, "Jiangou jiaoxue—lilun yu yingyong 建构教学—理论与应用 [Construction Teaching-Theory and Application]" *Taiwan: Wu-Nan Book Company, 2001*, 16.

are to be solved, this being the reason schools exist. However, current school education has distorted the original form of student learning and diverted student development in the opposite direction. Therefore, re-verification of the original meaning of learning and reconstruction of the concept of learning becomes the major theme of contemporary education research.

The issue questioning what learning is has been touched upon above, in elaboration of the characteristics of knowledge acquisition. What kind of activities can be called learning? Generally, it is believed that learning works through experiences, resulting in a process by which continuous change in behaviors, skills, abilities, attitudes, personalities, interests, knowledge, comprehension, and others, may take place. The basic connotations and characteristics of learning can be summarized as follows.

Firstly, learning means a change in behavior. Traditional psychology often defines learning as changes in behavior. However, from behaviorism to cognitivism and to constructivism, the basic trend of historical inquiries into learning shows that changes happen with the focus on external behavior (events outside the skin) being switched to internal psychology (events within the skin), and then to interactions between human psychology and the environment. In other words, the focus is first on external conditions of the behaviors concerned, then on internal conditions of the behaviors concerned, and afterwards on the connection and interaction of external and internal conditions of the behaviors.

As a representative of constructivist psychology, situated cognitive theory contends that cognitive behaviors are not based on certain objectives, plans, or knowledge in one's mind, but on a set of behaviors for adaptation to the situations one is in, hence known as situated cognition. This, at first glance, looks similar to behaviorism. Nevertheless, cognition in situated cognition theory is believed to not simply be responses to rewards and punishments. Rather, cognition is formed under the social and cultural influences that have included interpersonal relations and other tools. Furthermore, unlike epistemology that stresses the flanks of information processing (for example representation, concepts and knowledge) in the human mind, and considers learning as the formation of knowledge structure in the learner's mind, situated cognition theory believes that what learners acquire is not a cognitive structure relevant to the environment but an activity mode (contextual learning) in the environment.

Secondly, learning is the formation of meaning. In humanistic psychology the view of learning stresses subjective experiences of learners, and considers meaning as the essence of learning. Therefore, learning is defined as individual learners' discovery of meaning or the formation of meaning in the subjects' mind. Meaning can be divided into social meaning and personal meaning.

Social meaning has been established so that individuals cannot interpret it arbitrarily. In the history of education, learning means acquiring social meaning in a correct manner. However, in the new way of education, personal meaning gets more attention. The personal meaning is a reflection of individuals' specific findings of the relations between a variety of objects, events, and views. Meaning is not conferred by external authorities such as books and teachers, but conclusions are drawn by the learners themselves.

In this commentary, a personal field phenomenon draws attention. In the field phenomenon, the learner is the world he can experience, here and now, and he himself is also included in this world. From teachers and other learners' perspective, a child's field phenomenon might be full of errors, illusions and incomplete explanation of the facts, but for the child, the field phenomenon at that moment is the only reality he is able to know. Outsiders can hardly find what meaning he has identified exactly, because changes in behaviors are explicit outcomes of learning, while the process of one person's learning is hard for another person to control. However, this does not mean that the formation of meaning in children's minds is totally incomprehensible. Since all behaviors are the learners' own unique performance and it is possible to track children's field phenomenon and understand how the objective world is experienced, children's behaviors might be better understood. As the field phenomenon is often formed in the relationship with learners themselves, learning is often related to learners themselves. Learners' understanding of themselves (or their self-concept) restricts the significance of their experiences.

Thirdly, learning is sentiments (insights) about survival in life. It is believed that the human intellect works in two ways. The first is substantive thinking via the use of language and images in order to understand the world. The second is external behaviors, for example, putting the world under learners' control via calculating and writing. Planned school education is built on the base of the latter. However, the theory of arousal claims that there is a concept, sentiments (insights), which exist between substantive thinking and external behaviors. Sentiments are a sense of awareness created when learners make direct contact with the objective world, which comes to be when learners are in a high level of concentration. These are direct experiences of the reality in an objective world before the infiltration of thinking in terms of conceptualization, interpretation and evaluation. Sentiments indicates that the original interpretation schema has been broken, and fundamental changes have occurred in the relation between a person and the objective world. Thus, sentiments cannot be explained as a causal product. Instead, it is a great leap associated with events in relation to the subjective learner, and the thawing experiences of the mind, unconsciously. Educational activities on the one hand are involved

CONCEPTUAL RECONSTRUCTIONS

in the acquisition and exchange of information available. On the other hand, it is connected to the live world that creates the activities. The reason is that, sentiments are a sort of stimulation that accommodates the natural side of human biology, and human beings live in the objective world as an integrated whole and keep accompany with the objective world. This is the first point. Secondly, there is a tacit knowledge theory. The characteristics of tacit knowledge have been mentioned above. The reason why students discover knowledge and realize that what has been discovered is true, is that they have dynamically developed or integrated their own experiences into learning. Whenever a problem arises, students have to find resolutions one by one through thinking for themselves—what we can know is more than what we can say. It might be difficult for students to express in words, but great learning potential exists in their experiences: What he can get to know is more abundant and deeper than what he can express. Thirdly, there is a conditional knowledge theory. Knowledge always contains both theoretical and practical knowledge. These are the two sides, I. Scheffler claims, "knowing what" and "knowing how."[8] These two sides of knowledge have a similar structure, and one aspect cannot exist without the other. Thus the ability to understand certain information is equal to the ability to correctly use this information. However, understanding the information may not ensure correctly using the information. Although a concept is clear, if the relation between the concept and the student is not made clear, the concept will not affect the student's behavior. In reality, it is extremely complicated and difficult to turn the understanding of a concept into its use.

Fourthly, learning is a dialogue of wisdom. The practice of learning is complicated practice of dialogue. Classroom teaching is not a teacher's monologue but should be a dialogue of wisdom. "Where there is no dialogue, there is no communication; where there is no communication, there is no real education."[9] "In dialogue we are not against each other but collaborate with each other."[10] "Dialogue seems to be a stream of meaning flowing among people. It enables all speakers to participate and share the stream of meaning, which potentially inspires new understanding, and consensus will be reached in the group."[11] The classroom, as the platform of classroom activities, features an extremely complicated situation. In a classroom there is often a teacher and

---

8   Saeki, *Learning Community*. Tokyo: Tokyo University Publishing House, 1999, 92–93.

9   Paul Freire, *Pedagogy of the Oppressed*, trans. Gu Jianxin 顾建新, Zhao Youhua 赵友华, & He Shurong 何曙荣. Shanghai: East China Normal University Press, 2001, 93.

10   David Bohm, *On Dialogue*, trans. Wang Songtao 王松涛. Beijing: Educational Science Publishing House, 2004, 7, 6.

11   Ibid, 11.

dozens of students. People come from different backgrounds, behave differently, and form different understanding and emotions.

Although teaching activities are generally based on a teacher's intent, and carried out according to the teacher's design, not a single senior teacher would arrange teaching activities exactly as present in lesson plans. Teachers should always revise lesson plans timely and in accordance with student responses. Teaching and learning cannot happen if there is no intent and plan, but the intent and plan should be continuously changing, depending on teachers' decisions and realizations. In teaching, it is the process, not the results, that are essential. Keeping that in mind though, individual students' activities are extremely complex, because each student has his or her personality.

In response to the teacher's words and behaviors, students will have a variety of representations and emotions, react differently, and form a different understanding. Of course, a teacher cannot manage these entire complex occurrences in the classroom. Nevertheless, if the teacher does not know what a certain occurrence means, and the teacher and the students face a dilemma, teaching activities cannot be carried through. Occurrences in the classroom also happen in complex relations and networks, and while classroom events are accidental, understanding classroom events gives insight into conversations and behaviors in real life relations.

Fifthly, learning is a cultural practice. In traditional cognitive psychological research, mental activities and knowledge acquisition are attributed only to individual cognitive change. In the 1990s, with a strong tendency to revise the emphasis on individual factors, learning activities began to be studied in their social and cultural contexts. American education scholar M. Tomasello is a typical example, believing that almost all learning is "cultural learning" which should be studied as a "cultural practice."[12] Manabu Sato, a Japanese educationist, studies classroom teaching from the perspective of "cultural practice," releasing learning practice from the restraints of individualism, and redefining it as "collaborative practice" by which people resort to cooperation with others. In classroom teaching, practical activities containing complex elements cannot be covered by Soviet Kairov's pedagogy featured in mechanical indoctrination by Wang Cesan. Instead, classroom teaching aims at experiencing and creating a cultural community. Actually, cultural transmission and cultural creation are not isolated. Just as human activities for ideals are the process of collaborative practice, education or classroom teaching is also the process of transmitting and creating collaborative culture. That is to say, classroom teaching makes

---

12   Saeki Yuta, *The meaning of "learning."* Tokyo: Iwami Bookstore, 1995, 85–86.

CONCEPTUAL RECONSTRUCTIONS

meaning by the virtue of culture, science, art and other media, and then teachers and students exchange their views on meanings. In this sense, teachers and students are engaged in this cultural practice. On the one hand, Wang Cesan criticizes others for simply denying cognition and regarding classroom teaching as being too simple. On the other hand, he declares that pedagogy, in simple terms, means that teachers impart a ready-made knowledge for knowing outside world and developing students' inner world. Besides, his interpretation of the words—The essence of classroom teaching is communication and cooperation—is too simple. In fact, this sentence aims at the defect of traditional classroom teaching, and advocates a new classroom culture without denying role of cognition in learning. However, learning is limited to neither cognition nor knowledge cramming by teachers in classroom teaching.

In other words, we advocate that classroom teaching should be a practical process of dialogue so as to form meanings and connections in three dimensions. The first dimension is the cognitive (cultural) practice of dialogue between textbooks and objects. The second dimension is the interpersonal (social) practice of dialogue in communication with others. The third dimension is the existential (ethical) practice of dialogue in communicating with ourselves. These three dimensional dialogues are interrelated.[13]

There is no need to illustrate more about the first dimension. All teaching is based on specific contents and objects. For example, an object of fractional teaching is a fraction of the mathematical world, and a teaching object of the Renaissance is the history of the Renaissance. In the dialogue with the fraction, teachers help students to form a meaning of the fraction and involve students in the mathematical world of fractions. Students, with the help and explanation of their teachers, can form a meaning of the object and connect themselves to the mathematical world. Primarily, teaching is just such a cognitive practice.

The second dimension, social practice, shows the social nature of cognitive practice, similar to that in the first dimension. Class activities between teachers and students require the participation of both sides. Educational practice is not a monologue, but an interpersonal and social practice depending on communication. Each student in class is involved in social communication, weaving or cutting off a web of relationships. The classroom is a place for students with different emotions and ideas to learn and cooperate. When learning mathematical fractions, everyone in class has a different understanding. He or she can know others' ideas in communication without realizing it. On the

---

13   Manabu Sato, *The Joy of Learning-towards Dialogue*. Yokohama: Shizhi Study, 1999, 59–68, 155–156.

contrary, students who can neither adapt to class teaching nor participate well may continuously feel a sense of misfortune, even if they fully understand the textbooks.

The third dimension, ethical practice, refers to practices related to identity or self-existence identification. The classroom is a place to continuously show and confirm students' identities. Students who are unable to keep up with teaching will be puzzled by the difficult content and may experience a sense of estrangement and inferiority in class. Students talk to themselves in learning, with questions such as, What do I think? How do I think? What role do I play in class? How can I learn well?, and these inquiries form around questions of existence and ethics rooted in self-exploration.

In this way, the above research from psychology, sociology, and culture raise the question of how learning is initiated. Besides, it shows the characteristics of various learning activities at different levels. In other words, it demonstrates that the way for students to learn directly is not unitary but complex and various. Therefore, some simple and skillful learning goals may be achieved in accordance with behaviorism. However, more complex learning goals for advanced thinking are suggested to adopt methods of inquiry and constructive method, which are indispensable for constructing new learning concepts and curriculum concepts. It is true that there is no learning theory which can be applied to all situations. Then, with the guidance of learning theories, good teaching must employ different teaching methods so as to adapt to different situations because learning is the journey from a known world to an unknown world or a process of reconstructing experience and making sense rather than simply accumulating ready-made knowledge. Therefore, a good class should be the process of random and dynamic development rather than in a predetermined rigid framework. We know that one of the important qualities of human learning is to form, seek, and create meanings all the time. Besides, we should not neglect the development in scientific learning and curriculum theories in international education circles. If these theoretical development are compared with China's ancient learning concepts, it is easy to see that they can interact with each other although there are some obvious differences, for example, "Learning means consciousness,"[14] and "Teaching means learning.[15]

---

14   There are two words—学 and 习 in the Chinese phrase "学习" (learning). According to the *Origin of Chinese Characters* 说文解字, 习 counts the number of flies while 学 means imitation. The initial meaning of 学习 is consciousness. Knowledge is the foundation of understanding what you do not know.

15   What is 教 (teaching)? According to the *Origin of Chinese Characters*, 教 (teaching) means lessons, explanation, and enlightenment. It also means learning.

CONCEPTUAL RECONSTRUCTIONS   29

3   Reconstruction of Classroom Culture and Curriculum Innovation

In classroom teaching, teaching content imparted from teachers to students refers to the concepts and laws of knowledge. On one hand, knowledge, known to teachers but unknown to students, is discovered and recognized by one's forefathers, which means that students need to explore, construct and acquire it from their teachers. Students also acquire and internalize new knowledge via connections with existing knowledge and experience rather than only via their teacher's explanations. Thus, it is an implicit contradiction between the medium of knowledge and the acquisition of knowledge. Actually, this contradictory relationship is the root of all incorrect views in classroom teaching, especially cramming teaching which indoctrinates knowledge unilaterally and fails to abide by students' cognitive activities in accordance with their experiences. In fact, it is impossible for students to systematically acquire ready-made knowledge by repeating textbooks material issued by teachers. The cramming teaching excludes students from connecting their observations with experiences. Accordingly, it disregards the generation and development of new knowledge, which is the result of the interaction of observations and experiences.

"It is said that the history of teaching is a history of campaign and struggle for children's initiative in learning."[16] "The traditional teacher-centered teaching ignores individual differences among children. In this case, it is possible to neither expect children to exert subjective activeness nor cultivate their initiative and creativity."[17] Both global education and Chinese education have a common view in criticizing claims made by cramming style teaching, such as the dominance of teachers and the treasure box of knowledge which definitely could never internalize basic knowledge. Professor Qiu Chengtong, winner of the Mathematics Fields Medal warned, "People believe that Chinese students who don't play very well in innovation and creation have better scores in mathematics, physics and chemistry than American peers. They gain much more solid basic knowledge than American students in high schools. Actually, it has been a self-deception for many years!"[18] In *Cautionary Notes* written by Montagne, the pioneer of the new education, there is a very powerful paragraph against clichés like the treasure box of knowledge. "It is the custom of

---

16   Masao Sato, *Principles of Teaching*, trans. Zhong Qiquan 钟启泉. Beijing: Educational Science Publishing House, 2001, I, IV.

17   Ibid.

18   Yuan Xiaoming 袁小明, Huhuan jiaoyu zhidu de chuangxi 呼唤教育制度的创新 [*Calling for the innovation of the educational system*]. *Wenhui Daily*, 2004, August 24, 9.

pedagogues to be eternally thundering in their pupil's ears, as they were pouring into a funnel, whilst the business of the pupil is only to repeat what the others have said: now I would have a tutor to correct this error, and, that at the very first, he should, according to the capacity he has to deal with, put it to the test, permitting his pupil himself to taste things, and of himself to discern and choose them, sometimes opening the way to him, and sometimes leaving him to open it for himself; that is, I would not have him alone to invent and speak, but that he should also hear his pupil speak in turn...It is good to make him, like a young horse, trot before him, that he may judge of his going, and how much he is to abate of his own speed, to accommodate himself to the vigor and capacity of the other. For want of which due proportion we spoil all; which also to know how to adjust, and to keep within an exact and due measure, is one of the hardest things I know, and it is the effect of a high and well-tempered soul."[19]

Wang Cesan asked in his article: "Curriculum reform in every country attaches great importance to elementary learning ability and knowledge. Why doesn't our curriculum reform conform to the international prevailing trends? Why does our curriculum reform weaken knowledge and transform knowledge-oriented education?" In fact, there are different understandings of knowledge and elementary learning ability.[20]

The theories of taxonomy of educational objectives advocated by B. S Bloom and "achievement targets" by R. Stiggins indicate that knowledge includes "contents, understanding, reasoning, skills, completing work, attitudes, etc."[21] In addition, both the four categories in Japan's *Guidelines* or the three-dimensional Goals in the Chinese new curriculum make the same point. In the *Guidelines,* the four categories include knowledge and understanding, thinking and judging, skills and expressions, and interest, motivation and attitude. In the Chinese new curriculum, the three-dimensional goals contain knowledge and competence, processes and methods, emotional attitudes and values.

19　Tsukuba University Educational Research Association, *Foundation of Modern Education*, trans. Zhong Qiquan 钟启泉. Shanghai: Shanghai Educational Publishing House, 2003, 41.

20　What is 学力 (learning ability)? 学力means the power and competence of learning and research. Wang Ling (1032–1059), a Chinese poet in Song dynasty (r.960–1279 AD) put it as the study force with a deep and solid root, He said that poverty makes you know the heavy responsibility and illness makes you feel slack in study. 学力 is originally an inherent phrase in China. But it almost became a dead expression when Kairov's pedagogy swept across the educational academia in China. In the 1980s, it regained its status as an important educational term. The author once wrote in a paper saying that it is wrong for Japanese scholars to refer to 学力 (learning ability) as an inherent term in Japanese.

21　Tanaka Koji, *Theory and Method of New Education Evaluation*. Tokyo: Japan Standard Corporation, 2002, 40.

CONCEPTUAL RECONSTRUCTIONS

The knowledge both in Japan and China generally covers two aspects—to acquire facts, concepts, relationships, and principles, and to extract these facts, concepts, relationships, and principles as needed. This view stresses that knowledge is not isolated and can be incorporated into a system. Besides, it is structurally acquired with hierarchy—theory, principle, concept, theme, specific facts. What's more, it also stresses the need to observe, with the help of knowledge, the nature of things, to reason in problem solving, and to be concerned with interests, attitudes, values, and self-image. Indeed, Wang Cesan's view of knowledge is incompatible with this point. Emotion, will and value should be integrated into the goal of knowledge acquisition. Actually, this point criticizes the employment of useless knowledge in current test-oriented education. In this way, it doesn't degenerate knowledge but upgrades knowledge, which is exactly in line with international trends.

What is academic achievement? Generally, it is regarded as the ability to acquire wisdom through learning in school education. In global education, the definition of fundamental academic achievement is roughly divided into two. One is the substantial side, an explicit learning ability which can be easily measured by exams. The other is the functional side, also known as implicit learning ability, thinking and problem solving, interest and motivation. In fact, these two sides are interrelated, and the latter supports the former, an intelligent ability. We should know both and pay attention to their connection to each other.

Traditional education focuses on explicit learning ability which can be directly evaluated by examinations. In the past, teachers just imparted knowledge to their students as presented in textbooks. However, in the information society, it is more important to master attitudes and abilities to create culture (functional learning ability) than to master existing knowledge. This means it is necessary to decrease substantial learning ability and increase functional learning ability in education. Actually, classroom teaching that emphasizes functional learning ability is a collective practice which stresses, promotes and verifies critical thinking. In this way, the classroom can be seen as a place for cultural practice which enables students to construct new knowledge in accordance with their own experience. Students' thinking per se is a learning method, for which intellectual skills, new skills and a learning attitude are all important. In other words, the process becomes the content. However, in the current school education system, people only show interest in paper-and-pencil test for knowledge points in textbooks. It is true that a disadvantage reflected in exam-oriented education is the quick forgetting of the tested knowledge! This kind of teaching is criticized by Japanese scholars in that knowledge is stripped like gold plating. Blindly promoting the rationality of quickly forgotten knowledge in test-oriented teaching is detrimental to students.

A retrospective look at historical developments suggests that curriculum teaching theory has roughly three viewpoints on how to interpret basic learning ability and how to construct learning. From the first viewpoint, knowledge and skills imparted in school are regarded as a learning ability. From this perspective, people always keep their eye on how to remember knowledge and skills as accurately as possible. Therefore, exams are concerned so much that exam scores are always equated with learning ability that results in disregarding thinking and personality, and judging only by test scores. It is still an obviously prevalent error in the test-oriented education system. The second viewpoint, believing that explicit learning ability should contain more than just knowledge and skills, emphasizes problem-solving competence, attitude, and value. However, the second viewpoint excessively emphasizes psychology and intelligence such as the attitude of acquiring and applying knowledge and skills. Too much emphasis on mental functions would lead to ignoring in-depth study from textbooks. The third viewpoint, not attributed to knowledge and skills, does not underestimate attitudes and values, emphasizing learning ability as a whole. In other words, it attaches importance to the reconstruction of knowledge, while developing students' cognitive ability by acquiring these knowledge. Therefore, the third viewpoint discusses the acquisition of knowledge and skills so as to promote physical and mental development. It also explores how these cognitive abilities relate to personality such as motivation, emotion, attitude, and value. This is what the new curriculum holds. It is a matter of course that the new curriculum highlights emotion, attitude and value.

The fundamental point of curriculum innovation is the development of student holistic competence, rather than simply instilling knowledge in students' brains. In primary education, it is unnecessary and impossible for students to master all the knowledge needed in their future work. More importantly, students should know how to learn and how to develop intelligence. The new curriculum sets standards for content, achievements, and opportunities at respective educational phases. All these standards infiltrate into the tripartite educational goals of the new curriculum. The first goal is behavioral: mastering basic calculation for example. Generally, this kind of goal is expressed by "can." The second goal is cognitive, referring to the overall development of psychology and intelligence, such as perseverance. Generally, substantial learning abilities such as knowledge and skills belong to the behavioral goal, while the functional learning ability such as thinking, judging, motivation and attitude belong to the cognitive goal. The third goal is experience, referring to participating in activities such as social service. This goal does not necessarily aim at students' direct changes but rather at their experience. From a long-term perspective, it is crucial to develop students' personality by the accumulation of

CONCEPTUAL RECONSTRUCTIONS

emotions in their experience. Therefore, the new curriculum should not only take the first goal into account but also attach importance to the other two goals, which constitutes the dynamic knowledge source. It is the obvious progress of the curriculum theory. In other words, it is upgrading knowledge, while Wang Cesan regards it as knowledge degeneration. In fact, it involves an issue, how to understand the main battlefield in school education, or the essence of classroom teaching.

What is classroom teaching? It is defined as a complex process covering various elements. Moreover, teaching is not just a complex of various elements, but a complex of various processes. In these processes, dynamic structures develop in line with an internal logic. Therefore, over the years, many dialectical frameworks have been developed to analyze teaching structures, such as the Triangle Models, Quadrilateral Models, and Dynamic Models.[22] Actually, the cognitive mechanism is not strong enough to cover all the issues regarding student's growth and classroom teaching. It is not credible that Kairov's pedagogy could solve any issue related to the cognitive mechanism of student development. Nobody denies that classroom teaching is a process of cognitive development. However, the teaching epistemology we advocate is not Kairov's pedagogy. Classroom teaching can be seen as a complex activity with three categories. The first category refers to activities of teaching and learning in which personal relationships are formed. This process is viewed as social practice. The second category refers to the construction of activities involving interpersonal relations that share the borderline between teaching and learning cognitive processes, which forms the category of social practice of human interactions. The third category, composed of teaching and learning, refers to teachers and students. On the one hand, teachers and students connect themselves with object world and others. On the other hand, they explore and transform themselves in their own world.[23] In teaching and learning, as Sato criticized, "Traditional pedagogy is limited to the first category (cognitive process), neglecting the second category (social process) and the third category (introspective process)"[24] It just hit the crucial part of Kairov's pedagogy that in classroom teaching the relationship between teachers and students is interactive not dominant.[25]

---

22   Jun Yoshimoto, *Modern Teaching Research Events*. Tokyo: Meiji Books, 1987, 55–57.
23   Manabu Sato, *Curriculum and Teachers*, trans. Zhong Qiquan 钟启泉. Beijing: Educational Science Publishing House, 2003, 153–154.
24   Ibid, 154.
25   Zhang Hua 张华, Kecheng yu jiaoxue lun 课程与教学论 [*Curriculum and Teaching Theory*]. Shanghai: Shanghai Educational Publishing House, 2001, 358–361.

Teacher's responsibility is to create interactive learning environment which enables students to be the subject of learning activities. In other words, students shouldn't unilaterally recite and listen to teacher's explanations. Instead, they should actively respond to teachers. Therefore, in the information era, classroom teaching breaks through the Triangle Model, or the theory of teacher-student-textbook structure. On balance, classroom teaching transfers from person (teacher) -to-person (student) system to person (student) -to-interaction system. In other words, the former system is characterized by three centers: classroom, teacher, and textbook. In the former system, students are merely knowledge containers rather than spontaneous learners of knowledge. In the latter system, students, as the subject of learning, directly act on the interactive learning environment. That is to say, it is an interactive learning environment where students actively participate and show their personalities. Teachers play a role to create the interactive learning environment, covering learning issues. This environment contains teacher-based interpersonal learning and material learning,[26] which is the basic meaning of transformation from indoctrination-oriented teaching to dialogue-oriented teaching.

Perceiving the essence of classroom teaching from the perspective of teaching philosophy, we can find that classroom teaching is ultimately a place for personality development. Education is not a simple process of acquiring knowledge but the development or cultivation of personality. This development is entitled to further enriching the meaning of education and providing guidance for subsequent practice relying on experience reconstruction. In this situation, knowledge, a by-product of the inquiry process, can be seen as the product of intellectual reflection. The fundamental purpose of development is to reconstruct high-quality and substantial experience. As to reconstruction of experience, perceptual experience is of great significance because thinking is the interaction between people and the environment. When confronting specific situations, students are required to observe, listen, perceive, communicate, and cooperate, helping them obtain open experience from open disciplines, open classrooms and open schools that are connected with real social life. This openness is a kind of spiritual liberation and cultural reconstruction. In the context of curriculum innovation, the core of classroom teaching reform

---

26 Zhong Qiquan 钟启泉, Cui Yunhuo 崔允漷, & Zhang Hua 张华, eds., Weile Zhonghua minzu de fuxing, weile meiwei xuesheng de fazhan—Jichu jiaoyu kecheng gaige gangyao (shixing) jiedu 为了中华民族的复兴，为了每位学生的发展—基础教育课程改革纲要（试行）解读 [*For the rejuvenation of the Chinese nation, for the development of each student-Interpretation of the basic education curriculum reform outline (Experimental)*]. Shanghai: East China Normal University Press, 2001, 215–216.

CONCEPTUAL RECONSTRUCTIONS

is to transform students' individualistic learning into community learning because school is not a place to ration knowledge. Instead, school's primary task is to develop students. Knowledge should be acquired by students themselves rather than given by teachers. In order to promote students' development, teachers should guide them not to impart but to explore the existing truth.[27] "School's public mission is to cultivate each student into an independent, active and cooperative learner and to construct a cultural community which is synthesized by knowledge in and out of school education."[28]

It is not at all surprising that any reform, including the reform of the basic education curriculum, would inevitably encounter constraints and resistance from old concepts and old systems. Indeed, we confront with the severe task in both theoretical construction and academic style construction. Over the past few years, many organizations and frontline teachers have actively involved in curriculum innovation under the leadership of the Ministry of Education's Basic Education Department and Teacher Education Department. Those teachers, education researchers, young and competent with Ph.D.s in education are from more than a dozen research centers of basic education curriculum including Peking University, Nanjing University, Zhejiang University. With the principle of global vision, local action, they are committed to reconstruct a series of curriculum teaching concepts, and effectively participate in Chinese basic education curriculum reform. They have continuously gained practical experiences. In three years, they reconstructed a series of concepts on education and teaching in China. For example, the concept of curriculum in China's education sector has shifted from static plan to dynamic experience. Accordingly, teachers have been renewing their ides in four phases: presetting → generating → presetting and generating → presetting for generating. Obviously, this curriculum concept has far surpassed the presetting theory also known as theory of treasure box of knowledge which hammers existing knowledge into students' brains. Thus, China's curriculum innovation is advancing step by step: (1) from the Outline of Reform to Curriculum Standards; (2) from Curriculum Standards to Multi-version Textbooks in primary and secondary schools; (3) from Multi-version Textbooks to the implementation of the new curriculum. This innovation is not only welcomed by education circles in China and out of China, but also highly praised by international curriculum academia. In the past few years, the transformation of curriculum teaching began in theory and

---

27   Zhong Qiquan 钟启泉, Xiandai kechenglun (xinban) 现代课程论（新版）[*Modern Curriculum Theory (New Edition)*]. Shanghai Educational Publishing House, 2003, 452–535.

28   Manabu Sato. *The joy of learning-towards dialogue*. Yokohama: Shizhi Study, 1999, 59–68, 155–156.

moved to practice, a step in the right direction for Chinese basic education curriculum reform.

We may come to the conclusions: (1) The way out of China's basic education lies in its transformation from elitist to mass provision. In other words, it should be transformed from test-oriented to quality-oriented education. This is not only a common pursuit of the world's teaching reform, but also an inevitable result of Chinese education reform in accordance with practical experience. (2) China's scientific education research needs to eliminate old habits and seek for knowledge from the outside world, which means confronting the reality, advancing with the times, staying close to reform and academic frontiers, keeping up with international standards and practice. For China's education, especially in curriculum teaching, this is the right way to prosperity. (3) Both the curriculum reform outline or its interpretation should focus on the urgently needed talents in the new era when upgrading knowledge is the indispensable topic. It is believed that China's curriculum innovation put an end to the era of Kairov's pedagogy.

The prerequisite for curriculum innovation is the concept reconstruction, which needs a united organization to promote dialogues among different academic genre.[29] After all, we need to constantly challenge ourselves, renew ourselves, and surpass ourselves. "For us, the core of the previous course must be like a soul which is ferried to another shore and never comes back. Since the old has gone, we need a new one now."[30]

References

David Bohm. *On Dialogue*, trans. Wang Songtao 王松涛. Beijing: Educational Science Publishing House, 2004.

Kenneth A. Bruffee. Collaborative Learning and the conversation of mankind. *College English*, 1984, November, 635–652.

William Doll & Noel Gough. *Curriculum Vision*, trans. Zhang Wenjun 张文军. Beijing: Educational Science Publishing House, 2004.

Paul Freire. *Pedagogy of the Oppressed*, trans. Gu Jianxin 顾建新, Zhao Youhua 赵友华, & He Shurong 何曙荣. Shanghai: East China Normal University Press, 2001.

Jun Yoshimoto. *Modern Teaching Research Events*. Tokyo: Meiji Books, 1987, 55–57.

---

29 William Pinar, *Understanding Curriculum*, trans. Zhang Hua 张华. Beijing: Educational Science Publishing House, 2003, 875.

30 William Doll & Noel Gough, *Curriculum Vision*, trans. Zhang Wenjun 张文军. Beijing: Educational Science Publishing House, 2004, 31.

Manabu Sato. *Curriculum and Teachers*, trans. Zhong Qiquan 钟启泉. Beijing: Educational Science Publishing House, 2003.

Masao Sato. *Principles of Teaching*, trans. Zhong Qiquan 钟启泉. Beijing: Educational Science Publishing House, 2001.

Manabu Sato. *The Joy of Learning-towards Dialogue*. Yokohama: Shizhi Study, 1999.

William Pinar. *Understanding Curriculum*, trans. Zhang Hua 张华. Beijing: Educational Science Publishing House, 2003, 875.

Michael Polanyi. *The Tacit Dimension*. London: The University of Chicago Press, 1966.

Saeki. *Learning Community*. Tokyo: Tokyo University Publishing House, 1999, 92–93.

Tanaka Konji. *Theory and Method of New Education Evaluation*. Tokyo: Japan Standard Corporation, 2002.

Wang Cesan 王策三. Renzhen duidai "qingshi zhishi" jiaoyu sicao—Zai ping you "yingshi jiaoyu" xiang suzhi jiaoyu zhuangui tifa de taolun 认真对待"轻视知识"的教育思潮——再评由"应试教育"向素质教育转轨提法的讨论 [Treating the educational tendency of despising knowledge seriously—A revisit to the discussion about the proposal on the transition from exam-oriented education to quality Education]. *Peking University Education Review*, 2004, (3), 48–57.

Saeki Yuta. *The meaning of "learning."* Tokyo: Iwami Bookstore, 1995.

Tsukuba University Educational Research Association. *Foundation of Modern Education*, trans. Zhong Qiquan 钟启泉. Shanghai: Shanghai Educational Publishing House, 2003.

Yuan Xiaoming 袁小明. Huhuan jiaoyu zhidu de chuangxi 呼唤教育制度的创新 [*Calling for the innovation of the educational system*]. *Wenhui Daily*, 2004, August 24, 9.

Zhang Hua 张华. Kecheng yu jiaoxue lun 课程与教学论 [*Curriculum and Teaching Theory*]. Shanghai: Shanghai Educational Publishing House, 2001.

Zhong Qiquan 钟启泉. Xiandai kechenglun 现代课程论 [*The Study of Modern Curriculum*]. Shanghai: Shanghai Educational Publishing House, 1989.

Zhong Qiquan 钟启泉. Xiandai kechenglun (xinban) 现代课程论（新版）[*Modern Curriculum Theory (New Edition)*]. Shanghai Educational Publishing House, 2003.

Zhong Qiquan 钟启泉, Cui Yunhuo 崔允漷, & Zhang Hua 张华, eds. Weile Zhonghua minzu de fuxing, weile meiwei xuesheng de fazhan——Jichu jiaoyu kecheng gaige gangyao (shixing) jiedu 为了中华民族的复兴，为了每位学生的发展——基础教育课程改革纲要（试行）解读 [*For the rejuvenation of the Chinese nation, for the development of each student-Interpretation of the basic education curriculum reform outline (Experimental)*]. Shanghai: East China Normal University Press, 2001.

CHAPTER 3

The KAP Theory

Knowledge & Skills, Affective Attitude & Values, Processes & Methods (KAP), which was initiated in China's compulsory education curriculum in 2001, is a manifestation of progress in educational ideology. Ever since the inception of China's New Curriculum Reform ten years ago, there has been continual debates over the definition of KAP which indicates that some people are still adhering to Kairov's pedagogy and reject the new enlightenment in education. Under this discourse, China cannot make progress in the research on primary and secondary education, nor in the practice of subject teaching. As a matter of fact, the recognition of KAP has closely bonded with the reconstruction of modern subject pedagogy. This chapter aims to clarify the definition of KAP and its philosophy, and to cast some light on the framework of KAP Chain teaching design and its core tasks.

1 Definition and Significance of KAP

1.1 *Defining KAP*

1.1.1 Connotations of KAP

KAP is used to describe elementary learning ability. The first dimension includes the basic knowledge and skills human beings rely on for survival. The second dimension, affective attitudes and values, includes not only processes referring to the responsive learning environment and interaction, but also methods referring to the basic ways of learning and ways of life. The third dimension, processes and methods, includes affective attitudes and values[1]

---

1 People make value judgment of what is right or wrong and good or bad about things around them, which varies from person to person. However, everyone has their own inclination or paradigm known as "concept of value", or "consciousness of value". It is rather an operational concept than a substantive concept. The goal of education, in a sense, is to form personal concept of value. In school, moral and life education directly contribute to value formation. Besides, classroom teaching is directly or indirectly related to the formation of value. It should be said that classroom teaching is to answer all kinds of questions that children raise to teachers about textbooks. It is where their value entanglements and value judgments are triggered. From the perspective of sociology and psychology, a number of approaches concerning the interpretation of value are developed, such as behavior observation, participation observation, diary and letter analysis, content analysis of newspapers, magazines

© KONINKLIJKE BRILL NV, LEIDEN, 2022 | DOI:10.1163/9789004473300_004

THE KAP THEORY 39

referring to the interest in learning, attitude towards learning and life and the integration of personal value and social value. We should neither break away from process & methods, affective attitude & values in acquiring knowledge & skills in classroom teaching, nor should we discuss the development of processes & methods, affective attitudes & values without knowledge and skills. KAP's three dimensions are integrated and an inseparable whole. Those who oppose KAP think that it is the way to "weaken" knowledge and therefore a way to "despise or disdain" knowledge. Nevertheless, this is a typical expression of metaphysical thinking, for KAP is precisely the theory based on the definition of modern subjects that fully respects and treasures knowledge.

1.1.2 Metaphor of KAP

In order to accurately illustrate KAP, we would like to borrow Japanese scholar Kajita Eiichi's "four-layer iceberg model"[2] in the context of solid learning ability (elementary learning ability) to illustrate the metaphor of KAP. The theory suggests that an iceberg shows only a small portion of itself, leaving about ninety percent of its mass beneath the sea's surface. Similarly in KAP, the tip of its iceberg is the explicit learning ability which is characterized by knowledge and skills and understanding and memory while below the sea's surface lies the implicit learning ability—thinking and problem solving interest and motivation and experiencing and sensing. Elementary learning ability is the combination of explicit learning ability and implicit learning ability, which are mutually complementary, interdependent and inseparable as a whole. In order to carry out solid teaching that aims to better help students achieve elementary learning ability, it is necessary to fully grasp the two pathways that form elementary learning ability: (1) the bottom up formation pathway—a development pathway that starts from experiencing and sensing knowledge and skills and understanding and memory to "thinking and problem solving interest and motivation and experiencing and sensing; (2) top-down formation pathway—from knowledge and skills and understanding and memory thinking and problem solving and interest and motivation and experiencing and sensing. Eiichi Kajita emphasizes that these two top-bottom cycling developing patterns are crucial for cultivating comprehensive elementary learning ability.

---

and journals. Okuda Shinjou, *Chronological Events of Modern School Education*, Tokyo: Tokyo Administrative Publishing Company, 1983, 420.

2   Eiichi Kjita, *The Transformation of Views on Learning Ability and Value*. Tokyo: Kanekoshobo, 1994, 86.

40 CHAPTER 3

1.2 *Significance of Defining* KAP

KAP transcends the traditional theory of "Two Basics" and manifests a brand new view on learning ability. Borrowed directly from the former Soviet Union, the "theory of two-basics" was once criticized by the Russian *Teacher's Gazette* as running counter to Marxism because it denies the role of subjective initiative and it is a specimen of technological advancement. Education, a purposeful and planned activity, is practiced under the guidance of teaching goals by adhering to educational plans. Therefore, it is natural that teaching, as the basic form of educational practice, aims to fulfil educational goals and the principle of education is to cultivate personality. But the traditional theory of "Two-basics" equates training with education. Therefore, it is necessary to distinguish between cultivating students and improving scores. In this context, teaching practice, infused with the affects and attitudes is different from robotic learning and animal training because of its focus on society and values. In view of the pitfalls of test-oriented education, Japan's new edition of *Guiding Essentials of Learning* redefines the concept of elementary learning ability, which highlights the connotations of solid learning ability, as follows: (1) the development of language competence as the foundation of all learning, (2) the cultivation of mathematical ability in accordance with first-class international standard, (3) the inheritance of Japanese traditional culture accumulated throughout history, (4) the introduction of diversified experiences that modern Japanese children lack, including the experience of nature, welfare and labor, and (5) the implementation of English learning from primary school to be in line with the development of internationalization of education. In addition, solid learning ability is supported by moral forces like introspective ability and the sense of norms, and by a rich mind with qualities like artistic sense.[3] While learning does not take place without memorization and training, an overemphasis on training, or even equating training with education, is not acceptable. Some people take the Chinese saying for granted that "One will naturally have a clear understanding of a book after reading it one hundred times." In fact, to some extent obliterates the dialectic truth a Confucius saying, "learning without thinking is labor lost while thinking without learning is perilous." We cannot but say that this is a one-sided biased view.

As a solution of or a reaction against traditional view on subjects, KAP embodies the intrinsic value of the modern conception of subjects. A subject should be set in compliance with its educational goals and under the condition that it will expand and deepen the students' knowledge. A well-established subject

---

3 Human Education Research Council. *New Guidelines for Learning—Ideas and Subjects of Curriculum Reform.* Tokyo: Kanekoshobo, 2008, 10.

THE KAP THEORY 41

should never be composed of simple fragmented contents and segmented knowledge. Its structure must be logical. A subject needs to organize its teaching contents in order to manifest the system of knowledge and values according to the stages of student's physical and mental development and the reality of their ability development. Hence, each subject consists of three elements: (1) knowledge (system of basic knowledge and concepts constituting subjects), (2) methods (thinking mode and behavior patterns behind the system of basic knowledge and concepts of subjects) and (3) values (affects, attitudes and values behind the modes of thinking and patterns of behavior). In other words, KAP contains the construction of theoretical concepts, the teaching practice of knowledge, affects and will, which are linked to the seeking of truth, kindness and beauty, and the strategic educational plan for exploring the future and the unknown world. This kind of education mode that displays knowledge and value system in such a logical form is what we call subjects. Thus, KAP is not imposing something to subject teaching from outside subjects, but the cognitive value, social value and ethical value embedded in subjects themselves. If you take the Japanese new curriculum reform as an example, the *Guiding Essentials of Learning* attaches great importance to cultivating language competence which is regarded as the most basic topic to cultivate solid learning ability. This is not just reflected by an increase in the hours of instruction delivered in the Japanese language, but it also initiated a reform outline for teaching by (1) clarifying its attitude to give more stress on language education; (2) fostering students' interest in the Japanese language and a respectful attitude towards it; (3) mastering the basic language competence essential for further study of other subjects; and (4) cultivating the students' attitude of appreciating, inheriting and developing Japanese language and culture.[4]

KAP also serves as the antidote to counter-effect the poison of test-oriented education and serves as a real reflection of the dialogue between teaching and learning and essence of talent cultivation. Subject teaching, after all, is a process of learning in such forms as "dialogues" and "self-cultivation." The form of dialogue mentioned here refers to the act of exploring the unknown world and its meaning through interpersonal communication while self-cultivation refers to the act of self-perfection.[5] Philosophical epistemology defines the term knowledge the result of human cognition, which is passed down as human cultural heritage that has been tested by generations of systematic and rational thinking and preserved in the form of signs. This ontological view on

---

4   Ibid, 11.
5   Manabu Sato, *Pleasure of Learning—Toward Dialogic Practice*, trans. Zhong Qiquan 钟启泉. Beijing: Educational Science Publishing House, 2004, 10–11.

knowledge unveils the universal nature of human knowledge as a whole and provides us with universal value of outlook and methodology. Nevertheless, an indiscriminate copy of this ontological view on knowledge will render a teacher unable to identify the process of knowledge construction and reproduction of his/her students. Videlicet, the definition of knowledge in philosophical epistemology cannot completely replace the epistemology study in cognitive psychology and course teaching methodology. C. E. Silberman once said "The society is not static in that it needs education, not just training,"[6] because "Education is the cultivation of human souls, not the conglomeration of knowledge and recognition".[7] And "Training is an activity of isolated minds, while education is the harmonization of human spirit, the inheritance of culture".[8] There are some Chinese scholars who blindly emphasize the objectivist epistemology and applaud for the theory of treasure box of knowledge, which regards knowledge as an objective existence and universal truth for students. So learning is but a process of obtaining the ready-made knowledge from the treasure box. This theory preaches that course is knowledge and training is knowledge. The teaching only aiming at knowledge fragments is a kind of supercilious education, that ignores students' subjective initiative, violates the principle of education and development, and is, therefore, incompatible with the quality-oriented education. The practice of KAP indicates the downfall of test-oriented education. That is why KAP has been encountering resistance since the inception of the China's New Curriculum Reform.

2 Knowledge Philosophy of KAP

2.1 *KAP Manifests the Appeal for Human Science*
Educational research cannot be carried out without an overall understanding of human science. But what is human science? In brief, it is the study of human beings. To be more specific, it is the study of human phenomena which contain two dimensions: (1) a transparent dimension that manifests the superficial biological structure of human beings and (2) an opaque dimension that is the underlying psychological property of human beings. Researches that concern the opaque human property are generally known as soft science, which includes case studies in hermeneutics and field research on cultural

---

6 Charles E. Silberman, *Crisis in the Classroom*, trans. Tadashi Yamamoto. Tokyo: Saimaru Shup-pankai, 1973, 225.

7 Karl Jaspers, *What Is Education*, trans. Zou Jin 邹进. Beijing: SDX Joint Publishing, 1991, 4.

8 Ibid, 2.

anthropology. Hence, human science is a convergence of two fields, the transparency of the hard science and opaqueness of the soft science. Science is generally viewed as an objective activity, whereas soft science, often times deriving conclusion through subjective approaches is believed to be in disparity or inconsistent with the objective world. The reason behind this thinking is because, generally speaking, the more subjective an interpretation or explanation is, the farther away it is from the objective world. Therefore, case studies based on hermeneutics are often criticized by hard science for its lack of objectivity. Yet in anthropology, it is impossible to accept all these criticisms unconditionally. We cannot fail to see the trees for the forest and neither can we fail to see humanity for science.[9] Likewise, educational research on education not only requires the linear studies of hard sciences, but also the nonlinear study of soft sciences. KAP is a globally accepted curriculum. The theory of "behavior objectives" advocated by R. M. Tyler and B. S. Bloom, and the coordination theory of "behavior objectives, problem-solving objectives and expressive objectives" proposed by E. W. Eisner,[10] clearly indicate universal acceptance of the "soft objectives" and "hard objectives" (or "open objectives" and "closed objectives") in the international forum of education.[11]

2.2   *KAP Is Based on the New Philosophy of Knowledge*

Knowledge is not purely objective, but rather is constructed subjectively. Objectivist epistemology holds that the world is objective and structural, and its structure can be perceived and known. Therefore, there must be reliable knowledge about the objective world. Knowledge can exist objectively independent from human beings, and can only be obtained passively through lectures. Different from objectivist epistemology, constructivism believes that even though the world is objective, the perception and meaning imposed on it exist in the human mind. It is human beings who create reality, or at least, interpret reality in accordance with their own experience. It also believes that learning is a process of constructing internal psychological representation. Accordingly, teaching is not for teachers to transport knowledge from the outside world into a student's memory, but rather, it is an activity that enables the students to construct new knowledge by engaging them in interaction with

---

9   Takeo Saijo, *What is Constructivism?—Principles of Human science in the New Era.* Kyoto: Kitaojishobo, 2005, 7.

10   Elliot W. Eisner, *The Educational Imagination: On the Design and Evaluation of School Programs*, trans. Li Yanbing 李雁冰. Beijing: Educational Science Publishing House, 2008, 113–130.

11   Saburo Sato & Hiroo Inaba, *School and Curriculum.* Tokyo: Daiichihoki, 1984, 154–164.

the outside world in accordance to their own experience. This type of construction is not a direct reaction stimulated by the outside world, but a result of the student actively processing new information with the help of an existing cognitive structure. In other words, knowledge is a result of the student's "active construction" rather than something being hammered into their brains. These two views on knowledge result in two fundamentally different teaching modes: (1) cram teaching which is characterized by the dominance of teachers, and (2) constructive teaching which respects a student's initiative.

The constructivist view on knowledge is a philosophy of knowledge evolved from cognitivism. However, constructivism as a whole is undergoing a transition from individual constructivism to social constructivism. That is to say, its effect is now radiating from the individual personal domain to the social cultural domain. As a representative of individual constructivism, J. Piaget's cognitive development theories argues that human beings are capable of constructing knowledge actively. Most of the constructivists in the past are classified into this category. They placed individuals at the central position. From the perspective of individual constructivism, "I think, therefore I am" is the defining doctrine.

As the agent of cognitive structure, individual learners change and construct the cognitive structure (knowledge structure) by actively interacting with the environment. The change and construction are actually learning and development. It can be seen as constructivism based on cognitive structure. In addition, these qualitative changes of cognitive structure appear in development stages. The view of knowledge in the eyes of social constructivists can be expressed as "we think; therefore we are." Human knowledge exists widely in social and cultural environment and is "constructed socially" through interpersonal communication and exchanges. The first representative theory is the exchange theory of K. J. Gergen, a social psychologist, who once said that "we communicate; therefore we are." In a modern society dominated by the internet, it would be difficult to survive if we were constrained in our own individual knowledge isolated from the outside world. Therefore Gergen proposes that we "construct necessary knowledge in a social manner through mutual cooperation." The second representative theory is Vygotsky's developmental psychology theory, in which he proposed that human beings acquire knowledge through learning and experience, and then apply it in cognition and problem solving.

3   KAP Manifests the Law of Mental Development

The law of the development of higher mental functions, which was proposed by Vygotsky in 1931, covers the following points: (1) children acquire historical and sociocultural knowledge through group and social activities with adults,

THE KAP THEORY   45

especially teachers; (2) this knowledge acquisition is an internalized process. As a form of cultural heritage, knowledge can be understood and commanded only when children autonomously incorporate it in their own knowledge system, structuring it and applying it properly to solve problems or to communicate in new situations. A student can truly understand knowledge and form scientific concepts only when he/she finds consistency between facts and concepts being conveyed to or observed by him/her. "Scientific concepts do not come spontaneously, but generated consciously in the relationships between universal concepts established in the course of school education".[12] Once fully structuralized, new knowledge will be acquired and commanded with ease. As more knowledge is accumulated, it becomes easier for students to acquire and internalize new knowledge via its connection with the learners' existing knowledge. Curiosity would arise when new information is not in line with the student's existing knowledge system. It is necessary to spark students' curiosity in order to motivate them by giving them hints about information and ideas different from their existing knowledge. Promoting students' interest, motivation and attitude are prerequisite for knowledge acquisition and understanding.

Now we must guard against two extremes: Firstly, we must guard against knowledge cramming because students accumulate knowledge through interaction with the outside world. Knowledge is useless unless it is obtained in active interaction with other forms of knowledge, with knowledge restructuring and in problems solving. Comprehension is impossible if knowledge is crammed and the existing knowledge system and experience of students are ignored. Secondly, we must guard against the experiential teaching which disregards the construction of conceptual knowledge, because it fails to realize knowledge structuring. Therefore, the central issues for education are: how to activate students' hands-on experience; how to ensure they grasp concepts that cannot be naturally acquired through experiencing.

4 Framework and Task of KAP Chain Teaching Design

4.1 Teaching Goals as Hypotheses

Teaching goals refer to the hypotheses teachers make for teaching practice. As a fact, teachers can play the guiding role in teaching procedures, they have the ability to identify the potential direction of practical development, and can continue to promote that direction. While the effects of teaching practice

---

12   Kazuo Nakamura, *Psychology of Vygotsky*. Tokyo: New Reading Press, 2004, 31–32.

can be hypothesized, it cannot be predicted. In this sense, a teaching goal is merely a hypothesis, and it should be discussed and amended in practice, in order to function as a leading role in practice. It is through these discussions and amendments that teaching goals materialize. Without the materialization of teaching goals through the dynamic process of practice, the realization of a child's potential is merely empty rhetoric. If teachers are satisfied with a cut-and-dry teaching goal, they will find their professional development impossible, as following a goal blindly is not practice in its real sense. Here, practice means to put hypotheses and facts into the same context for consideration. The relationship between hypotheses and facts should be treated as the catalyst for mutual reference, amendment and development (i.e. a process or a procedure). Therefore, as soon as the goal is set, the process or procedure is determined and the revision of the goal starts occurs simultaneously. During the interaction of the goal and the process or procedure, once the goal is amended, it will function as it is meant to, that is, to guide the process or procedure in the desired direction. In fact, the teaching goal determines the process or procedure while the process or procedure in turn determines the value of the goals. The materialization of teaching goals is realized in the process or procedure of practice. Thus, when we say the materialization of teaching goals cannot be separated from the process or procedure, we mean that once the goals are materialized, teaching contents and methods will also materialize simultaneously. It is worth noting that the materialization of goals is endless, and so is their realization.

4.2   *Framework of the KAP Chain Teaching Design*

KAP implementation depends on teachers' insight. As there are more than one teaching goal, when teaching goal A is a "chain of teaching goals", the study of which cannot be divorced from research on teaching method, we will need to set up a couple of subordinate goals and sub-subordinate goals. The sophisticated system formed by interconnected goals is called theatricals and children's physical and psychological development. KAP in the context of China's New Curriculum bears a close resemblances to the cognitive goal, behavioral goal and experience goal acknowledged in the international education. In order to bring it into effect, however, teachers need to understand KAP as a whole and carry it out in the chain of curriculum goal—subject goal—unit goal—class goal.

Since the end of the 1970s, Japanese education experts began implementing KAP chain teaching design, they cover two dimensions—the hierarchy of goals and the domain of goals in order to construct a framework of analyzing

THE KAP THEORY

teaching goals (See Table 1).[13] They worked from more general hierarchies (the columns) to more specific ones, starting with ISubject·Domain the domain a cognitive goal (conceptual structure), working progressively downwards to IIUnit·Theme with the domain B behavioral goal (ability for problem-solving) and then to IIIClass·Segment with the domain C experience goal (emotion, will and attitude). These domains are represented in the form of rows in the table. Even the same cognitive goal will have a different hierarchy in I-A and III-A. Or, as is demonstrated in II-A, II-B and II-C, the goal of a unit and theme (small unit) requires not only the understanding of its cognitive goal like concepts and rules, but also the domain goal like the intention and research ability. In the analysis of teaching goal, teachers must take into account these nine "cells" (due to the fact that III-A is often included in II-C and in lower grade II-B is often merged with III B, there are less than nine categories or cells.) Meanwhile, emphasis should be placed on the interconnection among the three hierarchies and three domains, rather than solely on II-B or III-A.

TABLE 1   The hierarchies and domains of analyzing teaching goals

Hierarchies/Domains	A Cognitive goal	B Behavioral goal	C Experience goal
I Subject·Domain			
II Unit·Theme			
III Class·Segment			

SOURCE: MANABU SATO, *PLEASURE OF LEARNING — TOWARD DIALOGIC PRACTICE*, TRANS. ZHONG, QIQUAN 钟启泉. BEIJING: EDUCATIONAL SCIENCE PUBLISHING HOUSE, 2004, 116.

In the framework of teaching design of KAP chain, it is of great importance not to regard goals as something static. It is essential to understand the complex relationship between goals and processes. Since teaching practice is a dynamic flow, KAP can only be conducted according to the specific situation of the flow, rather than mechanically making one-to-one correspondence based on class hours. The "flow" here refers to the description of the process structure of teaching practice. It comes from the interactions of teacher and student behaviors.[14]

---

13   Mizukoshi Toshiyuki, *Views and Methods on Teaching Reform*. Tokyo: Mejitosho, 1979, 35.

14   The external part of this flow is reflected in the passage of time and the internal part is implied in the self-consistency with the passage of time. From the perspective of behavior, H. Meyer sums up the following behaviors of teachers and students which have appeared

4.3   *Core Tasks in Advancing KAP Chain Teaching Design*

The framework of KAP teaching design helps to disregard the restrictions of the traditional design, which is based on the instruction of knowledge points and thus contributes to the transformation of primary and secondary school education from merely training to a new height of human learning, which is the initial intention of promoting quality-oriented education. Classroom teaching reforms must start with the reform of teaching design and the implementation of KAP teaching design. The reform's core task is the shift from teacher-centeredness to student-centeredness. This shift can be further elaborated in the following three shifts:

1. The shift from a teaching plan design to a learning plan design[15] in order to unify teaching and learning. Teaching focused designs would easily

---

throughout the history of teaching methods around the world: (1) from partial to whole, or vice versa; (2) from simple to complex, or vice versa; (3) from known to unknown, or vice versa; (4) from explicit and clear to implicit, vague, contradictory and specious, or vice versa; (5) from abstract to specific, or vice versa; (6) from inductive to deductive, or from deductive to inductive; (7) developing in cycle or in spiral. That is, the setting of a subject can aim at higher and higher at the right time; (8) starting from teachers' guidance and ending with a student's keen participation of corresponding activities, or starting from spontaneous activities of students and ending with the realization of a teacher's predicted results; (9) starting from organizing specific activities to gradually leading students to internalize knowledge, or vice versa; (10) from teachers' and students' perceptual and emotional knowledge about the subject to rational and conceptual understanding of the subject, or vice versa. H. Meyer, *Chronological Events of Modern School Education*, trans. and ed. Harata Nobuyuki, Kitao jishobo, 2004, 114–115.

15   Japanese teachers focus on the design and implementation of a student's learning plan and place students at the central position. Throughout the teaching process, students are asked to think individually, think as a group and think as a class. Through repeated reading, thinking and discussion, students are led to achieve the goal expected by teachers. Chinese teachers, on the other hand, focus on the design and implementation of their teaching plan, which is teacher-centered and aims at bringing students into the study pattern pre-arranged according to the teacher's logic. As a result, Japanese classes end up with the viewpoints from students' discussion while Chinese classes end up with the viewpoints pre-arranged by teachers. A Ph.D. candidate under my supervision once conducted a "comparative study of Chinese and Japanese classroom teaching" in which he recorded what a Japanese teacher said after he watched the video of a Chinese classroom teaching: "It seems that the classroom instruction is too fast to follow. It may be good for 10–20% of the students, however, chances are that the rest of the students may be losers." He added, "It seems that Chinese classrooms are dictated by a force of control." "It was similar in Japan about thirty years ago. But nowadays it is not the teacher who pushes the class ahead. Students are the driving force to create teaching." Undoubtedly, different classroom cultures in different countries have their own strengths and weaknesses. China is no exception. I do not believe Japanese teachers are better qualified than Chinese teachers in general but I have to admit that in their teaching concepts they put

degenerate to the authority domination pattern where students are trained as passive receivers of knowledge rather than the new innovative pattern where free dialogues, self-cultivation and interactions are employed.

2. The shift from explicit learning ability to implicit learning ability in order to unify explicit and implicit goals. From the perspective of learning ability theories, the essential difference between test-oriented education and quality-oriented education lies in that the former lays biased emphasis on explicit learning ability and ignores implicit learning ability. The learning ability developed in test-oriented education lacks real vigor.

3. The shift from individual learning to collective thinking in order to unify individual and group development. Though the development of individual cognitive ability is of great significance, without collective thinking there will be no sound development for individual cognition.

What should be stressed here is that we must not confuse the concept of shift of emphasis with that of binary opposition, because the former actually serves to resolve the following relational oppositions in teaching designs: (1) the artistic property in teaching vs. technical property in teaching, (2) teaching materials on life-focused subjects vs. teaching materials on academic-focused subjects, (3) syllabus-oriented aspect in teaching goals vs. thinking-oriented aspect in teaching goals, (4) knowledge-oriented aspect in teaching goals vs. experience-oriented aspect in teaching goals, (5) teachers' control in teaching vs. children's autonomy in teaching, (6) focus on collective class teaching (universality) vs. focus on individual teaching (diversity), (7) intrapersonal focus in teaching vs. interpersonal focus in teaching, etc.

The process of teaching creativity consists of three phases, namely, (1) planning (or designing), (2) implementation (or practicing), and (3) evaluation (or reflection). However, in the teaching research of behavioral sciences, teaching creativity is regarded as a linear process of the three phases: planning, achieving and evaluating, in which planning is stressed and geared to evaluation of the teaching goals. However, the qualitative research method that arose after behaviorism follows a different approach by turning its focus onto

---

the children in a prominent place. According to the findings of the Ph.D. candidate, the role of Japanese teachers is to create a free learning atmosphere for students, predict the needs of students, lead students to think, and facilitate students' activities. They regard students as independent individuals with adequate cognitive and thinking capacity, and with different emotional experiences, ethical standards and codes of conduct. Therefore, in the eyes of these teachers, students should be fully respected. Even though students are imperfect and oftentimes immature, their imperfection and immaturity are due their experiences. Learning and growing, however, belong to themselves.

the research of the teaching process and its experience.[16] In this sense, teaching is conceived of as a process designed and developed by teachers, open for rectification in classroom activities. And in this process teachers create more meaningful experiences by reflecting on the issues from complex classroom events. The planning implementation and reflection in teaching are no longer a process of sequential stages, but a circulating procession. In addition, reflection ability becomes the core competence of expert teachers.

Constructivism holds that "I think, therefore I am," while social constructivism holds that "we think, therefore we are". Children's learning and the teacher's teaching designs should be in accordance with these sayings. Through thinking as "I" and thinking as "we", teachers can facilitate their ability of teaching reflection. This is the position of an innovative educator.

References

Eiichi Kjita. *The Transformation of Views on Learning Ability and Value*. Tokyo: Kanekoshobo, 1994.

Elliot W. Eisner. *The Educational Imagination: On the Design and Evaluation of School Programs*, trans. Li Yanbing 李雁冰. Beijing: Educational Science Publishing House, 2008.

Human Education Research Council. *New Guidelines for Learning — Ideas and Subjects of Curriculum Reform*. Tokyo: Kanekoshobo, 2008.

Karl Jaspers. *What Is Education*, trans. Zou Jin 邹进. Beijing, China: SDX Joint Publishing, 1991.

Kazuo Nakamura. *Psychology of Vygotsky*. Tokyo: New Reading Press, 2004.

Manabu Sato. *Pleasure of Learning—Toward Dialogic Practice*, trans. Zhong Qiquan 钟启泉. Beijing: Educational Science Publishing House, 2004.

Manabu Sato. *Education Methodology*. Tokyo: Sayusha, 2010.

Mizukoshi Toshiyuki. *Views and Methods on Teaching Reform*. Tokyo: Mejitosho, 1979.

Saburo Sato & Hiroo Inaba. *School and Curriculum*. Tokyo: Daiichihoki, 1984.

Charles E. Silberman. *Crisis in the Classroom*, trans. Tadashi Yamamoto. Tokyo: Saimaru Shuppankai, 1973.

Takeo Saijo. *What Is Constructivism?—Principles of Human science in the New Era*. Kyoto: Kitaojishobo, 2005.

---

16   Manabu Sato, *Education Methodology*. Tokyo: Sayusha, 2010, 116.

CHAPTER 4

On Integrated Practice Activity Course (IPAC): Contents, Characteristics, Values and Potential Misconceptions

The *Compendium of Curriculum Reform for Elementary Education* (*Trial*) (hereafter, referred to as *Compendium*) by the Ministry of Education clearly stipulates that activities associated with the integrated curriculum of practice must be included in compulsory classes in primary and secondary schools and cover information technology education, inquiry-based learning, community service, social practice, career, and technical education.[1] This is a prominent feature in *Compendium*. As a compulsory, cross-disciplinary course in the curriculum, what are the characteristics and values of IPAC? What are the implementing conditions and its potential misconceptions? This paper aims to deepen the understanding of IPAC and probe into the aforementioned issues.

1 Defining IPAC: A Model for Curriculum Development

IPAC, in short, can be defined as a model of curriculum development, which breaks the fixed structure of the traditional system of teaching: subjects, classroom activities and evaluation. IPAC is a course design or generation model that enables students to master the diversified knowledge, abilities and attitude necessary for the realistic and future world by putting them in real-life (or even virtual learning) environments. By means of this design, China's elementary education curriculum will not only cover subject curriculum, integrated subject curriculum (i.e. Life-oriented Moral Education, Society-oriented Moral Education, History and Society), but also multidisciplinary integrated practice activity courses, in order to achieve the simultaneous development of subjects

---

1 Zhong Qiquan 钟启泉, Cui Yunhuo 崔允漷, & Zhang Hua 张华, eds., Weile Zhonghua minzu de fuxing, weile meiwei xuesheng de fazhan—Jichu jiaoyu kecheng gaige gangyao (shixing) jiedu 为了中华民族的复兴，为了每位学生的发展—基础教育课程改革纲要（试行）解读 [*For the rejuvenation of the Chinese nation, for the development of each student-Interpretation of the basic education curriculum reform outline (Experimental)*]. Shanghai: East China Normal University Press, 2001, 21.

© KONINKLIJKE BRILL NV, LEIDEN, 2022 | DOI: 10.1163/9789004473300_005

and their integration.[2] The implementation of IPAC will bring a dramatic change to China's elementary teaching and learning.

1.1 IPAC and the Traditional Subject-Separation System are Motivated by Two Different Theories of Curriculum Development[3]

In the evolution of curriculum's definition from the systemic organization of teaching contents, proposed by H. Spencer, to the emphasis on life experience inherent in the postmodern definition, we can understand curriculum as not only containing school subjects, but also, within in the organization of these subjects, it ensures the construction of the relationship between human and knowledge and the social relationship among human beings, which constitutes the social background of education.

Manabu Sato, a professor at Tokyo University, distinguishes two models for curriculum development from the perspective of the relationship between teaching content and students.[4] The first model is the Tyler is going up stair model. In this model, each unit is separated into targets, targeted actions, and assessments. First the target is set and then effective actions are taken to realize the target during teaching; finally, assessments (i.e. test) are taken to ensure the target is being achieved. This model works well in conveying knowledge and skills, but its disadvantages are obvious, too. Students in this model are limited to narrow and similar experiences, and there is no difference in their assessments. For the sake of efficiency and benefits, this model divides study into several small steps, in order to reach the final goal. Its features are reflected in the current subject-separation teaching system: students make step-by-step progress in a one-way and linear process, and once they fail in one step they run the risk of not reaching the final goal. The Tyler model is a typical example of this teaching system, because of its clear specification of four componential parts: objective, choice, organization, and evaluation. Similarly, the "small-step principle" in "Programmed Learning" by B. F. Skinner, and the "formative evaluation" and "mastery learning" by J. S. Bloom belong to the step-by-step curriculum development. This model is compared to a factory assembly line, and such a comparison is coherent with historical facts.

The scientific movement in education, which was popular during the last half of the 1910s to the 1920s, was characterized by F. Bobbitt and W. W. Charters' "scientific curriculum design." These designs recognized teaching and

---

2 Ibid.
3 Manabu Sato, *Reforming Teaching and Changing School—From Integrated Learning to Curriculum Creation*. Tokyo: Shogakukan, 2000, 135.
4 Manabu Sato, *Pleasure of Learning—Toward Dialogic Practice*. Yokohama: Seorishobo, 1999, 177–183.

ON INTEGRATED PRACTICE ACTIVITY COURSE (IPAC)

learning as an assembly line where schools, teachers and students are regarded as factories, workers and raw materials, respectively. In this context, students are turned into products after going through the assembly line. The Tyler model functions well in respect to the uniform or unified treatment of course goals and teaching processes, as well as the realization of each student's individual accomplishments. However, to unify student academic achievements into the same grades is to place them in one series or the same mode. Just as Bloom's theory of mastery learning replaced the concept of student difference in competence with a corresponding concept of the difference in time, the individual differences in the Tyler model is no more than a time difference in their acquisition of knowledge.

The second model is "mountain climbing" pattern, which takes a major subject as a mountain and offers students several learning methods as climbing paths. Different from the structure of the "objective-choice-organization-evaluation" model, it follows the process of "subject - exploration (experiencing) - communication" by first pre-designing a subject, then engaging students in various exploration activities, and finally activating students to communicate and share information and learning outcomes with each other. This model of curriculum development not only takes the learning results into consideration, but also stresses the diversification and personality within the course design. In Tyler's model, the ultimate pursuit of learning lies in "result" (arriving at the destination), while in the "mountain climbing" model, in addition to the destination as its ultimate goal, the value of learning lies more in the experiences and pleasure obtained from "climbing up the mountain." In the "mountain-climbing" model, students can freely choose their individual learning method and speed. They can broaden their horizons while "climbing up the mountain" and reflect after climbing. In addition, dangers such as the failures in Tyler's model will not occur, as long as students avoid climbing paths that are too tough for them to handle. This unit-based curriculum is designed in accordance with the children-centered doctrine applied in Dewey's School, the prototype of the "mountain climbing" model. The following are some typical slogans, which have been used to advocate for this system in developed countries: "theme learning," "program learning," "problem-solving learning," "authentic learning," "service learning," "experiential learning," and "performance learning."

1.2 Two Models of Curriculum Development Based on Two Different Views of Learning

The Tyler model, which is based on the premise of individualism and individual competence in the psychology of learning, considers learning as an acquisition of response and knowledge and linear accumulations of personal knowledge, while ignoring mutual learning within a social network. The more delicate and organized the processes, the goal, the contents and the activities are, the more it reinforces the individualism and serialization of learning results. In China, the exam-oriented education system is still the mainstream, so when information technology is applied to teaching, it only results in the consolidation of the exam-oriented education stronghold. Perhaps, that is the reason for the current situation confronting China's education system: claiming quality-oriented education, while reinforcing exam-oriented education from the point of technology. By contrast, the view of learning in the "Mountain climbing" model conforms with constructivism, which is the basis of John Dewey's "Experience Theory" and L. S. Vygotsky's "Activity Theory." Different from "Behaviorist learning," which is modeled on the basis of animal experimentation by J. B. Waston and E. L. Thorndike, Dewey's empiricist learning advocates students' active interaction with the environment, and proposes the notion of "inquiry-based learning" based on "reflective thinking." Therefore, this kind of learning not only involves the acquisition of cognitive experience from the interaction between students and their environments, but also that of social experiences from their social networks. In this context, the curriculum emphasizes the "meaningful experience." In his Constructive Theory, in which the concept of "activity" constitutes the core, L. S. Vygotsky maintains that learning should not be constrained in knowledge alone, but should also be a mental construction by means of internalization. His term, "learning through activity," refers to the socialization or social mediating activity through the usage of "tools," such as language, logic, signs and concepts as its media. The most phenomenal feature of the view of learning in the "mountain climbing" model lies in its breaking of the binary opposition in the traditional conception of learning: concrete vs. abstract, experience vs. knowledge, emotions vs. rationality, and practice vs. theory. The "mountain climbing" model stresses the dialogue between learners and the objective environment, teachers and other learners, and with learners themselves. In this way, learners acquire and master knowledge by relying on those three "interactive practices": understanding the world (cognitive practice), building social network (social practice), self-improving (ethical practice).[5] This view of learning puts forward three research tasks or projects for teachers to realize the transformation of classroom activities—to employ "activity learning" as a means to ensure interaction between "knowledge, people and events," to employ "co-operative learning" as a means to ensure communication with other learners, and to employ "reflective learning" as a means to ensure sharing knowledge and skills acquisition

---

5   Ibid, 59.

ON INTEGRATED PRACTICE ACTIVITY COURSE (IPAC)

by abandoning feeding knowledge into learners. At present, some primary and secondary schools in China, according to the *Compendium*, have begun implementing the curriculum of integrated practice activity, which guides learners to explore the natural world, focus on the society, and apperceive self-development from the perspective of nature, the society and the learner himself. This is the typical case of tridimensional education.

2 Value of IPAC: Integration of Wisdom and Integration of Knowledge

2.1 *As a Brand New Model in Curriculum Development, IPAC Is Geared to a Contemporary Model of Knowledge Production*

British philosopher M. Gibbons (1997) holds that knowledge production (academic research) has two modes in terms of its relation with social reality. Mode I: modern (1840–1949) knowledge production is intra-disciplinary, linear, hierarchical, rigid and narrowly contained in one discipline; Mode II: contemporary (1949-) knowledge production is inter-disciplinary, non-linear, netlike, communicative and flexible. To some extent, the subject-separation system and IPAC are specific examples of the two modes in China's education system.

The traditional subject-separation system is the result of Mode I, which was established during the development of the public education system in the 19th century. During the first phase, there were only subjects like reading, writing, arithmetic, and moral education (religion) in modern European schools. In later years, the development of science created new subject systems in physics, chemistry, biology, history, geography and a series of artistic subjects in music, painting, and physical education (i.e. gymnastics and housekeeping). The construction of these new subjects were the result of scientific achievements in their corresponding fields and the formation of their own logical structures.

However, there are weaknesses and deficiencies in the traditional subject-separation system:

1. Scientific and social development and the increasing number of subjects added to the curriculum has resulted in an overload of learning tasks for students, and mutually unrelated subjects make the integration of knowledge difficult.

2. The principle of prioritizing logical or analytical subjects over other subjects brings no benefit to student learning. Thus, there is a disconnection between knowledge in the textbook and from life experience.

3. The evaluation places an overwhelming amount of stress on knowledge, understanding and skills, while ignoring potential learning factors, such

56   CHAPTER 4

as interests, motivations, logical thinking, critical judgments, idea presentation and problem solving.

4. A disproportionate distribution of learning focuses on traditional academic achievements and tends to derail from more practical subjects such as information, global issues and the environment, all in which are becoming prominent in contemporary studies. As a result, this leads to the phenomenon of course arrangements that are "hard, complicated, biased, and outdated."

The traditional subject-separation system is built on the premise of scientific knowledge in modern Europe (Mode I) with the idea of "Essential Reductionism"[6]: decomposing the world into minor elements before the comprehensive illustration. In other words, modern science prefers the sub-classification of natural, social and cultural phenomena and encourages the acquisition of objective knowledge through experiments and observations of definite objects. Similarly, it is the case with the learning of subjects that aim to interpret and explain knowledge, which is produced by scientism, concerning various phenomena. Proponents believe that the whole is equal to the sum total of its componential parts (elements), and any action of human beings or everything in the world can be explained and manipulated once people grasp the whole of the componential knowledge (in fact fragmentary knowledge). However, the paradigm shift in thinking, recognition and value from the 1960s to the 1980s motivated criticisms of scientism: the whole is not simply equal to the sum of its parts, and the whole is irreducible: the decomposed parts reorganized or reconstructed would not become the same whole as it was. The counter "essential reductionism" advocates the learner's perceptual development through observation and experiment in science learning. It also enhances both sense and sensibility about the self and the world by interacting with the natural world, the society and the culture. The notion of scientific quality cultivation contains the essence of IPAC.

The foundation of modern Europe's scientism is dualism, which separates material and spirit, viewing them to be independent, unrelated and often opposed to each other. According to Plato, the universe contains "the perceptual world" or "the visible world" and "the rational world" or "the intelligible world." "The perceptual world," namely the world perceived by our senses, is not the true world; it is a changing, unpredictable world, or it is one thing today, and something else tomorrow. The "the rational world," on the other hand is actually a conceptual world comprised of abstract ideas from concrete

---

6   Association of Subject Education in Japan, *Developing New Curriculum*. Tokyo: Kyouikushuppan, 2001, 11–12.

materials. Plato over-emphasized the objectivity of the intelligible world to be the only genuine and eternal world and negates the reality of the perceptual world and regards it as a derivative of intelligible world. Plato's ideas dominated the western philosophy until F. Nietzsche proposed differing ideas at the beginning of 20th century. F. Nietzsche ideas were later debunked by M. Heidegger, a German philosopher, who focused on the visible physical world and believed it to be the only genuine world, as human understanding and knowledge of the world is acquired through our experiences with the physical realistic world, rather than a result of mental abstraction. By centering on "the theory of ideas," Plato established "rationalism," while Heidegger constructed "existentialism" whose central concern was the problem of "being." Plato's rationalism has profoundly affected the history of western philosophy and the traditional subject-separation system, as well. According to the traditional belief, only derivative qualities deserve scientific enquiry and scientific methods (hypothesis, experiments, observations by senses, recording and the quantification of the experimental results) are encouraged to discover the rationality of the research objects. This tradition also separates conceptual and perceptual knowledge in accordance with dualism by partially observing abilities in direct connection with conceptual knowledge.[7] That is to say, only conceptual forms of knowledge, such as intellectual power, rationality, conception and reasoning (scientific wisdom), are believed to be of universal, objective and logical value or significance. In contrast, perceptual forms of knowledge, such as perception, representation, intuition, and emotion (artistic wisdom), are believed to be individual or personal, subjective and illogical. The perceptual competence ought to be discarded, because it is a distraction of the pursuit of conceptual knowledge. Following this observation, curriculum development in elementary education should pay more attention to such subjects, such as language and science, which are closely related to intellectuality, rationality, conception and reasoning. Subjects concerning sensibility, representation, intuition and emotion, which cultivate artistic performance and cognition, are considered to be futile in developing conceptual knowledge. Therefore, artistic subjects are marginalized.

In the elite education system, the majority of students are confronted with fierce competition and live in the horrid shadow of classroom instruction, curriculum and school. In fact, the subject-separation curriculum transforms education into a monotonic, scary and self-abusing process and deprives learners of confidence, which, in turn, results in mediocrity, deformation, or

---

7   Ibid, 13.

even impaired personality. Toyoda Hisakame, a Japanese professor, indicates that in the history of the development of public education, teaching that treats students as real human beings has never been easily achieved. Rather, public education tends to impede the development of humanism and suffocate the students.

Teacher domination still widely existed in the 19th century, although ferules, beatings and other physical punishments were not openly practiced. Even today, teaching suffocation remains eerily similar to the 19th century. Nowadays, it is common to see students bustling in the grueling 'suffocation' and even at the sacrifice of their life."[8] The Wholeness Education Ally, a non-government organization which has been active globally since the 1990s, calls for a return to children's nature, arguing that "without sound and healthy human nature, there would be no healthy society and economy."[9] Based on wholeness and monism, IPAC advocates for the integration of rationalism and existentialism, emphasizing the harmonious development of morality, intelligence, body and knowledge, emotion, volition.

Built upon Mode II, IPAC is a contemporary concept of knowledge production and a mode of curriculum production designed on the basis of multidisciplinary problem-solving. It aims to satisfy the need for talent cultivation in the new century- knowledge builders (knowledge creators) who are independent, cooperative, humane and adaptive to the changing times. The new curriculum production model will definitely act as a detonator, a stimulant or a catalyst to shake the very foundation of the subject-separation curriculum.[10]

2.2 *IPAC: "Not Just a Formal Structural Change in Curriculum Development, but a Profound Substantial Innovation of Curriculum Values"*[11]

IPAC primarily pursues the integration of scientific wisdom and artistic wisdom. Against the notion of the dualism of capability, IPAC appeals to

---

8   Tadao Sato, *Teaching Principles*, trans. Zhong Qiquan 钟启泉. Beijing: Educational Science Publishing House, 2001, 2.

9   Whole-Person Education Alliance, *Whole-Person Education Principles*. Tokyo: Hakujusha, 1995, 93–113.

10   Zhong Qiquan 钟启泉, *Xueke jiaoxuelun jichu* 学科教学论基础 [*Basis of Disciplinary Teaching*]. Shanghai: East China Normal University Press, 2001, 209.

11   Zhang Hua 张华, Zonghe shijian huodong kecheng de benzhi 综合实践活动课程的本质 [On The Nature of Integrated Curriculum of Practical Activity], in Zhong Qiquan 钟启泉, Cui Yunhuo 崔允漷, & Zhang Hua 张华, eds. Weile Zhonghua minzu de fuxing, weile meiwei xuesheng de fazhan—Jichu jiaoyu kecheng gaige gangyao (shixing) jiedu 为了中华民族的复兴，为了每位学生的发展—基础教育课程改革纲要

understanding anew the significance of artistic wisdom, in direct relation to art activities: the two wisdoms should not be separated but integrated as a whole. In other words, the learner's ability in the rational cognition (scientific wisdom) and perceptive cognition (artistic wisdom) dimensions are inseparable and interactive, as well.[12] Human cognitive and expressive abilities develop only when artistic and scientific wisdoms impose influence upon each other. The difference between rational and emotional recognitions lie in that symbols in rational recognition stand at the center of scientific thought, while materials, such as sound, color and body movements, dominate the way of artistic thinking. In addition, scientific conclusions, as a result of rational recognition, are a significant asset for further cognition. In contrast, artistic wisdom, as represented by emotional recognition, may not be significant in drawing conclusions for artistic expressions, but significant for the perceptual cognition of art as a whole. However, in scientific or artistic activities and in creative activities where knowledge and experience interrelate, transform and disintegrate to generate new knowledge, the artistic wisdom like perception, representation, intuition and emotion plays a pivotal role. Fortunately, IPAC enables students to realize the value of the immediate experience: an integrated art and lifelong physical education, which is neglected in their interactions with nature, the society and culture (the outside world). In this way, learners are enthusiastic about practice. They raise questions, design creative tasks, and apply knowledge, emotion, and volition when solving problems. In this way, they develop in various aspects, such as rationality, sensibility and technical skills, to fulfill the integration of scientific wisdom and artistic wisdom.

Secondly, IPAC seeks for the integration of academic knowledge and life experience. The four ingredients of IPAC: information technology education, research-oriented learning, community service and social practice, and labor and technology education- demonstrate to the students an extensive virtual world and connect them with reality. In essence, learning is no more than a process of experience reconstruction—direct and immediate experience, indirect and mediate experience, and the outcomes of learning in the broader sense.[13] IPAC aims to develop learners in two stages: immediate-experience

---

（试行）解读 [*For the rejuvenation of the Chinese nation, for the development of each student-Interpretation of the basic education curriculum reform outline (Experimental)*]. Shanghai: East China Normal University Press, 2001, 72.

12   John Dewey, *Democracy and Education: An Introduction to the Philosophy of Education*, trans. Wang Chengxu 王承绪. Beijing: People's Education Press, 1990, 82.

13   Takuro Iwane, *My Theory of Education—Trinity Education of Truth, Kindness and Beauty*, trans. He Jian 何鉴. Nanjing: Nanjing University Press, 1999, 49–93.

stage and problem-solving stage. At the immediate experience stage, learners are in direct contact with nature, society and culture, and take actions and command things by using their perceptual senses. As immediate experience is perceptual, easily commendable and conveniently demonstratable by formal representations, it is a comprehensive experience that can be developed anywhere and at any time. Ultimately, IPAC aims to strengthen problem-solving learning ability—solving real-life problems, in order to form networks of learning activities. IPAC takes advantage of the knowledge and experience that learners have acquired from their previous immediate experience and subject-separation learning. Then, learners are motivated to conduct investigations and experimentations to solve problems that they find interesting in the first stage of the immediate experience, and ultimately acquire problem-solving competence. Exploring and discovering the laws, rules and logic of the experience and recording them through words or symbols constitute the problem-solving process of scientific research, while revealing eternal experiences, such as emotions and moods, which are beyond the use of words or symbols, by using sounds, colors and body movements, which constitutes the problem-solving process of artistic expressions. The knowledge and experience previously acquired from real-life situations and the subject-separation learning is activated and reconstructed with fresh during the problem-solving process and, at the same time, the simple and first-hand life experience raise the profile of the learner's rational and emotional recognition.

The integration of wisdom and knowledge required by IPAC should meet the following preconditions: Firstly, teaching should be problem solving oriented. In other words, learners should engage themselves in problem-solving activities. However, the problems involved should not simply come from *Teachers' Reference Books* or *Exercise Books,* which are compiled to categorize points of knowledge and problems in accordance with the corresponding teaching units in the textbooks. Small, isolated fragments of knowledge do not result in knowledge integration. It is in the process of solving comprehensive problems like environment protection that the integration of knowledge across disciplines and beyond textbook units can be achieved. Secondly, teaching should target life-oriented problems. If learners are unaware of the realistic nature of the problems, they will most likely to fail to exert significant efforts into the problem-solving process. Hence, the real purpose of IPAC lies in breaking away from Mode I, which is rigid, formalized and isolated classroom teaching and learning, and restoring learning to what it should be- active and combined with rationality and passion. It is true that comprehensive problems that are connected with authentic life do not always lead to the final and ideal solution, for there is usually more than one correct solution to a comprehensive problem. In fact, whether or not the problem is clearly solved is not important, a concept which is completely different from the questions in *Teachers' Reference Books and Exercise Books,* in which the answers are important simply because the questions and answers are particularly designed for learners to acquire knowledge and skills. What IPAC pursues is not an exact answer to questions or a solution to problems, but rather the learners' experience during the course of problem-solving, which promotes a broader view of the world from global, historical and cultural perspectives in order to achieve knowledge integration during problem-solving process. Thirdly, teaching should build up a network of cooperative learning. In order to realize this goal, it is necessary to organize activities to facilitate learners to solve problems of common interest in a cooperative way. Learners are encouraged to communicate with and learn from each other, obtaining inspiration, and thus forming a network of cooperative learning. Without such a network, learning becomes mechanical and loses its vitality. Just as the human body grows by way of metabolism, the human mind matures by obtaining, digesting, and absorbing updated knowledge in a learning network, particularly the cooperative learning network.

2.3 Systematic Research on the Modern Knowledge Production Model Provides the Theoretical Basis for the Simultaneous Development of the Separation and Integration of Subjects

Based on a deep analysis of two modes of knowledge production, Gibbons negates Mode I and asserts that Mode II will eventually replace Mode I in the future. However, the significance of Mode I cannot be negated completely, as we cannot simply separate these two modes. Therefore, some foreign scholars have proposed Mode III,[14] which explores problems by using Mode II, analyzes and theorizes these problems by using Mode I, and then returns to Mode II. Thus, we can formulate an infinite cycle of knowledge production (II → I → II...). In other words, we need to construct a knowledge production system composed of Mode I, II and III, which provides the theoretical basis for the simultaneous development of the separation of subjects and their integration proposed in the *Compendium*. Multidisciplinary IPAC is bound to facilitate curriculum integration in curriculum development. It is not only a way that embraces the separation and integration of subjects, but also a way of learning that incorporates scientific wisdom with artistic wisdom and book knowledge with real-life knowledge.

---

14   UNESCO headquarters Chinese Language Division 联合国教科文总部中文科 trans., Learning: The Treasure Within. Beijing: Educational Science Publishing House, 1997, 79–88.

3 Implementation of IPAC: Strengths and Misconceptions

As Chinese essential education is based on the subject-separation system, IPAC does not have a solid foundation in China's primary and secondary schools. Fortunately, its distinctive strengths are becoming increasingly prominent, since its implementation as a relatively independent curriculum. First of all, IPAC has opened up new horizons to cultivate living skills for learners. Knowledge-oriented education is not sufficient to support people living in the modern society of information, globalization and high technology, unless it is paired with developing living skills. Learners are taught to equip themselves with such qualities, as exploring and discovering problems, making judgments, taking actions and solving problems, no matter how dramatically the society changes, and practicing self-discipline, caring for others, enables a strong ability to adapt to social reforms. It is not an exaggeration to say that IPAC is designed for living skills cultivation. Secondly, IPAC supplies learners with a platform for learning how to learn. Research-oriented learning, the foundation of all learning activities, is now being treated as a means or an approach, which penetrates the practical activities of IPAC and even subject-separation learning as an exploration method. IPAC is also an exercise for the cultivation of the mind, intelligence, curiosity, innovation and encouragement for self-challenge. It contributes to independence and a sense of responsibility and self-efficacy. It also cultivates verbal communication and team spirit. Thirdly, IPAC injects fresh energy into the new teacher-student relationship, in which teachers are not the single source of knowledge, but partners in constructing knowledge.

Unfortunately, because of the deep-rooted, dominance of subject-separation education and the intangible shackles of exam-oriented education, educators have misconceptions regarding the implementation of IPAC, especially in regards to practicing research-oriented learning, which should be guarded against.

First of all, there is a blind emphasis on utilitarianism and elitism. The charm of research-oriented learning lies in its exploration and its research focus on realistic subjects. However, some schools, especially in key high schools, consciously or unconsciously confuse the notion of exploration with research as a professional term for the sake of reputation and quick profits. Some media organizations have aggravated and intensified this already complicated situation by claiming that the exploration learning implemented in kindergartens is an act like cultivating postgraduates in universities. Certain teaching and research institutes show intense interest in the fastidious differentiation of exploration-oriented learning and research-oriented learning in order to overstate the aim and purpose of research-oriented learning. Consequently, research subjects selected by some schools are detached from the learner's real-life interests and tend to pursue "highly sophisticated scientific subjects," which fail to spark the child's interests and do not take realistic meanings into consideration. They compete with each other in inviting academics and scientists as their consultants, showing that they are committed to those scientific subjects. This is unnecessary, because it is like putting the cart before the horse, and marginalizes the importance of students in learning. This is has become one of the major pitfalls of elite education.

Secondly, there is an unbalanced emphasis on either theoretical knowledge, or practical skills. Research-oriented learning does not design a new set of subjects, but rather an activity that cuts across disciplinary boundaries and encourages learners to self-determine learning subjects and content. For a long time, curriculum has been mistakenly equated with subjects and textbooks. The result has been research-oriented learning textbooks that show no genuine differences from the traditional subject-separation textbooks. In addition, some schools mistake IPAC as a subject, which results in either subject-separation teaching, or in the dissection of the overall target of IPAC into separate individual subject targets, thus depriving learners of free choice and their central position in learning.

Thirdly, there is an unguided emphasis on activities and experiences. Autonomous learning, featured by autonomous planning and autonomous problem solving, is not the kind of learning that school authorities are supposed to organize. Schools are places where each individual learner should realize cooperative learning with the help of teachers and classmates. Therefore, teachers should never evade their responsibilities in recommending learning topics and expanding learning content under the excuse of respecting learners' autonomy and subjectivity. Unfortunately, some teachers disregard this responsibility—believing that subject learning is acquisition of systematic knowledge and research-oriented learning is the accumulation of life experiences. Greater still, some educators are even unable to tell the difference between quality-enhancement education and anti-perceptionism. They are content with singing and dancing in the name of reform and call these activities and experiences.

The root of these three aforementioned misconceptions lies in the long-held subject-centered tradition in education. In the context of a school culture dominated by exam-oriented education, China's elementary education has long attached importance to the subject-separation model and shown preference for receptive learning. This is true even with quite a number of the best high schools in China where more than 95% of the students can go to their expected universities. There is nothing wrong with respecting subjects and their status within the curriculum, but an absolute and exclusive focus on subjects does not work, because it severs the interdisciplinary connection between courses. The tendency of "subject first" is fully demonstrated whenever there is a new curriculum reform- people argue against each other about the status of different courses and class-hour allocation, which demonstrates the narrow-minded self-centeredness of teachers, who neither have no sense of disciplinary groups, nor that of overall curriculum development.[15] This is a stumbling block in implementing IPAC.

The implementation of IPAC facilitates reconstructing the concept of subjects and curricula, and reforming curricula and teaching among front-line teachers. Thus, it is of much significance to have the right interpretation of the differences between subject curriculum and IPAC, and to understand their respective values. People tend to distinguish them as being either knowledge-centered, or experience-centered. They believe that the former is founded on the basis of knowledge (skills) learning and the latter is founded on the basis of experience learning. These understandings are both inadequate. In essence, both of them design courses and curricula for learners' subject learning in accordance with their own knowledge or experience. Otherwise, neither of them is real learning, as knowledge isolated from experience is nothing but flat information, and experience without acquiring knowledge is no more than experience itself. Therefore, the difference between the two curricula lies in the combination of knowledge and experience in the formation of the teaching unit.[16]

Subject curriculum arranges its knowledge and experience by focusing on content or topics, while IPAC focuses on themes or issues related to real life. From the perspective of curriculum development, the subject-separation system and IPAC represent two different modes and independent curriculum structures. However, they are not separate, but mutually reinforcing in the context of the overall curricular framework. In their implementation, they may clash with each other in terms of teaching content. In order to resolve this, educators must employ out of the box thinking and identify their complementary aspects. We argue that educators can organize IPAC activities involving themes that might be irrelevant to, or overlapping with subject curriculum. We

---

15   Zhong Qiquan 钟启泉, Xueke jiaoxuelun jichu 学科教学论基础 [*Basis of Disciplinary Teaching*]. Shanghai: East China Normal University Press, 2001, 206.

16   Manabu Sato, *Reforming Teaching and Changing School—From Integrated Learning to Curriculum Creation*. Tokyo: Shogakukan, 2000, 135.

believe that IPAC activities are valuable, as long as learners and teachers show interest in the themes, even if they overlap with those in subject curriculum. As long as China's elementary education curriculum fulfills the general format of the simultaneous development of subject-separation and integration, we have taken a serious step forward in enabling learners to integrate textbook knowledge with life experience and scientific wisdom with artistic wisdom, thus accelerating the unique characteristic enhancement of school curricula. We will ultimately realize our ideals of a quality-oriented education curricular development.

References

Association of Subject Education in Japan. *Developing New Curriculum*. Tokyo: Kyouikushuppan, 2001.

John Dewey. *Democracy and Education: An Introduction to the Philosophy of Education*, trans. Wang Chengxu 王承绪. Beijing: People's Education Press, 1990.

Michael Gibbons, *Creation of Modern Society and Modern Knowledge—Discussing Theory of Modes*. Tokyo: Maruzen Kabushikikaisha, 1997.

Manabu Sato. *Pleasure of Learning—Toward Dialogic Practice*. Yokohama: Seorishobo, 1999.

Manabu Sato. *Reforming Teaching and Changing School—From Integrated Learning to Curriculum Creation*. Tokyo: Shogakukan, 2000.

Tadao Sato. *Teaching Principles*, trans. Zhong Qiquan 钟启泉. Beijing: Educational Science Publishing House, 2001.

Takuro Iwane. *My Theory of Education—Trinity Education of Truth, Kindness and Beauty*, trans. He Jian 何鉴. Nanjing: Nanjing University Press.

UNESCO headquarters Chinese Language Division 联合国教科文总部中文科 trans. *Learning: The Treasure Within*. Beijing: Educational Science Publishing House, 1997.

Whole-Person Education Alliance. *Whole-Person Education Principles*. Tokyo: Hakujusha, 1995.

Zhang Hua 张华. Zonghe shijian huodong kecheng de benzhi 综合实践活动课程的本质 [On The Nature of Integrated Curriculum of Practical Activity]. In Zhong Qiquan 钟启泉, Cui Yunhuo 崔允漷, & Zhang Hua 张华, eds., Weile Zhonghua minzu de fuxing, weile meiwei xuesheng de fazhan—Jichu jiaoyu kecheng gaige gangyao (shixing) jiedu 为了中华民族的复兴，为了每位学生的发展—基础教育课程改革纲要（试行）解读 [*For the rejuvenation of the Chinese nation, for the development of each student-Interpretation of the basic education curriculum reform outline (Experimental)*]. Shanghai: East China Normal University Press, 2001.

Zhong Qiquan 钟启泉. Xueke jiaoxuelun jichu 学科教学论基础 [*Basis of Disciplinary Teaching*]. Shanghai: East China Normal University Press, 2001.

Zhong Qiquan 钟启泉, Cui Yunhuo 崔允漷, & Zhang Hua 张华, eds. Weile Zhonghua minzu de fuxing, weile meiwei xuesheng de fazhan—Jichu jiaoyu kecheng gaige gangyao (shixing) jiedu 为了中华民族的复兴，为了每位学生的发展—基础教育课程改革纲要（试行）解读 [*For the rejuvenation of the Chinese nation, for the development of each student-Interpretation of the basic education curriculum reform outline (Experimental)*]. Shanghai: East China Normal University Press, 2001.

CHAPTER 5

Dialogues and Texts: The Transformation of Teaching Norms

If we take a realistic view of teaching, we can say that the fundamental feature of teaching lies in communicative practice. Teaching cannot exist without practices of interpersonal communication. Therefore, illustrating the essence of teaching and probing into the significance and projects of the transformation of teaching norms, from the perspective of communication theories, are conducive not only to a further understanding of the guiding principles of teaching, but also to the transformation and innovation of the front-line teacher's classroom practices.

1   Teaching: Activities of Communication and Cooperation

Anyone calling for education and teaching progress is fully aware that the journey from test-oriented education to quality-oriented education is never smooth. As far as classroom teaching innovation is concerned, the most difficult point begins with the innovation of teaching concepts. Hence, this chapter attempts to give a theoretical account of teaching norms from the perspective of communication and language.

It is generally acknowledged that "there is no teaching without communication."[1] Teaching cannot proceed without communication or social interaction. Teaching is an intensive, high density and multivalent communication activity, in which various types of multi-level and multi-dimensional communicative relationships are formed. Similar to other social interactions, teaching and learning in classroom situations are interconnected in a network of objective conditions and subjective factors. Generally speaking, the basic concern in the theoretical discussion of teaching and learning is the relationship between teaching and learning; in fact, all teaching theories can be reduced to the relationship between teaching and learning, which is a special type of social relationship. In addition, regardless of the form teaching activities may take, they are involved in the fundamental relationship between teaching and learning.

---

1   Yuriko Kinoshita, *Study on Teaching Communication and Teaching Language.* Tokyo: Kazamashobo, 1996, 316.

© KONINKLIJKE BRILL NV, LEIDEN, 2022 | DOI: 10.1163/9789004473300_006

From this perspective, teaching and learning are a pair of relational concepts. Learning is an integral part of teaching, which in turn, is an integral part of learning. The relationship between them is demonstrated as a behavioral relationship, or a social interactive relation between educators and learners under certain objective circumstances. Therefore, teaching and learning in classroom situations is a special social phenomenon of communication and cooperation. The study of this phenomenon is the starting point for the theoretical discussion of teaching practices.

Teaching and learning form a person-to-person relationship that is not only between teacher-student and student-student at the personal level, but also between teachers-students and students-students at the collective level. Classroom activities are conducted among these complicated networks of relationships. Therefore, the various types of relationships amongst teacher and students in communication create complicated relationships of roles. In this network of relationships and roles, teachers and students are collective subjects who occupy their own respective subjective positions. In traditional teaching theories, teaching and learning are generally regarded as a recognition process, stressing the peculiarities of the recognition process. Therefore, in many situations, practical classroom instruction cannot perform well, because of restrictions in the traditional theory, in which knowledge is regarded as a medium. However, in the theory of life-long learning, the transmitting function of knowledge is marginalized, expelled from its previous central position, and replaced by functions of information as the medium of communication, and evaluation functions of critical thinking, judgment and knowledge exchange as indices of assessment. Thus, in the new functional teaching theory, teaching is primarily regarded as the social process in which educators and students, in the face of a tremendous amount of information, not only focus on information analysis, processing and integration, but also the synthesis of classroom teaching and out-of-school learning, which has become the new and the most fundamental function in teaching activities.

Language serves as a medium of human communication and cooperation. Therefore, teaching is heavily influenced by language in most situations. Teaching should also be manipulated as a linguistic process (i.e. teaching is by verbal means), because teaching occurs throughout the entire process of a child's language development. On the one hand, teaching develops a child's language competence for everyday use and academic written purposes, which contributes to a child's language development. On the other hand, teaching helps children consciously use verbal forms as a cognitive and communicative tool. In addition, the teaching of all subjects is represented by language as the medium. The teaching task is to help children acquire scientifically social insights and ideas in natural and social processes, as well as knowledge, notions, values and norms. Teaching materials are mainly special texts that have been technically treated according to the principle of education. Moreover, teaching particularly reflects and develops students' cognitive and communicative styles. Teaching and language usage are mutually complementary and interdependent. From this viewpoint, "teaching of all subject is an organized social communication phenomenon, and a language teaching. There is no such thing as subject teaching without communication and language."[2] It should be pointed out that stressing the importance of medium functions of language does not negate the functions of non-linguistic media. From the perspective of the essence of language, we can probe into the social dimensions of teaching. Language, as a materialization of the distinctive nature of human beings, is an indicator of human nature and social development. In fact, as educational history shows, there are people who have indeed placed excessive stress on the role of language. For instance, there are cases in which students engage in the route memorization of words without understanding their contextual meaning, ignoring the dialectic relationships between words and thoughts, contents and forms, cognition and value. Some students can produce flowery language by parroting fluently without truly understanding the connotations of words. In the current era of information overflow, language, sometimes to some extent, counter-educates our students with clichés, nonsense and false stories, thus distorting values and poisoning the minds of the young people.

Teaching not only creates language and communication culture, but also lays the foundation for the development of learning ability and personality. Teaching can be conceived as a communication culture between theoretically competent teachers and their students and, as such, this type of culture is an interactive relationship between realistic subjectivity. As predecessors and successors respectively, educators and students possess their own language and communication cultures. As adults and representatives of the new generation, as well as individuals in the present society, they have opportunities to engage in spiritual communication to explore the world, themselves and each other. Klingberg believes that the intersubjectivity learning ability,[3] and all other qualities required by modern society, can only be developed through activities that exercise the relationship between communication and cooperation. American scholar E. L. Boyer[4] believes that the school should be a

---

2 Ibid, 3.
3 Ibid, 143.
4 Ibid, 186.

"learning commonwealth" formed by teacher and students in their interactions; the crucial mission of this commonwealth is to entitle all children to receive high-quality education. The education goal should be geared towards a child's whole-personality growth, specifically it should be designed for a child's educational, social, emotional, physical and moral demands. For this reason, the learning commonwealth should firstly create a cooperative environment where members can enjoy cooperation and attentive care. Through participation, equal dialogues, sincere communication and mutual trust, all the members can hope to develop the spirit of cooperation, stimulate moral power and courage, share experiences and knowledge, and thus achieve self-transcendence. In addition, the fundamental task of this commonwealth should develop children's oral and written language abilities, as childhood is the right time for language learning and language competence is the basis of all learning. However, the language abilities that should be developed in the commonwealth are broadly defined. It includes verbal, mathematical and artistic language. The three language systems have distinctive features, but are also closely related. Teaching must lay a foundation for each individual student to develop their learning competence and personality growth during the process of creating language and communication culture.

2 Dialogues and Texts: Conceptual Reconstruction of Teaching and Teaching Materials

Defining teaching as linguistic communication or linguistic activity is a prerequisite for the study of the essence of teaching phenomenon. This signifies that more attention should be given to the teaching of language. Just as L. Klingberg points out, "to involve all teachings with 'dialogues' in the broadest sense...no matter which teaching method dominates, the interactive dialogue is an essential identification of excellent teaching."[5] He holds the viewpoint that teaching, by its essence, is composed of various kinds of dialogues, which is the "Teaching Dialogue Principle."

The concept of "text" might be used in the process of the teaching "dialogue," namely, teaching "dialogue" is based on the whole process of "text generation, texts and text reception." Texts in teaching activities are contextual and unique. Therefore, "texts" in this context refers to teaching texts, rather than those in a general sense. Teaching texts are produced and accepted during the

---

5 L. Klingberg, *Pedagogical Application and Initiatives in Socialist School.* Berlin: VEB Dt. Vrlag der Wissenschaften, 1962, 86.

process of teaching communication, and can be regarded as a general term for texts for conversation and texts for reading and writing, dialogue texts and monologue texts.[6] Teaching texts are extremely complicated products that are co-produced by teachers and students. While research on teaching texts is still in the preliminary stage, research findings have shown that texts can contribute to the studies on function mechanism and design principles of teaching, which can produce great influence on the language for teaching. Texts that may influence language for teaching are primarily as follows:

1. Texts concerning guidelines for education reform or consulting reports;
2. Texts concerning educational policies that guide teaching directions as represented in the "Disciplinary Curriculum Standards";
3. Texts guiding teaching activities as represented in the "Reference books for teaching and learning";
4. Texts concerning scientific and cultural knowledge, which provides input for teaching contents;
5. Professional texts based on teaching theory represented by textbooks and teaching materials;
6. Audio and visual texts represented by televisions, videotapes and broadcasts;
7. Teaching design texts- communication strategies and plans represented by teaching plans;
8. Texts concerning teachers' language behaviors, such as questions prepared by teachers in teaching design;
9. Texts concerning language behaviors represented by students prepared speeches, such as assignments and survey reports;
10. Texts concerning teachers' language usage during the teaching process;
11. Texts concerning students' language usage during the teaching process;
12. Texts produced after classroom teachings, such as teaching records and student compositions.

The aforementioned texts can be classified into four types, as they relate to teaching activities—the perspectives of planning (P), demonstration (D) and assessment (A), which are illustrated as follows:

1. Ready-made texts that are not directly developed by teachers themselves, which correspond to numbers 1–6 in the list above.
2. Texts designed by teachers for teaching purposes, which correspond to number 7 in the list above. These texts are the teaching plans made by teachers according to the students' actual condition. Since there are

---

6 Yuriko Kinoshita, *Study on Teaching Communication and Teaching Language*. Tokyo: Kazamashobo, 1996, 181.

72   CHAPTER 5

some differences between the designed texts and the implemented texts, it is significant to explore the relationship between the two.

3. Texts made in the course of actual teaching correspond to those in numbers 8–11 in the list above. These texts can be further classified into two kinds: (1) the texts selected from existing documents, such as course books, resource texts, reports or exercises produced by students, or texts combined with multimedia, through which teachers impart and students acquire knowledge; (2) the various texts produced in the course of classroom teaching communication, such as blackboard-writing, instructing, dialogues, discussions, notes, abstracts or cues and directions for students participate in classroom activities. Teaching primarily relies on the first kind of texts, and improves them in the creation of the second kind of texts, in order to produce new communication products. The combination of the two kinds of texts generates teaching content. Therefore, teaching content comes from the teaching process.

4. Texts produced by teachers and students after class correspond to number 12 in the list above. In this process, texts related to the first ones are produced, such as the texts produced by teachers in their analysis of teaching practice (teaching recordings). If we use teaching languages as teaching texts, we can open up a brand-new domain to examine teaching theories. Such teaching texts are produced dynamically, and the producers and receptors of them are students and teachers, as well. However, the dynamic teaching texts are produced under the condition of specific social history, especially under the condition of the educational and teaching environment. Therefore, it is an important task to analyze the relationship between the conditions and the way in which these texts are produced and received. In terms of the mechanisms for the production and reception of the teaching texts in China, we believe that these two problems urgently require further studies.

The first issue is about the broad definition and production of teaching materials. Teaching is a complicated dynamic process, and it is structurally composed of three main factors: teachers, students and teaching materials (teaching media), which is probably the most classical model that we have used to master teaching structure since Herbart's time. In other words, teaching must contain teachers, students and the third party—teaching materials to be used by both teachers and students. Teaching without the third party is inconvincible. However, as one of the three main elements, the meaning of "teaching materials" is ambiguous. Nevertheless, the most general and broad definition of teaching materials covers all source materials and means used in teaching activities, not only including the standard textbooks, but also a variety of books, audio-visual and electric teaching materials, of which textbooks are the most representative core of teaching materials. In other words, the concept of "teaching materials" encompasses "textbooks"- the core teaching materials. There are two strategies concerning textbook reform: (1) a quantitative strategy, which seeks to simplify textbooks by cutting out the superfluous parts, and (2) a qualitative strategy, which seeks to enact a structural reform. In the past half century, each round of textbook reform in China has been confined to the quantitative strategy and taken the old disciplines and their content for granted. It was believed that "thinner textbooks" could alleviate the burden of students, as if the weight of a child's schoolbag is equivalent to the burden of their learning efforts. On the contrary, the burden of a student's learning efforts depends on his/her level of cognitive structure and learning motivation. Subjectively speaking, students with adequate cognitive potential and strong learning motivation can attain a certain goal through his/her efforts regardless of their textbook size. In contrast, students lack learning interest and lower cognitive potential will not attain a certain goal and will feel overwhelmed even if they carry only one textbook in their schoolbag. Objectively speaking, vivid textbooks with abundant resources and information are more attractive than those with dogmatic and boring content. From this perspective, textbook development requires a series of intellectual and technological preparation.

We could draw inspiration from "core knowledge" and "core knowledge courses" developed from E. D. Hirsch's concept of "cultural literacy."[7] Boyer pointed out that school authorities must define "core knowledge" before working on disciplines. The "core knowledge" refers to the universal experience of all people and the indispensable conditions that make human existence meaningful.[8] It includes the "life cycle," "use of symbols," "group member," "spatial consciousness," "aesthetic response," "mutual dependence between man and nature," "production and assumption," "noble living," etc. The eight types of "core knowledge" represent the sequential order of the journey of human life. The "life cycle" starts from birth and is followed by language (use of symbols). Then, children start to identify themselves as "group members" and acquire "spatial consciousness." Next, children "respond" toward aesthetic aspects and gradually learn where food comes from, as well as come

---

7 Gao Wen 高文, Xiandai jiaoxue de moshihua yanjiu 现代教学的模式化研究 [*Modern Instructional Model Studies*]. Jinan: Shandong Education Press, 2000, chapter 11.
8 Ernest LeRoy Boyer, "Latest Proposal for School Reform" in *The Basic School*, ed. Akio Nakajima. Tokyo: Tamagawadaigakushuppanbu, 1997, 107–131.

to understand the relations between man and nature, and learn to make and use of tools as they grow older. Children will naturally think about "the significance and purpose of life." The eight types of "core knowledge" are based on a universal human experience, and contribute to the integration of traditional disciplines, as well as help students better understand the relevance of all disciplines and enhance their awareness to relate theoretical knowledge in books with real life. Boyer posits that foundational schools should design disciplines or create domains centering on the "core knowledge," and form a set of logically consistent courses in a spiral sequence of sophistication. There are three concepts at different levels, including "cultural contents," "educational contents," and "teaching materials (text books)" in the educational processing.[9] In accordance with the mission of education, we should first select the core knowledge of educational contents from the vast expanse of cultural contents, then collect and organize data by concentrating on the core knowledge, and finally develop teaching materials (text books). For many years, China's course material reform did not pay adequate attention to the distinction among cultural contents, educational contents and teaching materials (text books) and its operational procedure.

The reform of teaching material today has already been expanded to include the development of a set of teaching media. Apart from textbooks, teaching materials should be abundant and colorful. The exploration of these teaching resources depends on front-line teachers. Textbooks for elementary education, especially those for compulsory education, are directly under the control of the Chinese government, which carries a strong sense of political and historical characteristics. These textbooks are authoritative, because they have been approved by experts and government officials. However, the development of various kinds of teaching materials lies in the professional domain of teachers.[10] The scale that differentiates teacher professionalism is how they use teaching materials (textbooks) to "teach what is in the textbooks" or to "teach by using the textbooks."[11] Teaching what is in the textbooks is the characteristic of the traditional "teach-book-smith" model, while "teaching by using the textbooks" is the characteristic of the modern education model.

The current teaching environment is undergoing tremendous transformation. The immense knowledge, supported by the Internet, is re-editing the

---

9   Shinjo Okuda, *Encyclopedia of Modern School Education*. Tokyo: Gyosei kabushikikaisha, 1993, 254–255, 348–350.
10   Hitoshi Yoshimoto, *Encyclopedia of Modern Pedagogy*. Tokyo: Meijitosho, 1987, 80.
11   Zhong Qiquan 钟启泉, Xiandai xueke jiaoyuxue lunxi 现代学科教育学论析 [*On the Modern Pedagogy of Disciplines*]. Xi'an: Shaanxi People's Education Press,1993, 185.

definition of texts to enrich their meanings and provide unlimited resources. Teaching materials are by no means equaling to knowledge points. As carriers of certain disciplines (or realms), teaching materials have two basic features. The first one is the typicality of teaching materials. Since students acquire academic knowledge from teaching materials, they must be comprehensive, stable, progressive and accurate. The second one is the concreteness of teaching materials. Since students utilize teaching materials for analysis, learning and generalization, after they have acquired some professional knowledge, they must be reliable, concrete and enable students to carry out intellectual activities. Essentially speaking, teaching materials consist of three basic properties: (1) provide facts, concepts, rules and theories, in order to construct the student's knowledge system; (2) be closely related to knowledge, in order to help students command various abilities and skills, and be familiar with the steps, working mechanisms and techniques of psychological and practical tasks; and (3) be closely combined with the knowledge and ability systems, in order to construct cognition, concepts and norms that lay foundations for world outlook, belief, political ideology and moral standard.[12] The traditional view of teaching materials strictly confines teaching materials within the framework of factual knowledge, or principle-knowledge (concepts, laws), ignoring the ability system, ways of thinking and moral principles. The new view of teaching materials highlights the knowledge of methodology and ethical knowledge, because teaching materials designed for didactical purposes around knowledge points are insufficient, fragmentary and deviate from the track of quality education.

The second issue is regarding the information-based and life-like teaching environment. Teaching is not a simple process of knowledge cramming, or knowledge transfer. As has been noted above, the real teaching process should be an inter-subjective process of learning that involves students and teachers, along with teaching environments. In the 20th century, teaching was classroom-centered, teacher-centered, and textbook-centered, which is a style of teaching that is appropriate for teachers to pass on knowledge (i.e. propagate the doctrine, impart professional knowledge and resolve doubts). With this style, teachers are able to control students and pass a ready-made book of knowledge to them. In the 21st century, the mission is to develop students' survival ability, in order to adapt themselves a dynamic and rapidly changing society, and design and organize a respondent learning environment, in which students are the subjects of learning activities. As a result, the future teaching

---

12 Yukitsugu Kato. *On Creating Learning Environment*. Tokyo: Kyouikukaihatsukenkyujo, 1997, 11–12.

model would transfer from a system of "man-to-man" to that of "man-to-environment."[13] The traditional "three-centeredness" classroom teaching system is known as "man-to-man" system, in which the first "man" refers to the teacher who orally passes on knowledge and skills to the second "man"—the students. In this system, a teacher teaches students synchronously, and is effective in passing on ready-made knowledge. However, students must respond to the teacher passively. Rather than active independent pursuers of knowledge, students are made to be no better than "receptacles." In order to help students to become active independent "pursuers" of knowledge, it is necessary to construct a new type of system, known as "man-to-respondent learning environment." In this context, "man" refers to students. Students directly interact with the environment, and solve their learning problems. In this teaching environment, students are encouraged to play active roles and respect students' individuality. In this environment, classrooms and teachers are not the sum total of the learning environment, and classroom teaching is not limited to traditional media, such as textbooks, blackboards and chalk. In addition to traditional means, the new system is supported by multimedia and the Internet. In the future, it is not difficult to predict teaching that will be supported by diversified media and human resources, in order to become an arena for students to exercise independent autonomous learning.

The logic of the teaching process is that it promotes the communication between teachers and students in a unique and realistic way (mainly through dialogue). With the gradual realization of an "information-based" teaching environment, it is increasingly important for teachers and students to engage in direct dialogues to fulfill communication. Of course, this process is not free of contradictions and complications. The "receptive texts" refers to "text understanding." The first prerequisite for understanding texts is that the receptor should be able to extract information from texts intuitively and obtain information indirectly. The second prerequisite for understanding texts is that the receptor should be able to evoke information by means of the texts from what he/she has acquired, memorized, and stored in his/her mind. The second prerequisite is a result of the receptors' attitude, prior knowledge and exploration of the texts.[14] The latter constitutes the inner knowledge structure of the receptors' brain. However, the psychology is still unclear on the working mechanism for the formation of this structure, which is complicated and

---

13 Yuriko Kinoshita, *Study on Teaching Communication and Teaching Language*. Tokyo: Kazamashobo, 1996, 127.

14 Zhong Qiquan 钟启泉, Xiandai xueke jiaoyuxue lunxi 现代学科教育学论析 [*On the Modern Pedagogy of Disciplines*]. Xi'an: Shaanxi People's Education Press, 1993, 38.

includes cognition, emotion and imagination. Therefore, the receptors' understanding of the texts is not determined by the intention of text compilers. In other words, it is not a mechanical accurate duplication of what is in the original text, but a construction of knowledge. Therefore, it is important to encourage teaching communication.

Effective teaching should not be content with indirect experience and virtual communication, because knowledge construction depends on knowledge and direct experience. The usage of language and dialogue in teaching has become popular due to three factors: (1) first, with the development of the information society, digital media has opened up new dimensions for communication, which has produced substantial changes to the world, and virtual communication is playing an increasingly more dominant role. In fact, teaching takes place in an artificial environment—people acquire human natural ability and develop their personality traits through the medium of teaching. Today, this artificial environment is more complicated, abstract, technical and increasingly artificial in nature. Second, the rapid changes of society tend to isolate teenagers from their homes and communities, which reduces their exposure to shared experiences. While their social communication decreases, their demand for dialogue increases. Third, teaching cannot fully meet all of these requirements, due to the exam-oriented education system and examinations' function as an assessment. Hence, it is critical for teaching to return to life and come close to life. In other words, teachers are required to design simulated real-life situations, draw practical experiences from students' personal lives, and conduct face-to-face dialogues with students. Thus, students will be able to acquire authentic, dynamic and vigorous knowledge and effectively cultivate their personalities.

3   Transformation of the Teaching Paradigm

In fact, the above observation covers two discussion topics: (1) the inadequacies of traditional teaching communication, and (2) the innovation of teaching communication.

The form of teaching communication is an institutionalized form. The traditional form of teaching communication is adapted to teaching as a system. It is formed and developed along with historical and social developments. Although the form of teaching communication is constantly changing and developing, the communication "model" remains stable and, some aspects of it, have evolved into a "ceremony." These forms are passed down by teachers from generation to generation. Although education is future-oriented, more often than not, it does not draw lessons from the past to predict the present and future. Rather, it tends to follow past examples. Therefore, some past experiences have been accepted without conditions, which leads to considerable problems in teaching communication.

First, lecture-centeredness, a classical classroom arrangement, aims to synchronize teaching. The arrangement with seats facing teachers is a typical example of teacher-oriented learning.

Second, the question-answer ceremony, in which the teacher asks questions, students raise their hands, then the teacher appoints students to give short answers, and finally the teachers make supplementary explanations. Then, the same cycle repeats. This is a typical example of the question-answer teaching ceremony.

Third, the teacher monopolizes communication within his/her own preset framework. In this context, teachers are unable to tolerate questions and proposals for dialogues raised by the students.

Generally speaking, problems that arise during the course of teaching, such as the authority and roles of teachers endowed by the traditional system, are connected with this style of communication. These problems within China's teaching system must be reformed. From the traditional perspective, the relationship between teaching and learning is not on an equal plane; in fact, the relationship between teachers and students is liken to that of guiders and the guided, or the action of commanding and obeying. The authority of teachers permeates this kind of relationship. In other words, in the traditional teaching model, teachers are the embodiment of authority. As an expert, the teacher forcefully instills experiences, concepts, principles, and theories into the minds of his/her students, who then memorize and recite the readily available knowledge. However, a teaching analysis shows that teaching is a kind of communication. More precisely, the relationship between teaching and learning should be the interaction in communication, and the relationship between educators and students should be that of an inter-subjective partnership. This inter-subjective interaction is carried out and achieved through the style of teaching. Students play the dual role of learners and communication participants. If this type of balanced teaching style is not implemented, the authority of teachers cannot be maintained. The majority of teachers understand that if they do not engage in dialogues and show no respect for communication partners (students), there will be no guarantee of their authority. A good teacher is a reliable and respectable professional in the eyes of his/her students. The teacher's authority is not imposed externally, but cultivated internally. That is, authority is not built on the ground of the system, but established by the teaching style of the teacher—a kind of creed for educators.

Student-centered teaching has been a slogan since the beginning of children's epoch. It represents a developmental trend in pedagogy and teaching theory. Today, people use this slogan to advocate "student-oriented teaching" and autonomous learning. But what kind of teaching conception is student-oriented teaching? It is neither a teacher-centered theory, nor a student-centered theory. Although teacher-centered and student-centered are the two propositions proposed from teaching and learning respectively, each side has its basis. However, these two propositions are two antinomies, and cannot exist together. A popular theory in Chinese education claims, teachers are leading factors and students are focal factors that endeavor to reconcile the conflict between teacher-centered theory and student-centered theory. If we want to solve problems caused by the conflict between these two propositions, we need to introduce the medium of these two propositions, namely, a third proposition. Based on the above considerations, L. Klingberg put forward the "syllogism" teaching theory, as the medium to solve the problems in these two propositions:[15]

1. Teaching is the process that occurs under the guidance of the teacher, which is the principle of the teacher guidance effects;
2. Students must be in an active and self-conscious condition during the learning process, which is the principle of students' autonomy;
3. The guiding role of teachers and students' autonomous participation in activities are two aspects of teaching. They can be held in a paradoxical relationship for teachers to conduct critical analysis and use, and such a paradox constantly arises, gets negated and arises again, which is the basic nature of teaching theory.

This syllogism contains valuable theoretical information for teaching. What is the guiding role of teachers? What is the autonomy of students? However, the fundamental problem is the relationship between them, which is precisely what has been ignored in previous teaching theories. From the view of syllogism, we can dialectically grasp the problems in teaching practice. The center of the teaching process is neither a simple concept of students, nor that of teachers. The dialectical relationship of teaching is that teachers and students are central figures in teaching or learning. Therefore, our observation must start from the relationship between teaching and learning, and the relationship between educators and learners. Teachers should give guidance to students, in order to influence students through teaching's mission and strategy, which puts students in the central position and provides a space for them to

---

15 Yuriko Kinoshita, *Study on Teaching Communication and Teaching Language*. Tokyo: Kazamashobo, 1996, 342.

be actors of learning. In other words, students should be regarded as the central factor of communication and activities. Only when the teacher places his/her students in the central position can his instruction be regarded as teaching under the guidance of the teacher. This is how teaching communication is achieved through the cooperation of the involved corresponding parties. During this process, teachers and students share their thoughts, ideas and knowledge, exchange emotions, concepts and ideas of each other, enrich the teaching content, seek for new discoveries, and ensure the mutual benefits for teachers and students.

For a long time, classroom teaching in China has consciously or unconsciously followed the ethics of "teacher's authority," which adheres to the principle of prioritizing knowledge and elitism. Classroom teaching that integrates the three educational values negates the essence of classroom teaching as communication and cooperation, deprives students of their rights as independent learners, and thus ultimately denies the real guiding role of teachers in actual teaching. China's new curriculum reform poses challenges to each teacher as he/she attempts to transform teaching norms. However, the dominant teaching design theory to date is still the rationalist theory, namely, the adoption of the model of scientific management and analysis in teaching design. At its core, this teaching theory is still prescriptive. W. E. Doll, a representative of postmodern curriculum theory, puts forward a different view. He stresses the progressive value of disorder, transition, imbalance, and gradual progress. Drawing on chaos theory, he believes that a small, seemingly unimportant local change is likely to produce a profound impact. His theory may look as if it lacks structure, but there is actually a universal structure within chaos theory. Curriculum design aims to eradicate the traditional 3R (reading, writing and arithmetic) model, transcend the modern Taylor model, and produce the unbalanced, inter-related and contextualized curriculum structure.[16] The teaching plan should be diversified, flexible and productive, in order to broaden the students' horizons. Imbalance and re-balance are necessary components in teaching design. The new teaching paradigm should have the "4R," which comprises "richness," "recursion," "relations," and "rigor," as pointed out by Doll. In this context, "richness" means that the course should be deep and meaningful, capable of various possibilities and interpretations with appropriate degrees of chaos, imbalance and vivid experiences, that allow for dialogues, interpretations, assumptions and categorizations. "Recursion" refers to the process of reflection, the discussion, exploration and research of meaning

---

16   William. E. Doll, *A Post-Modern Perspective on Curriculum*, Trans. Wang Hongyu 王红宇. Beijing: Educational Science Publishing House, 2000, 248–261.

DIALOGUES AND TEXTS: THE TRANSFORMATION OF TEACHING NORMS   81

constructers and the texts in question, with the aim to develop abilities of organization, integration, inquiry and interpretation. "Relations" refers to the internal structural connection of courses, and their relationship with culture. "Rigor" refers to the exploration of the underlying assumptions and the coordination of these assumptions to turn dialogues into meaningful dialogues. Doll's proposition provides us with a new theoretical basis for curriculum and teaching reform.

References

Ernest LeRoy Boyer. "Latest Proposal for School Reform." In *The Basic School,* ed. Akio Nakajima. Tokyo: Tamagawadaigakushuppanbu, 1997.

William. E. Doll. *A Post-Modern Perspective on Curriculum,* trans. Wang Hongyu 王红宇. Beijing: Educational Science Publishing House, 2000.

Gao Wen 高文. Xiandai jiaoxue de moshihua yanjiu 现代教学的模式化研究 [*Modern Instructional Model Studies*]. Jinan: Shandong Education Press, 2000.

Hitoshi Yoshimoto. *Encyclopedia of Modern Pedagogy.* Tokyo: Meijitosho, 1987, 80.

L. Klingberg. *Pedagogical Application and Initiatives in Socialist School.* Berlin: VEB Dt. Vrlag der Wissenschaften, 1962.

Shinjo Okuda. *Encyclopedia of Modern School Education.* Tokyo: Gyosei kabushikikaisha, 1993.

Yukitsugu Kato. *On Creating Learning Environment.* Tokyo: Kyouikukaihatsukenkyujo, 1997.

Yuriko Kinoshita. *Study on Teaching Communication and Teaching Language.* Tokyo: Kazamashobo, 1996.

Zhong Qiquan 钟启泉. Xiandai xueke jiaoyuxue lunxi 现代学科教育学论析 [*On the Modern Discipline of Pedagogy*]. Xi'an: Shaanxi People's Education Press, 1993.

CHAPTER 6

Towards a Humanistic Curriculum Evaluation

Quality-oriented education and exam-oriented education are two entirely different and irreconcilable pursuits of educational values. The study of curriculum evaluation in quality-oriented education is designed to answer two questions: first, how to help educators change the outdated learning and evaluation perspectives of the exam-oriented education system; second, how to establish the theory and methods of curriculum evaluation in quality-oriented education. At the primary and secondary level, curriculum and teaching under China's exam-oriented education system has led to misguided approaches to children's learning and development, which is primarily due to an inadequate amount of focus on individual personality and growth. Curriculum evaluation reform not merely focuses on technology or efficiency, but also on the transformation of educational thought, educational philosophy, curriculum mode and education methods. Quality-oriented education aims to fundamentally transform the evaluation concept and system towards the humanistic curriculum evaluation.

1 Curriculum Evaluation: Redefining the Concepts

1.1 *Defining Curriculum Evaluation*
In China's primary and secondary schools' exam-oriented education system, there is no concept of curriculum, let alone of curriculum evaluation. Primary and secondary schools have always attached great importance to the evaluation of students' academic performance and achievements. In addition, public opinion demonstrates that university enrollment rates are one of the only accepted measurements to evaluate schools, which means that schools have always paid attention to the institutional evaluation outside the educational system—a kind of recruitment evaluation. While high school and college entrance examinations have become an increasingly hot topic in public discourse about education, curriculum evaluation, which is a major issue for China's education system, has largely gone ignored. Thus, China urgently needs to introduce the concept of curriculum evaluation, without which educators would be doing an injustice to China's education system, because the current system is seriously imbalanced and distorts the functions of education.

© KONINKLIJKE BRILL NV, LEIDEN, 2022 | DOI:10.1163/9789004473300_007

TOWARDS A HUMANISTIC CURRICULUM EVALUATION

As the term implies, educational evaluation is the act of evaluating educational activities. In this context, education plays an influential role in promoting children's learning and development. Educational evaluation, in a broad sense, refers to the practice control and value judgment directly or indirectly related to educational activities. If recruitment evaluation is characteristic of the administrative behavior for China's national education scheme, then developmental evaluation is characteristic of the professional behavior for schools and teachers. Therefore, from the perspective of education, solid recruitment evaluation requires support from a solid developmental evaluation. Although the former is important in its own right, the latter is the obligation of primary and secondary education. In the exam-oriented education system, the heavy emphasis on evaluation in China's primary and secondary education must be corrected; instead, there should be a transfer of focus from recruitment evaluation to developmental evaluation.

The developmental evaluation, referred to here as curriculum evaluation, is advocated in Europe, the United States and Japan. It is an activity that evaluates courses, "which targets at a series of courses and their contents developed for learning activities and judges their advantages, values and significance."[1] However as an activity to "confirm education success, and improve education quality," the superordinate concept of curriculum evaluation is school evaluation, and its subordinate concept or hyponym is classroom evaluation, teacher evaluation, learning-competence evaluation, etc. These concepts are similar to Russian Matryoshka (nesting) dolls, with each concept being placed one inside another. Therefore, curriculum evaluation, as a complete set of concepts, can perform evaluation activities designed for different purposes at different levels, such as classroom evaluation, which includes education objectives, teaching methods, instruction processes, learning patterns, and learning-competence, as well as the structure of teaching units. This kind of evaluation is primarily based on the evaluation of classroom achievements or learning competence, and can be used to discuss the characteristics of course goals and the configuration of course content. The core of curriculum evaluation, as the evaluation of classroom results, after all, is learning-competence evaluation. In brief, curriculum evaluation could be expressed as evaluation activities involving the following levels of structural contents: the core of school evaluation is curriculum evaluation; the core of curriculum evaluation is the classroom evaluation or teacher evaluation; the core of classroom evaluation is the learning-competence evaluation.

---

1   Toji Tanaka & Tomomi Netsu, *An Introduction to Curriculum Evaluation.* Tokyo: Keiso Shobo, 2009, 31.

1.2 *Focus of Curriculum Evaluation and Its Innovation*

The focus of curriculum evaluation is children's learning and learning ability or learning competence. The learning evaluation or learning-ability evaluation in China needs to break the shackles of "Two basics" (mastery of basic knowledge and training of basic skills). Learning-ability evaluation covers three basic categories. The first category is the evaluation of knowledge (i.e. long-term memory of concepts and definitions of things and natural phenomena), understanding (i.e. grasp of knowledge, theories and principles) and skills (i.e. application of theories and principles). It is a pivotal task to accurately evaluate children's knowledge, understanding and skills, to advocate the teaching adapted to different personalities, and to avoid mechanical training; The second category is the evaluation of thinking, judgment and expressions. It means that children, on the basis of situations and experience, creatively apply different kinds of knowledge to make judgments, or express themselves. The mastery of these abilities must be defined as the goal of school curriculum; The third category is the evaluation of students' interests, hobbies and attitudes. How to develop children's interests, hobbies and attitudes as the prerequisite of teaching before class, in class, and after class is an important project.

In the final analysis, the value and success of school curriculum is neither judged by revealing the ideals and ideas, nor by the teaching methods that teachers expect. It must be judged by educational achievements—the progress each child makes. Hence, teachers must have a good command of children's growing processes, the academic foundation for their future development, and then evaluate the changes according to the education values and goals. This is the responsibility that teachers supposed to take for parents and the whole society. If traditional curriculum evaluation has emphasized the process of "Plan-Do-Check-Act" (referred to henceforth as PDCA), the innovative curriculum evaluation begins with the in-depth observation of the current situations of children's learning experience, namely "Check-Act-Plan-Do" (henceforth as CAPD). Thus CAPD is the pillar that supports school management activities. With positive evaluation of children's strengths and their progresses as its starting point, CAPD is able to grasp the achievement of educational goals, explore the reasons for possible failure in achieving goals, reveal the logic of reform from the cause-effect analysis and keep track of the progress of education reform.

2 Humanistic Curriculum Evaluation: Blueprint of the Reform

2.1 *Transformation from Cumulative Learning to Constructive Learning*

N. A. Kairov's idea of education has been dominating the educational circle in China for many years. Where the significance of curriculum research is neglected, there would be no place for curriculum evaluation. The real genuine curriculum research did not take place until after China's reform and opening up to the outside world in the early 1980s. Thus, it is easy to understand the backwardness of learning and evaluation reflected in China's primary and secondary school curricula or classroom evaluation. There is a brilliant episode of criticism on cumulative education (cramming education) by J. P. Freire in his influential work—*Pedagogy of the Oppressed*, which reveals the defects of school education. He criticizes that school education has become an act of depositing—banking form of education, i.e., students are considered to be empty receptacles or bank accounts that keep receiving the one-way indoctrination made by the teachers or the depositors. The more the students work at storing the deposits entrusted to them, the less they, the innovators of the future world, develop their critical consciousness and competence. This cumulative or "banking education" exposes ten features.[2]

1. Teachers teach while students are taught;
2. Teachers know everything while students know nothing;
3. Teachers think while students are thought about;
4. Teachers talk while students listen—meekly;
5. Teachers discipline while students are disciplined;
6. Teachers choose and enforce their choices on students who just comply;
7. Teachers act while students have the illusion of acting through the action of their teachers;
8. Teachers choose program contents while students (who are not consulted) to adopt them;
9. Teachers confuse the authority of knowledge with their own professional authority, ignoring the freedom of the students;
10. Teachers are the subject of the learning process, while students are mere objects.

These features are a true portrayal of the dominant lecture style of classroom teaching in China's exam-oriented education. In primary and secondary schools in China, in the face of learning difficulties, most of the students are blamed for their immaturity or idleness. As a result children are classified into top students and poor students and teachers are inclined to adopt the cramming teaching method that aims to overcome their students' learning difficulties. Such a teaching method implies the "blank slate" view of learning which considers students' mind to be in a condition of blank slate and their acquisition of knowledge is just like the accumulation of bank deposits. This is the view of the cumulative learning.

---

2 Paul Freire, *Pedagogy of the Oppressed*, trans. Gu Jianxin 顾建新, Zhao Youhua 赵友华, & He Shurong 何曙荣. Shanghai: East China Normal University Press, 2001, 25–26.

Along with the reform of China's curriculum, constructive learning, a new concept of learning takes over as the mainstream in education and children are the center and decisive factor of learning. The reason that children would encounter learning difficulties lies with the children themselves. The "Naive Theory" is a typical example. The special way in which children understand the world is not an indication of their incapability, but rather a demonstration of their capability. Thus, the central idea of constructive learning is founded on the belief of children's capability, and their mechanism of cognition. J. Dewey, J. Piaget and M. C. Vygotsky are the advocates of constructivism who highlight one common proposition that knowledge is not acquired by passive transmission, but is constructed by active learners in learning. Children form their own way of interpretation to construct and learn about this world by their own experiences and interaction with the environment. Constructivism asserts that knowledge is constructed by individuals' communication and collaboration with surrounding people and events, rather than something that is stored in the brain.

What constructive learning emphasizes is the construction of cognitive activities, but this does not mean rejection of the role of responses. In fact, as one of the representatives of constructivism, J. Piaget also recognizes cognitive activities as an interaction between assimilation (responsive learning) and accommodation (constructive learning). Therefore, we can say that constructivism does not take the position of binary opposition between construction and response as its theoretical presumption, but considers their relationship as that between the two sides of the same coin with construction on the positive side and response on the negative side so as to seek a dialectical balance between the two systems.

This constructive view of cognition suggests the necessity of study on children's developmental learning. First of all, it should be acknowledged that heretofore children possess knowledge acquired from life experiences. Secondly and more specifically, the interrelation between children's knowledge acquired from life experiences and knowledge instructed at school, i.e. the dialectical balance between construction and response should be identified. Thirdly, we need to analyze the recycling process of children's acquired knowledge and unacquired knowledge to identify how the knowledge is reconstructed in their mental schema. Besides, scholars in the Bloom school of psychology and education have investigated the significance of feedback in the course of education evaluation, and concluded that feedback does not simply mean approval but appraisal of all kinds of realistic situation by consciously making contrasts with reference to educational aims and objectives.

2.2 Transformation from Evaluation for Score Purpose into Evaluation for Learner Purpose

As a consequence of long-term test-oriented education, the convention of highlighting score-raising rather than talent-cultivating education has been established. For instance, score-raising education emphasizes the mastery of subject knowledge and basic skills, and considers the sum of all subject scores as the only standard for ranking students and the students' status in the ranking list is also accepted as the real and actual reflection of their learning achievements. However, information is by no means equal to knowledge, knowledge is by no means equal to wisdom, and wisdom is by no means equal to morality. The sum of subject scores does not equate with the person as a whole. Of course, evaluation for score purpose should not always be seen in a negative light as far as learners are concerned, but the problem is that the classification of top and poor students by using ranking scores in this evaluation obviously deviates from the principle of education.

Firstly, evaluation for score purpose misplaces the relation between the educational end and evaluation means by treating examinations as the end and children's learning (development) as a means that serves the end of examinations. In other words examination score is the recognized measurement that labels children's ability dictated by teachers.

Secondly, evaluation for score purpose confuses the concept of exam-adaptive ability with that of basic learning ability. Theoretically, the two concepts are not absolute antonyms or entirely opposing to each other and are even partially overlapping. However, it is extremely necessary to distinguish the two abilities in education. Ogi Naoki, a Japanese scholar, defines children's abilities in exam-oriented learning as follows. (1) Learners' passive receivers whose thinking abilities are narrowly constrained by the intentions of exam generators who leave no room for children's doubts, refutation and creativity. (2) Learning themes and topics come from teachers' tactful guesses based on the intentions of test generators. Children are trained as the mechanical robots with conditioned reflex, while their problem-finding ability and comprehensive analytical ability are completely ignored. (3) Test-oriented learning deviates the normal principle of education. Having been exposed to thousands of questions in the sea of exam preparation exercises, children would develop the cognitive ability called test-oriented learning ability—the scoring ability acquired by repeated mechanical trainings.[3] Obviously, the test-oriented learning ability is not the ultimate purpose of education. However, many

---

3   Ryosuke Kikuchi, *The Construction of Learning Ability*. Tokyo: Minshusha, 1992, 95–96.

primary and secondary schools in China complacently satisfied with the learners' achievements of test-oriented learning ability, neglecting their elementary learning ability. To make things worse, public media join the massive gossip about "Top scorers or number one scholars of CEE (College Entrance Examination)". It is time we began to reflect on such a situation.

Evaluation for learner purpose, in contrast to evaluation by means score, considers examination evaluation as a tool, and children's learning (development) as the aim and objective. To abandon evaluation for score purpose does not mean to deny the value of examinations and evaluations themselves. In fact, evaluation for learner purpose advocates that there is no guarantee of *excellent* education where there is no evaluation. This is true especially under the new circumstance of interdisciplinary research-oriented learning recommended in the new curriculum, evaluations are of great importance in systemizing education implementation because of the shortage of shared textbooks (the standard of evaluation). In quality-oriented education, the evaluation is not equivalent to "examination" or the ranking of students' academic performance. It fully focuses on developing each individual learner's personality, and makes flexible use of the information collected from evaluation for score purpose (paper and pencil test). This evaluation aims to enrich children's learning process, guiding and monitoring their learning. Evaluation for learner purpose, with distinctive innovations, stands out in sharp contrast with evaluation for score purpose in the following essential features.

(1) Evaluation for learner purpose is based on the wholeness of children's life for the full development of their personality.

(2) Evaluation for learner purpose is interested in the end result of education as well as the process of learning.

(3) Evaluation for learner purpose is not only conducted by teachers, but children's self-evaluation is also an important factor.

(4) Evaluation for learner purpose keeps track of children's growing course from the perspective of long-term development.

What we need to do is to develop children's basic learning ability. What we hope is to see children pursuing knowledge rather than being enslaved to knowledge.[4] Evaluation for learner purpose is an indispensable part of effective curriculum and education activities.

---

4 Tobin Hart, *From Information to Transformation: Education for the Evolution of Consciousness*, trans. Peng Zhengmei 彭正梅. Shanghai: East China Normal University Press. 2007, 30.

3 Transformation of Curriculum Evaluation from Utilitarian Consideration into Humanistic Consideration

We should not take a lopsided or extremely utilitarian view towards children's education, but a developmental view of children's whole personality education based on their learning ability. E. L. Simpson says that utilitarian education is "counter-humanistic education" or "pseudo-humanistic education" while humanistic curriculum education is a real humanistic education.[5] (N1) For many years people in Chinese education have held the tenet that education equates training, which is theoretically supported by N. A. Kairov's supercilious pedagogy, a typical extremist education model for test purpose and with counter-humanistic characteristics. It is Kairov's pedagogy that narrows curriculum down to subjects, subjects down to textbooks, textbooks down to

---

5 E. L. Simpson in her Humanistic Education: an Interpretation (Ballinger, 1976) clearly distinguishes three kinds of education: "anti-humanistic education", "pseudo-humanistic education" and "real-humanistic education". "Anti-humanistic education" herein refers to the education tenet with the purpose and objective of human education being not derived from people's internality, but imposed by the external authority. Children's learning and development are based on the recall of the past and the expectation of the future, while the present process of experience is totally ignored. Human beings, believed to be no different from animals, are driven by evil instinct. Thus the society is believed to be a well-ordered pyramid with an internal system of mutual interacting and disciplining functions to continuously suppress the "animalistic instinct" inherent in human beings. In this way, the purpose of such education is not to establish a commonwealth to support each individual's growth, but to form a social group to be maintained by obeying the authority. Contrary to "anti-humanistic education", "pseudo-humanistic education" not only neglect the past and the future, but the traditionally accumulated wisdom is also denounced as useless. The social collective group becomes an instrument to chase individual benefits and interests, rather than an organization which can bring about intimacy and cooperation. The "humanity" here is interpreted as nothing but an extreme egoistical propensity that only pays attention to one's own achievements and social status in complete disregard of others. There are five basic ideas concerning "real-humanistic education". (1) The process of learning involves the cognitive subject's active exploration of the objective world. Based on this kind of learning, learners gradually acquire the ability to show themselves in world arena by their self-discipline. (2) Traditions, beliefs and values should be selectively retained, changed and amended. (3) It is inadequate to place emphasis on one certain element of the emotional, spiritual and rational wisdom that are inseparable from the whole person. (4) Although the reality that everybody faces takes its root in current experiences, it is still necessary for us to look into the future and live in memory of the past, without which, the real meaning of "here and now" cannot be clearly defined. (5) Self-discipline can be demonstrated only in the context of the social group, and creativity can be realized only in pursuit of collective interests but not selfishness. For more detailed information, please see The Humanity of Education, edited by Eiichi Kjita on special issue of Japan Human Education Association. 1989, 9–10.

knowledge points, and ultimately teaching down to indoctrination of knowledge points. Thus, education evaluation has been narrowed down to the measurement of "the pure memory rate of knowledge points". However, there are kaleidoscopic facets in children's learning and development. Education is a process designed to improve human behaviors which are rather complicated and hence the evaluation of human behaviors should be varied accordingly. Therefore, it is extremely hard to grasp the diverse profiles of children's learning and development by means of paper-pencil tests organized by teachers in limited time, opportunities and perspectives.

Children's education in China should return to its tradition of humanistic education, the essence of education thought rooted in Chinese culture. Education cannot deny the involvement of "training", which should not be equated with animal training after all. The long-standing domination of test-oriented education in China has forced children to bear the overloaded mechanical training. Instead of creating the effect of "practice makes perfect", it results in "practice makes tedious", "practice makes foolish", and even induced tragedies such as self-mutilation and suicide occur from time to time. Test-oriented education has been vividly portrayed as "tests and examinations are teachers' magic weapons; scores are students' destiny", but in fact it is a crooked and misleading practice of children's education, characterized by "counter-children", "counter-humanistic" and "counter-education".

As a matter of fact, the same curriculum program would be endowed with different functions and meanings in the process of implementation due to different social backgrounds and teaching standpoints.[6] Thus, the benefits that children gain from the same curriculum are undoubtedly different. With the increase of school knowledge commercialization, unified school culture could never produce the same effects or results. Therefore, concepts such as "equality and uniformity", "diversity and discrepancy" and "course selection and talent selecting" have become distinctive defining terms that separate new education from backward education. The practice of the new nine-year curriculum reform in China shows that even the new curriculum reform cannot save China's education from the mire of "knowledge commercialization" and "curriculum utilitarianism". Therefore, the study of curriculum evaluation should focus on such problems as the causes of the differences and the influential factors leading to these differences. The simplified mechanical mediation treatments like the test-oriented education plus quality-oriented education are not able to innovate the curriculum evaluation. The challenge that we face in implementing quality-oriented education is that we need to accumulate new energies

---

6   Akio Nagao. *Curriculum Reform on "School Culture."* Tokyo: Meijitosho, 1996, 129.

TOWARDS A HUMANISTIC CURRICULUM EVALUATION

and make new efforts to launch an earth-quaking campaign in curriculum evaluation, a transformation from utilitarian curriculum evaluation towards humanistic curriculum evaluation.

4 Humanistic Curriculum Evaluation: A Qualitative Description

Children are initiators of learning and development. According to UNESCO, the term children is defined to indicate those whose ages range from o to 18. Children defined here is not an abstract word, but refers to the live and concrete beings. To better understand children's world, we must approach them, respect them and trust them. That is the essence of children education and of humanistic curriculum evaluation as well. The following are the essential features of humanistic curriculum evaluation.[7]

First, authenticity. It means that the subjects and activities evaluated must be authentic. That is, authenticity evaluation is the evaluation conducted on the children while they are solving realistic problems, which stresses the authentic society, real life and practical projects. Obviously, this evaluation is a critical reaction against the artificial and procedural properties of the "standard tests".

"Reality" herein is close to the logical meaning of children's life, while the "authenticity" of evaluation corresponds to the implications of two high-level objectives—"application" and "synthesis" proposed by B.S. Bloom in his taxonomy of educational objectives. Wisdom refers to the ability to make sensible judgment and decisions when encountering problems and ability to solve problems successfully by integrating previous experiences and continuously absorbing knowledge. According to G. Wiggins, "comprehensive questions" refer to newly-emerging problems in teaching which provide learners opportunities to conduct experiments by using textbooks, reference books and other relevant resources. Therefore, evaluation authenticity means that the problems designed for children to handle must constitute certain degree of difficulty. As a matter of fact, the problems, especially those which reflect life, are familiar to children which contributes to motivating them to take up challenges. However, to solve these problems, children are required to have deep and comprehensive knowledge. It is crucial to know that "familiarity" and "difficulty" are a pair of important concepts in correctly understanding "authentic evaluation".

---

7 Koji Tanaka, *Theory and Methodology of New Education Evaluation*. Tokyo: Nihon Hyojun Press, 2002, 24–30.

Second, children's involvement and decision-making in class. Children are decision-makers and initiators of learning rather than recipients of teaching. Thus, to implement this privilege, we need to ensure children's involvement. By children's involvement, we mean that children have a role to play in the process of school management and even school decision-making, under the condition that they are given enough necessary information. As active participants and collaborators of education rather than simple-minded passive recipients, children could cultivate their abilities to exercise their learning rights. Having this sense of participation is the prerequisite and foundation for children to be capable learners. Of course, how to participate and to what extent to participate deserves careful discussion. To answer the question "to what extent the learners are supposed to participate", some scholars argue that a distinction should be made between "children's involvement" and "children's co-decision". The former means that teachers have the authority to carry out decisions after consulting children for their opinions, while the latter, as the term indicates, means that decisions can be made only after a thorough negotiation between teachers and students, and the realms and contents of involvement must be separately arranged in line with the development characteristics of each individual child.

In the 1970s American researchers on education evaluation have been using the term "evaluation participants". Evaluation used to be the magic weapon representing teachers' authority, which is now challenged by children as the evaluation participants. Essentially, children won't be really involved in learning when their participation in evaluation is constrained. Thus, some scholars suggest that the notion of participants of evaluation can be extended to include people such as guardians and community residents. However, if various kinds of people are involved in evaluation, we need to redefine teachers' professional identity and expertise and explore a new model of co-decision. The concept of "evaluation participants" is bound to yield a reform on evaluation characteristics and even school systems.

Third, children's expression and educational appreciation. By "expression", we mean to say that children express their thoughts and emotions by way of gestures, drawings and language as well. Taking challenges to confront "realistic projects", teachers could contemplate the evaluation methods to understand children's colorful learning expressed by their physical senses, and to enable the children to select the right ways to express their academic achievements. Children should be free to choose their own medium of expressions, not only in compositions but also in pictures and oral descriptions. Once their "productive works" (children's expressions) are presented in the class, children would surely be surprised and fascinated by the various expressions of thoughts of other children and re-consider their own interpretation. That is what we call "alienation effect". By consciously embedding "expressions" in the context of evaluation and teaching, children's involvement in teaching will be further enriched.

Both the theory of behavioral objectives advocated by R. W. Tyler, B. S. Bloom, and the co-occurrence theory of behavioral objectives, problem-solving objectives and expressive objectives claimed by E. W. Eisner clearly demonstrate the appeal and urge for an integrated command of "soft objectives" and "hard objectives" in global education. E. W. Eisner also stresses the significance of developing teachers' appreciation of complicated classroom life in curriculum design and evaluation. That is to say, we need to develop teachers' ability to listen to children's opinions, interpret children's life experience and promote children's self-evaluation, just as E. W. Eisner once said that education appreciation is the guarantee or necessary condition of efficient education evaluation.[8]

Fourth, children's self-evaluation and mutual evaluation. Self-evaluation refers to the situation in which children make assessments of themselves, and with the information they gain, they identify themselves and adjust their learning and actions. Mutual evaluation means that children mutually evaluate their learning in group activities. The educational values of self-evaluation are shown in the following. (1) Providing children with opportunities to introspect themselves. (2) Helping children overcome their tendency of unbalanced development. (3) Enabling children to objectively analyze and position themselves if they can evaluate themselves from diverse perspectives. (4) Cultivating children's positive emotions, including sense of efficiency, achievement and confidence if they can make best use of self-evaluation. (5) On the basis of self-evaluation, children can be expected to strengthen determination and willingness to make incessant progress.[9] In short, self-evaluation helps to develop children's initiative and meta-cognition of learning. Accordingly, the ability of self-evaluation can be named as "meta-cognition ability" or "monitoring power". And this meta-cognition ability can be further classified into meta-cognitive knowledge (the knowledge of self-cognition, knowledge about subject matter and knowledge about learning strategies) and meta-cognitive activities (meta-cognitive monitoring and meta-cognitive controlling). The educational value of mutual evaluation helps to develop children's cooperative spirit and estimation of mutual knowledge and thoughts.

---

8 Elliot W. Eisner, *The Education Imagination: On the Design and Evaluation of School Curriculum Programs,* trans. Li Bingyan. Beijing: Educational Science Publishing House, 2008, 226.
9 Eiichi Kjita, *An Introduction to Education Evaluation.* Tokyo: Kyodo Shuppan Press, 2007, 122–126.

Modern education aims to enable children to form the ability of self-evaluation, because more and more children who are entangled in the maelstrom of exclusive egocentric competition end up in losing their confidence. One of the ways to regain confidence is to provide children with a teaching context in which they could discover their values and ensure their progress in "self-exploration" and "self-decision". With the development of information society and lifelong learning society, there is an increasing demand on children to acquire self-education ability when they are at school. Graduation from school does not indicate the end of learning. This is the age by which we can reformulate school learning styles, as well as the age in which we expect to create a glorious future by lifelong learning. Thus, there is no doubt that self-education ability will come to naught without the ability of self-evaluation.

In the final analysis, the innovation of curriculum evaluation goes hand in hand with children's self-evaluation ability, aiming to facilitate self-evaluation that can moderate the contradiction between the "known" and "unknown", and integrate the various forms of representations of self-evaluation. In order to prevent self-evaluation from being closed by limited personal frame of reference, it is necessary for children to expose themselves to the outside world so as to support children's "involvement" and "expressions". As a form of evaluation, authentic evaluation has attracted much attention for its "productive works" accumulated in the learning process, and on the other hand, it can promote self-evaluation in the context of discussions involving teachers and students, in which children's self-evaluation ability will be steadily formed.

5 Humanistic Curriculum Evaluation: A Cultural Renovation

5.1 Transformation from Credential Society into Learning Society

According to N. Noddings,[10] "The traditional organization of schooling is intellectually and morally inadequate for contemporary society. We live in an age of social problems that force us to reconsider what we do in schools". Humanistic curriculum evaluation is a cultural renovation, certainly involving the activities of curriculum evaluation.

The deeply rooted social convention that worships examination scores in primary and secondary schools results in the infinite amplification of credential value. And the defect hidden in test-oriented education intensively reflects the

---

10   Nel Noddings, *The Challenge to Care in School: An Alternative Approach to Education.* Beijing: Educational Science Publishing House, 2003, 220.

intrinsic social structure of the credential society.[11] The positive and negative effects that the credentialized education system creates on the society can be summarized as follows. (1) Promoting social mobility, wherein individuals can achieve their promotion as long as they strive regardless of their social status or background. (2) Extensively discovering elites and cultivating talents. However, the society witnessed the tremendous drawbacks of its vicious development as well: (a) The education system fails to develop personal characteristics, changing schools into organizations develop "individuals who distinguish themselves" and "social talent placement". (b) The rigid classification of social hierarchy due to overemphasis of elite schools amplifies the real value of examination scores and academic attainments. In other words, the deformed curriculum evaluation of test-oriented education in China has distorted students' development. "Credential society" becomes a "diploma disease".[12] The transformation from credential society into learning society is the new trend of social development, and the humanistic curriculum evaluation is the requirement of the new era.

5.2 Transformation from Unilateral Lopsided Development into Holistic Development

The "wholeness" of curriculum evaluation is an indispensable prerequisite for the development of curriculum as well as children's learning ability.[13] Against the background of test-oriented education, the view of subject separation has long prevailed, which results in weak awareness and general lack of "wholeness" in the conceptualization of curriculum evaluation. The problems are represented as follows.

(1) Neglecting the holistic consideration of children's personality formation. Each child is a whole person, not an assembled robot nor animal.

---

11 According to the researches of educational sociology, "credential qualification" has the following three values or functions: (1) Instrument value. It means that credential qualification helps to qualify someone to engage in professions, such as doctors, lawyers and teachers. (2) Social order value. "Credential qualification" can serve as a guarantee for certain social status, and promises the holders the permanent license to engage in one profession. In this way, credential qualification functions to classify people into different social status. (3) Selection and replacement value. It can be used for the purpose of selecting rare talents in the realization of the above two values. These three values constitute a trinity, known as "credentialism", which is worshiped by the "credential society". For more information, please refer to *Modern School Education Code*, eds. Shinjo Okuda et al. Tokyo: Tokyo Administrative Publishing Company, 1993, 401–403.

12 Ronald Dore, *The Diploma Disease: Education, Qualification and Development,* trans. Tadahiko Abiko. Tokyo: Iwanamishoten, 1978.

13 Tadahiko Abiko, *To Promote the School Reform on the Basis of Curriculum Development.* Tokyo: Meijitosho, 2003, 152–154.

There should be an intrinsic difference between human education and animal training. Apart from that, what differentiates elementary education from common education is that the former lays foundation for learning ability development and personality development, with personality development as its ultimate purpose. Thus, its emphasis should be placed on personality construction without affecting the formation of learning ability, especially on the comprehensive development in elementary education. The comprehensive development in this context means the holistic development, which aims to develop the wholeness of every child, rather than in the simple sense of "all aspects" which is another term for "biased fragmentary development" or "mediocre development".

(2) Neglecting the equivalence and diversity in subject education. From the perspective of pedagogy, although human competence or aptitude differs from person to person, but such difference does not imply difference in value judgment, with one kind of competence superior to another. For instance, it is unreasonable to compare children good at logical thinking with those good at artistic thinking, and claim that the value of the former is greater than that of the latter. The Theory of Multiple Intelligence proposed by H. Gardner deserves our attention. Teachers of different subjects ought to be equally treated, for their respective unique roles in maximally developing children's abilities of all kinds.

(3) Neglecting specific analysis of learning stages and value hierarchy in course contents. A change should take place from a description of course contents into a description of course objectives, through which we can clarify learning stages, including such programmed procedural learning as "logical analysis" and "behavior analysis", and "subject analysis" in a general broad sense. In this way, course contents could be redacted in line with the logic stages of gradation and according to course objectives. Another point that cannot be ignored, however, is children's developmental stages. Thus, it is of great importance to design learning stages that are compatible with both the logical stages and developmental stages. In addition, the value hierarchy in course contents should be taken into consideration. For instance, we need to consider talent-cultivating value and degree of pertinence when selecting textbooks.

(4) Neglecting the consistency and optimization in children's learning. The consistency in learning process herein refers to the correlation of teaching objectives, teaching contents and teaching methods in the whole process of teaching. No matter how fantastic and glamorous the teaching

objectives may seem to be, they serve no good purpose unless the contents and methods are suitable for students. Consistency in this context depends on how to clarify the implicit internal relationship among the teaching objectives, contents and methods. This clarification of different stages is what "optimization" is all about, which means that when we design teaching contents and methods based on teaching objectives, we should make different choices with different learners, rather than treating them alike as a unified whole.

5.3 Transformation from Black-Box Evaluation into Evaluating Evaluation

The innovation of curriculum evaluation covers a wide range of improvement at different levels and from different aspects, such as curriculum measurement technology, curriculum operation management and curriculum evaluation culture, none of which could be accomplished overnight and it is unrealistic to complete the curriculum evaluation of quality-oriented education by conducting only one research. Thus, the construction of curriculum evaluation in quality-oriented education relies heavily on the innovative implementation of evaluation by frontline teachers.

Teachers are the main force in curriculum evaluation. The core competence they need to possess is the ability to observe, to judge and to appreciate. More specifically, first of all, observation ability means that teachers must know whether the current courses can meet learners' education demands, which are probably not perceived by learners themselves. The "eye of observation" is not simply the ability to assess the written education syllabus, but the ability and skill to diagnose and amend the curriculum from the perspective of education demands. Second, judgment is the ability to reassess curricula, and discover their effects and limitations. To acquire this ability, rich experience on curriculum evaluation should be accumulated. Third, appreciation is the communicative ability to share and appreciate the achievements of curriculum evaluation, the ability not endowed by individual units, but by the organized units in the form of a school.[14] This means the rebirth of a brand-new curriculum evaluation culture.

However, the construction of any curriculum evaluation system is based on assumptions, which should be improved in the process of implementation and testified against children's resistance and conflicts as well as the reprehension

---

14   Toji Tanaka & Tomomi Netsu, *An Introduction to Curriculum Evaluation.* Tokyo: Keiso Shobo, 2009, 22–24.

from public opinions. Thus, we need a mechanism to evaluate evaluations.[15] The curriculum evaluation system in quality-oriented education is never a secrete black-box evaluation, but a system that could open to the public to gain approval, understanding as well as support from all the children and adults.

References

Akio Nagao. *Curriculum Reform on "School Culture."* Tokyo: Meijitosho, 1996.

Ronald Dore. *The Diploma Disease: Education, Qualification and Development*, trans. Tadahiko Abiko. Tokyo: Iwanamishoten, 1978.

Eiichi Kjita. *An Introduction to Education Evaluation.* Tokyo: Kyodo Shuppan Press, 2007.

Elliot W. Eisner. *The Education Imagination: On the Design and Evaluation of School Curriculum Programs,* trans. Li Bingyan. Beijing: Educational Science Publishing House, 2008.

Paul Freire. *Pedagogy of the Oppressed*, trans. Gu Jianxin 顾建新, Zhao Youhua 赵友华, & He Shurong 何曙荣. Shanghai: East China Normal University Press, 2001.

Koji Tanaka. *Theory and Methodology of New Education Evaluation.* Tokyo: Nihon Hyojun Press, 2002.

Nel Noddings. *The Challenge to Care in School: An Alternative Approach to Education.* Beijing: Educational Science Publishing House, 2003.

Ryosuke Kikuchi. *The Construction of Learning Ability.* Tokyo: Minshusha, 1992.

Tadahiko Abiko. *To Promote the School Reform on the Basis of Curriculum Development.* Tokyo: Meijitosho, 2003.

Tobin Hart. *From Information to Transformation: Education for the Evolution of Consciousness,* trans. Peng Zhengmei 彭正梅. Shanghai: East China Normal University Press, 2007.

Toji Tanak & Tomomi Netsu. *An Introduction to Curriculum Evaluation.* Tokyo: Keiso Shobo. 2009.

---

15   When evaluation activities become popular, evaluating evaluation would be necessary. There is no absolute exclusive evaluation procedure in the world. To improve the quality of curriculum evaluation and evaluators, it is indispensable to create a valid evaluation model to support "evaluator B to evaluate the evaluation made by A". In other words, just as the chasing experiment is essential to keep track of the results of previous experiments, "chasing evaluation" is also important to keep track of the results of curriculum evaluations, also called "meta-evaluation". For more information please refer to *An Introduction to Curriculum Evaluation*, eds. Toji Tanak et al. Tokyo: Tokyo Keiso Shobo, 2009, 45.

CHAPTER 7

Innovation in the Teachers' Education System in China

After years of reform, on the one hand, as public opinion on teacher education becomes more and more explicit, relevant policies are becoming clearer and clearer. On the other hand, teacher education has not received due attention as a top priority project in the national education development, with no reform measures taken and no financial support obtained. Now the development of teacher education in China is in a critical period of transformation from quantitative expansion to qualitative improvement. It can be said that with the upgrading, transformation and enrollment increase in China's higher institutions, teacher education development also faces the risks of lower standard, lower educational requirement, lower educational curriculum for teachers and lower financial support. In short, teacher education will be marginalized. Therefore, it is a matter of the utmost urgency to promote the system design and curriculum construction of teacher education under the guidance of the scientific view of development.

1 Historical Development of Teacher Education

The origin of the concept of teacher is as old as human history. Moreover, there are different images of teachers at schools at all times and in all countries, so a historical perspective is indispensable when discussing the quality of teachers. Teaching as a profession can be traced back to ancient Greece. According to Herodotus' *History*, as early as around the 5th century, private family-run teaching and public schools had been established in Ionian Islands of ancient Greece for teachers to teach sports, music and grammar.[1] The idealistic quality of teachers has also changed with the development of times and society, and this is true even with teachers who take education as a career: the requirement for a qualified teacher changes along with the different missions and characteristics of different schools. Western secondary school education originated in the Middle Ages, and its long history is second only to university education.

---

1 Hitoshi Yoshimoto, *Encyclopedia of Modern Pedagogy*. Tokyo: Meijitosho, 1987, 573.

© KONINKLIJKE BRILL NV, LEIDEN, 2022 | DOI: 10.1163/9789004473300_008

This kind of schools, known as grammar schools in the western countries, offered courses in liberal arts. From this basis teaching concept I—teachers who taught arts emerged. Elementary school education, however, was the product of modern public education, which came into being as part of the compulsory education system due to the intervention of public power. Teacher schools (or normal schools) established in this context were to teach theories and techniques concerning educational methods to ensure enough teachers to work in compulsory education schools. Teacher's school education of the time provided modern pedagogy, especially using Pestalozzi's pedagogy as a guiding principle. In particular, the Prussian teacher's schools in the 19th century closely integrated their teaching materials with Pestalozzi pedagogy, which was followed as an example of good teacher's education around the world. This is how teaching concept II—teachers who taught methods emerged. With the rapid development and popularity of secondary education in the 20th century, there was an increasing need for the integration of the above two types of teacher education. Particularly in the United States, teachers were expected to be familiar with arts as well as methods, so teaching concept III emerged; one that aimed to produce teachers within a learned profession—professional teachers.

The traditional teacher's school education being gradually replaced by the policy and system of the teacher education marks the development of contemporary international education. Essentially, it reflects the innovative process of teacher professionalization. It is a consistent demand of UNESCO and a common course of teacher education development in developed countries to move from distinguishing the conceptual differences between vocation and profession to advocating the professional status of teachers and professional development of teachers. In fact, it took western countries one century of arduous work to realize a transition of teacher education from non-profession to semi-profession (quasi-profession) to professionalization. The ideal image of teachers in East Asian countries including China also experienced three evolutionary steps from sanctification (teacher as a sacred career) to craftsmanship (teacher as a worker) and to professionalization (teacher as a profession). Eventually, the professional image of teachers was established.

Teaching is a profession. According to *Education as a Profession* (1956)[2] written by Lieberman, there are 8 criteria to define a profession: (1) Clearly defined realm and monopolistic engagement in work indispensable to society; (2) Use of highly intellectual techniques; (3) The need of long-term professional

---

2   Tsukubadaigaku Pedagogical Research Association, *The Basics of Modern Pedagogy*, trans. Zhong Qiquan 钟启泉. Shanghai: Shanghai Educational Publishing House, 2003, 452–453.

education; (4) Having self-discipline either as an individual or as a group; (5) Bearing direct responsibilities for making judgments and taking action within the professional self-control domain; (6) Non-profit driven and service motivated; (7) Forming a comprehensive self-government organization; and (8) Using workable and specific ethics guidelines. *Proposals Concerning the Status of Teachers* (1966) of UNESCO and ILO points out that "teaching should be regarded as a profession, and it is also a public service that requires teachers to acquire and maintain professional knowledge and expertise after a rigorous and continuous study, and it also requires an individual as well as a collective sense of responsibility for the education and welfare of the students". It also stresses the following features of technical work: (1) Long-term rigorous practice and continuous study; (2) Professional knowledge and expertise; (3) A form of public service; 4. An individual and a collective sense of responsibility for the public service. *Teaching is in Crisis: Calling for Action* (2004) written by National Board for Professional Teaching Standards (America) even emphasizes that teaching is the most valuable profession of a country, a profession that makes all other professions possible.[3]

Teaching is a learning profession. *World Education Report 1996—Teachers and Teaching in an Innovative World* of UNESCO points out that "teaching, like any other profession, is a 'learning' profession, and teachers always have chances to regularly update and supplement their knowledge and skills in career".[4]

Teaching is a "lifelong learning profession". UNESCO emphasizes that "youth education and adult education should be seen as a lifelong process",[5] and "teachers should treat students as their main concerns throughout their lives so that they can fully immerse themselves into the global knowledge-based society in the future", and "all institutions of higher learning that train kindergarten teachers and primary & secondary school teachers should formulate clear policies, encourage continuous innovation of the curriculum, use the best methods and familiarize themselves with different learning styles".[6] Education and teaching are creative activities in essence. Years of rich teaching experience and self-conscious research are the two indispensable parts to form excellent

---

3 Wu Gang 吴刚, Jiaoshi zhuanye fazhan: Huhuan xingdong 教师专业发展：呼唤行动 [Developing Teacher Education: Calling for Actions]. *Shanghai Education Research*, 2005, 1.
4 Li Qilong 李其龙 & Chen Yongming 陈永明, Jiaoshi jiaoyu kecheng de guoji bijiao 教师教育课程的国际比较 [*Global Comparison of Teacher Educational Courses*]. Beijing: Educational Science Publishing House, 2002, 388.
5 Zhao Zhongjian 赵中建, Quanqiu jiaoyu fazhan de yanjiu redian 全球教育发展的研究热点 [*Popular Topics of Global Education*]. Beijing: Educational Science Publishing House, 2003, 341.
6 Ibid, 401–416.

teaching practices for teachers. В.А. Сухомли́нский, known as Макаренко II in the Soviet Union, once said that "giving students sparks of knowledge requires teachers to constantly absorb every ray from the eternally shining sun composed of knowledge and human wisdom".[7] The nature of teacher learning and training is different from that of general academic research.

The professionalism of teaching mentioned above is expounded from the perspective of the nature and value of educational practice. It provides a frame of reference for China to think about the professional characteristics that teachers should possess as professionals.

Teacher education requires a system innovation of lifelong learning. Since the 1980s, China has been advocating the concept and policy of teacher education, which means the transformation of both development concept and development mode rather than a game of words. Teacher education implies the objective of development: First, teacher training changes from a mono-channel mode to a multi-channel mode and requires overall planning (not only teacher's colleges and universities, but also comprehensive universities are involved); second, teacher training process changes from pre-service training to lifelong development and requires a whole-process (integrated) design and multiple design (the whole-process and multi-level design in system); third, the image of teachers changes from teaching technicians to reflective teaching experts who pay great attention to professional quality. UNESCO points out that "the common pursuit of the world is to establish a mode of teacher education that integrates cultivation and training".[8] In this way, where teacher education mode is different from teacher's school mode, the objective of development for teacher education can be deduced from three basic points: (1) It is not a closed and conservative system, but one that seeks for openness and progressiveness; (2) It is not intended to train accomplished teachers, but rather to train "to-be-accomplished teachers"[9]; (3) It is not confined to the

---

7   Keiichi Takano, *On Modern Teachers*. Tokyo: Daiichihoki, 1984, 102.

8   Zhao Zhongjian 赵中建, Quanqiu jiaoyu fazhan de yanjiu redian 全球教育发展的研究热点 [*Popular Topics of Global Education*]. Beijing: Educational Science Publishing House, 2003, 468.

9   Modern science points out that human beings are born prematurely and biologically unfinished. UNESCO stressed, "...One might say that he never does become an adult, that his existence is an unending process of completion and learning. It is essentially his incompleteness that sets him apart from other living beings." See *Learning to be: The World of Education Today and Tomorrow* written, UNESCO, 157. Dietrich Benner, a German educator, also emphasized the "incompleteness" of human beings while discussing the concepts of "practice" and "educational practice". He said that the human beings are different from animals or plants, and "human beings are the only 'unfinished' or 'incomplete' creature". See *Allgemeine Pädagogik* written by Dietrich Benner.

development of teachers as individuals, but aims to form teachers as a group. In this respect, the teacher education theory of Kojiro Imazu is enlightening. He points out that there are two modes of teacher education research so far. One is individual teacher mode, which means qualified teachers are mainly recognized by their knowledge and skills as well as attitudes; the other is school education improvement mode, which is intended to improve the professional behavior of teachers centered on the teacher-student relationship as well as to pursue quality improvement of school education. These two modes have provided a theoretical basis for teacher education research and become a new thinking method. He also explores the basic concept of "school education improvement mode" theory and compares the differences between the old and new teacher education modes to suggest the direction of mode transformation from the following three principles:[10] (1) Principle of professional teachers. The concepts of accomplished teachers and to-be-accomplished teachers represent the different principles of professional teachers between old and new modes. In the traditional society, teachers who have commanded the required professional knowledge and skills are called accomplished teachers, and to have completed teacher school education is equal to have accomplished education; while in an information society, teachers are required to be able to reflect on their own behaviors in the interactive relationship with students and they should cooperate with colleagues and never stop learning. This is what we call to-be-accomplished teachers in China. When confronted with various kinds of problems, teachers are required to constantly develop themselves. (2) Principle of school organization. Rigid schools and flexible schools respectively indicate the old and new school organizations. The former have a closed teaching system where knowledge is delivered to all students in an efficient and unified way, while the latter have an open teaching system where teachers flexibly respond to the changing environment with new curricula and facility and they not only help students gain knowledge but also study the way of learning, and at the same time, teachers adopt collaborative and constructive teaching methods to adapt to the individual personality development of each student. (3) Principle of developing environment. The old education mode aims to train teachers in rigid schools with a closed teaching system, which centralizes the thinking mode of accomplished teachers and attaches great importance to the cultivation and employment of teachers, and the quality of teachers relies exclusively on their personal quality. The new education mode on the other hand, aims to develop teachers in flexible schools

---

10   Kojiro Imazu, *Teacher Education in Changing Society.* Nagoya: Nagoyadaigakushuppankai, 1996.

with an open teaching system. This system focuses on the thinking mode of to-be-accomplished teachers under the belief that teachers' quality relies on the improvement of a teaching-prioritized school education system, and that the professional development of teachers is determined to a great extent by in-service education.

With the continuous progress of society and the constant advancement of reform in basic education, the development of teacher education is facing new opportunities and challenges and there is an urgent need to transform from quantity expansion to quality improvement. It should be said that after years of reform, on the one hand, as the public opinion of teacher education is better and better prepared, ideas for relevant policies are becoming clearer and clearer. On the other hand, though teacher education is of top priority for the national education development, it fails to attract due attention in that no significant steps of reform are taken nor are affirmative educational finances affected. Now the development of teacher education in China is in a crucial stage of transformation from quantity expansion to quality improvement. It can be said that with the expansion of the open pattern and quantity of higher education brought about by the upgrading, transformation and enrollment increase in China's universities, the development of teacher education faces risks of lower standard of running schools, lower educational requirement, lower educational curriculum for teachers and lower financial support. In short, teacher education will be marginalized. Therefore, it is a matter of the utmost urgency to promote the system design and curriculum construction of teacher education under the guidance of the scientific view of development. In other words, efforts should be devoted to overcome the drawbacks and problems in the existing teacher education system and its curriculum, and establish a new teacher education model. This means to establish the modern teacher education system and its curriculum that are both featured with the contemporary knowledge-based economy and can adapt to even lead the reform and development of basic education curriculum in China. The main contents of *Project for Teacher Education's Curriculum Reform* of Ministry of Education include: issuing *Curriculum Standards of Teacher Education*, constructing a modern curriculum system of teacher education, building up a database of national excellent curricula, advocating model reform of teacher education's personnel training, setting up the assessment system of teacher education. Such demand for system innovation and curriculum construction is necessary for the implementation of quality education and the construction of a harmonious society.

2   Curriculum Standards of Teacher Education: Key to System Innovation

2.1   *Diagnosis of the Current Situation of Teacher Education in China*

Professionalism is the foundation of teachers, and the curriculum of teacher education plays an irreplaceable role in developing the professionalism of teachers. Therefore, the key to the system innovation of teacher education is to clarify the professional standards of the teacher education's curriculum. There are more than 10 million teachers in China, and this is the largest domestic professional team responsible for the largest primary and secondary education system in the world. Although it is stipulated in *Teachers Law of the People's Republic of China* (1993)that "teachers are professionals who perform the duties of education and teaching", and even though the Ministry of Education has implemented a reform plan for teaching contents and curriculum system of higher institutions of teacher education facing 21st century

Since 1997, some curriculum plans and teaching material modules have been engendered that broke through the old modes, but not resulting in any fundamental change on the whole. Now there still exist problems such as weak professional awareness, the neglect of children' value, weak teaching practice, disconnection between development and training and so on in the curriculum of teacher education, and they are specifically demonstrated as follows:

(1)   Teacher research is relatively underdeveloped. Teachers act as facilitators of children learning in propagating doctrines (*chuandao* 传道), imparting professional knowledge and resolving doubts rather than police and preachers who place themselves above students. Teaching in European and American countries started to shift from research on process-output to research on hermeneutics in the 1980s, when research on process-output based on behavioral science was criticized for its lack of the three Cs, (content, cognition and context).[11] More specifically, research that does not inquire into the value and meaning of educational content, the cognition of teachers and children, and the context concerning class and society can hardly be regarded as teaching research in its real sense. This kind of research interest branched into three subtypes of research endeavors — studies on teachers' thinking, studies on teachers' knowledge and studies on reflective practice. Studies on teachers' thinking concentrated its analysis on the core elements of teaching—the choices

---

11   Manabu Sato, *Curriculum and Teachers*, trans. Zhong Qiquan 钟启泉. Beijing: Educational Science Publishing House, 2003, 386.

and judgments made by teachers during their teaching process are thinking activities from which they could accumulate abundant samples of teaching design. Studies on teachers' knowledge discussed the knowledge foundation that constitutes the contents of teacher's professional education and the connotation and characteristics of practical knowledge in the teaching process. Studies on reflective practice aims to reveal the new professional image of reflective practitioners, which sheds valuable light on the redefinition of the professionalism of teachers. The efforts invested in teacher research have steadily produced solid results in accumulating rich academic and practical experience. Influenced by Kairov's Pedagogy, Chinese educators have always considered educational process as one during which teachers instill knowledge into students and restrict their behaviors. Teachers are treated as police and preachers who are in a dominant position where they can control and shape students. However, it is an indisputable fact that the role of teachers thus defined runs counter to curriculum reform.

(2) Research on children is relatively underdeveloped. Children are departures as well as destinations of education, and essentially the profession of teachers is a profession of child research. It is, therefore, the central theme of teachers' educational research to know what characteristics children have, what children's learning is, and what features children's development are. It is also the basic function and basic value of child education to explore children characteristics, respect children, protect the rights of children, and promote the development of children. Teachers are henceforth required to listen to children and understand children, and they should not only comprehend the differences in childhood behavior during the different developmental stages, but also understand the uniqueness of every child's personality development. However, the most notable characteristic of Kairov's Pedagogy lies in not taking children into account, which is a significant reason leading to the problem that most teacher colleges and universities pay insufficient attention to studies on child development and studies on child learning. Children are the main part of learning and development, and the communication activities of children are the form and foundation of their learning and development. However, the teaching of learning theory in China is still entangled with operational learning and excludes inquiry learning and expansive learning. It is clear that the pernicious influence exerted by Kairov's Pedagogy on China's pedagogical research has not yet been removed.

(3) Research on learning is relatively underdeveloped. Research on the science of learning I with brain science and cognitive science as its main

emphasis is just beginning in China while the science of learning in other countries has made remarkable progresses in the past 25 years. In fact, issues in educational practice such as what are the necessary conditions for learners to have a deep understanding, what is effective teaching and what are the adequate environmental conditions that support teaching and learning have made use of the latest achievements of the science of learning. Of course, deep explorations of themes like learning process, learning environment, teaching methods, as well as socio-cultural process still require the further explorations of fieldwork studies and laboratory studies in science of learning. Research in the science of learning in the United States involves studies in 6 fields of the learning process of students—the role of previous knowledge in learning, the effects of early experience on the development of brain and the possibility of learning, learning as a dynamic and initiative process, the learning based on understanding, competent learners with high proficiency, learning requiring long-term consistent practice. In addition, it also involves research in 5 fields about the teaching methods and learning environments that support learning—significance of socio-cultural context, conditions for the extensive application of the transfer and learning, unique features of disciplinary subject learning, evaluation aimed at supporting learning, new information technologies. What is learning? According to Professor Engestrom at University of California, learning activities of human beings can be classified into three levels. The first is the operational level—S-R learning or learning by stimulus-response; the second is the behavioral level—S-R purposeful and situational learning; the third is the personality level—fundamental self-change. For sure, these three levels cannot be separated or exist independently. Without learning II and learning III, it is incomprehensible for one to learn, even when one learns mechanically and repeatedly. Operational learning, centered on adapting to survival, was necessary in the pre-industrial society (learning I). In the early part of industrial society, inquiry learning (learning II) was necessary, as it is aimed at applying science to answer questions in the problem situation; but in the late part of industrial society (post-industrial society), expansive learning has become the core of learning society (learning III).[12] The situation in China which is still under the domination of the learning theories based on Pavlov's dog and Skinner's lab rat must be changed.

(4) Research on practical issues is relatively underdeveloped. The profession of teachers is characterized by practicality and innovativeness. The pro-

---

12   Yoshinobu Shoi, Development Aid of Finland Today. *Tokyo Education*, 2005, (6), 66.

fessional practice of teachers is an interpersonal communicative activity which boasts of the educational wisdom of teachers either as individuals or as a group in solving real and complicated problems in practical educational situations. It is the lifeline of teacher education to improve the core competence of teachers—educational practice competence with the help of research on practical issues. However, the biggest drawback of the traditional teacher education curriculum lies in despising experience, reflection and the reflective practice of teachers. The research on practical issues, first of all, is different from theoretical research in that the former aims to find out problems in practice (research content) to improve performance in practice (research purpose). Second, it refers to the research methodology on practical issues. The characteristics of research on practical issues are manifested not only in the research purpose and research content being directly related to practice but also in the wide varieties of research methods that can be employed in accompaniment with the practical studies. The process of educational research on practical issues can be divided into three stages: the pre-reflection stage where subjects and objects are not differentiated; the in-reflection stage where subjects and objects are differentiated and the post-reflection stage where subjects and objects are recombined in practice.[13] The idea of reflective practice infuses vitality into the professional development of teachers, and directs the way for the professional development of teachers. Such an idea can be traced back to Dewey. The "practice" concept of Kant, however, can also offer basic clues to educational research on practice issues. In his *Critique of Judgment*, he divided practice into technical practice and moral practice. The former is a kind of practice aiming to achieve proficiency of goals and dealing with routine work; the latter is a kind of practice that qualifies a freeman and a disciplined people. The reform of international teacher education curriculum breaks the boundary of a discipline system, strengthens the studies on the science of learning and curriculum and teaching theory, pays closer attention to practical teaching, case teaching and internship, focuses on the training of educational practice competence of teachers, and so on. These measures are close to the formation of teachers' teaching behaviors, and they are exactly what is needed to promote the professional development of teachers.

(5) Research on textbooks is relatively underdeveloped. Curricula and textbooks are the media and guidelines that instruct students to start

---

13   Seikichi Takaku, *Thoery of Education Practice*. Tokyo: Kyouikushuppan, 1990, 235–239.

cultural dialogues, and a good set of curricula and textbooks of educational disciplines demonstrate the basic experience and core values of children education. They not only reflect educational knowledge with enduring value, but also present the latest findings of contemporary science of learning and child research, and contain many vivid cases of the development of modern children. From the 1980s to the late 1990s, studies in pedagogy worldwide, underwent a transformation from quantitative studies on behavioral science to qualitative studies based on cognitive science, cultural anthropology and ethnography Likewise, studies on school reform also experienced a transformation from discussing concepts, systems and policies to analyzing the effects of those concepts, systems and policies on real school and classroom teaching. However, the existing curricula of educational disciplines and its contents in China has barely changed for decades. Both the development system and textbook system are seriously undeveloped, which not only affects their leading role in curricula reform, but also fails to meet the demands of curricula reform. Although there are over 500 textbooks on pedagogical principles and more than 200 textbooks on public pedagogy available, the disciplinary framework is established generally by following the ideas of Kairov's pedagogy—teacher-centered, classroom-centered and textbook centered. Additionally the professional curricula of teachers are still the three old disciplines—pedagogy, psychology and methodology. The unchanged and inflexible curriculum fails to not only inform the advantages of professional education of teachers, but is even against curricula reform. Consequently, when they start to teach, young teachers will be surprised to find that everything in real classrooms, including curriculum, teaching methods and educational resources are different from what they have learned at university. These problems send prospective teachers a message that the educational knowledge acquired at university has nothing to do with primary and secondary education. Therefore, there is no need to delve into the curricula of educational disciplines for it is not conducive to the lifelong learning of teachers.

The underdeveloped state of all the above mentioned studies indicates that authoritative teacher professional standards or curricula standards of teacher education are important to regulate and lead the theoretical studies and reform practice of teacher education. Additionally, the lack of these standards inevitably causes the distortion of the professional image of teachers in China. It is time to draft the curriculum standards.

110 CHAPTER 7

2.2   *Discussion on the Framework and Core Contents of Curriculum*
       Standards of Teacher Education

The curriculum of teacher education refers to all varieties of educational curricula which aim to train qualified teachers for kindergartens, primary, and secondary schools. Such curriculum planning can never be separated from the establishment of teacher image. That is to say, only when the general outline of teacher image is established, planning the specific contents of educational curricula could be possible. Many educational doctrines in history have described the ideal state and real state of teacher image. Soviet pedagogy, for example, has described teachers as engineers of human souls, and Japanese pedagogy has depicted the historical development of teacher image as public servants, workers, technically proficient people, or reflective practitioners. However, just as *Teacher Education*, the annual reports (1963 and 1975) of National Education Association in America, lamented, "the studies on teacher education were in such poverty in 19th century and the first half of 20th century".

However, the establishment of teacher education standards has become a controversial topic of discussion since the late 1980s. The international education community has so far produced considerable information in relation to the definition of the factors of teacher image, along with research findings on the teaching sociology of the teacher specialization index. *A Nation Prepared: Teachers for the 21st Century* (1986) and *Tomorrow's Teachers* (1986) of America clearly put forward teacher professionalization as that which turns education from a vocation to a real professional specialization. Likewise, *Outline on Teacher Specialization Benchmark* (1989) formulated by the National Board for Professional Teaching Standards in America is the most explicit expression of the teacher specialization benchmark. The five propositions stipulated in it clearly reflect the professional characteristics of teachers and show the professional development direction of teachers as reflective practitioners. Proposition 1 states that teachers are committed to students and their learning indicates that the primary responsibility of teachers is helping the learning and growth of children rather than digesting curricula. Proposition 2 states that teachers know the subjects they teach and how to teach those subjects. Proposition 3 says that teachers are responsible for managing and monitoring student learning which indicates that the professional contents and knowledge basis of teaching are the core of teacher profession, and the generative understanding of knowledge is close to the integration of knowledge. Proposition 4 states that teachers think systematically about their practice and learn from experience, and proposition 5 assumes that teachers are members of learning communities which highlights the professional characteristics of teachers as reflective practitioners.[14] Since the late 1990s, almost all the countries in the world have made the professional development of teachers a task of top priority of educational development. The United States Department of Education submitted *Meeting the Highly Qualified Teachers Challenge: The Secretary's Annual Report on Teacher Quality* to the Congress for four consecutive years from 2002 to 2005. The world-famous educational and academic organization American Educational Research Association (AERA) has made the professional development of teachers one of the major topics for discussion in recent years. Additionally, in June 2005, the OECD also published a report on issues on educational policies of 25 countries *Teachers Matter: Attracting, Developing and Retaining Effective Teachers. On the Establishment of Multi-level Teacher Education System* and *The Standards of Discipline Orientation and Professional Classification for Higher Vocational Education* were issued by the Russian government in 1992 and 1994 respectively in order to constantly improve the specialty catalog and curriculum establishment of teacher education. According to the study[15], different countries share the same philosophy on the reform and practice of teacher education, namely, (1) emphasizing the principle of being child-centered for the purpose of promoting their learning and improving their lives; (2) focusing on practical teaching and educational practice itself which has an obvious practical orientation; (3) laying emphasis on training teachers' lifelong learning ability and their lifelong professional development.

It is easy to learn from the stipulations of teacher professional standards (curriculum standards) of developed countries that crafting the *Curriculum Standards of Teacher Education* in fact is what is required to define the professional standards of teachers. The standards describe what the high-quality teacher role that can meet the requirements of the times and society is, and how to construct teachers teams in possession of such high-quality teachers. Therefore, the research on curriculum standards of teacher education needs to focus on three issues: the background qualification of teachers, the concrete standards of teacher's quality, and the implementing scheme of teacher training curriculum.

---

14   Manabu Sato, *Curriculum and Teachers*, trans. Zhong Qiquan 钟启泉. Beijing: Educational Science Publishing House, 245–246.

15   Zhong Qiquan钟启泉, Mianxiang xinshidai shizi peiyang de gaishan fangce—Jizi Riben de jiaoyu baogao (zhi san) 面向新时代师资培养的改善方策—寄自日本的教育报告（之三）[Innovation strategy of teacher training in the new era—Education Report from Japan]. *Education References*, 1998, (3), 40.

In the framework of curriculum standards of teacher education, the central idea is to define what professionalism of teachers is: the sum total of knowledge and skills supported by dedication, pride and a sense of belonging that teachers display towards the specialized profession—the profession of teachers, and it's an acquired quality as opposed to being an inborn quality.[16] It can be assumed that the qualities defined here refer to the universal requirements for teachers that go beyond the limits of times. And at the same time, based on such general requirements, these qualities examine problems existing in society, schools and teachers in order to define the particular qualities of teachers in the future. Japanese scholars have worked out a specific criteria for describing the professionalism of teachers: the abilities to act locally and think globally (qualities required for the understanding of the world, nation and mankind); the necessary abilities of social creatures living in a changing society (problem-solving ability, interpersonal skills, and the knowledge and skills that allow a person to adapt to the changing society); the abilities required by the profession of teachers (proper understanding of students and teaching, dedication, pride and a sense of belonging of the profession of teachers, and knowledge, skills and attitudes). The profession in which teachers are engaged is complex, dynamic, diverse and constantly developing. The Kurosawa Hidefumi study group of Musashi University in Japan in 1991, 1993 and 1999, conducted a series of surveys to investigate the qualities required of teachers in the new age among university teachers, with in-service primary and secondary school teachers and the students who took curricula of teacher education as the respondents. The survey showed six key points in the qualities of teachers (listed in order of priority): (1) Possessing a rich sense of humanity and a wealth of knowledge of human and educational ability to understand people; (2) Possessing the ability to deeply understand children and educate them according to their status as well as physical and mental states; (3) Possessing a broad international vision in the age of globalization and the ability to be engaged in international education; (4) Possessing the educational ability that can give full play to self-innovation and cultivate the creativity and imagination of children; (5) Possessing the ability to show their personal charm and cultivate children's individual personality; 6. Possessing the ethics and sense of mission as an educator.[17] The professional abilities of primary school teachers

---

16   Wang Ling 汪凌, Faguo zhongxiaoxue shizi biaozhun he zhuanye peixun de yuanze yu kecheng moshi 法国中小学师资标准和专业培训的原则与课程模式 [French teachers' qualifications and professional training principle and curriculum]. 2005, unpublished.

17   Fang Mingsheng 方明生, Xinshiji Riben jiaoshi jiaoyu mianlin de keti yu daxue de yingdui 新世纪日本教师教育面临的课题与大学的应对 [Problems and strategies faced by Japanese teachers in the new era]. 2005, unpublished.

defined by the Ministry of Education of France include the following four aspects: (1) ability of multi-disciplinary teaching, (2) ability of organizing and analyzing teaching situations, (3) ability of handling class activities and understanding the differences among students, and (4) educational responsibility and professional ethics. However, the professional abilities of secondary school teachers highlight the responsibilities they should shoulder in the educational system, in the schools and classes. These professional abilities represent the professional image of teachers featured with proactivity, openness, self-knowledge, multifaceted abilities and good management abilities.[18] The National Research Council (U.S.A.) has summarized six qualifications an expert teacher is required to have from the perspective of learning science. They are, (1) teachers need expertise in both subject matter content and in teaching; (2) teachers need to develop understanding of the theories of knowledge (epistemologies) to guide the subject-matter disciplines in which they work; (3) teachers need to develop an understanding of pedagogy as an intellectual discipline that reflects theories of learning, including knowledge of how cultural beliefs and the personal characteristics of learners influence learning; (4) teachers are also learners and the principles of learning and transfer suitable to student learners are suitable to teachers as well; (5) teachers need opportunities to learn about children's cognitive development and children's development of thought (children's epistemologies) in order to know how teaching practices can be built on learners' previous knowledge; (6) teachers need to develop models of their own professional development that are based on lifelong learning, rather than on an "updating" model of learning, in order to have frameworks to guide their career planning.[19] Undoubtedly, studies on the professionalism of teachers in the new age in developed countries provide enlightenment regarding China's issues on building up ideal teacher images.

To formulate the *Curriculum Standards of Teacher Education*, Chinese education should fully implement the philosophy of quality education to achieve the professional development of teachers by following the requirements of the times and the status quo of teacher team spirit. Firstly, the professional development of teachers should refer to the overall development of individual teachers rather than the accumulation of linear knowledge and skills. Therefore, emphasis should be put on the principles of children-centeredness,

---

18 Wang Ling 汪凌, Faguo zhongxiaoxue shizi biaozhun he zhuanye peixun de yuanze yu kecheng moshi 法国中小学师资标准和专业培训的原则与课程模式 [French teachers' qualifications and professional training principle and curriculum]. 2005, unpublished.

19 American Research Promotion Association, *Transforming Teaching*, trans. Toshiaki Mori. Kyoto: Kitaojishobo, 2004, 254.

practice-centeredness and lifelong learning to overcome the drawbacks in the traditional format, and train the professionalism of teachers by focusing on educational innovation and practical ability in teaching. Secondly, teacher professional development is not molded by relying on external technical input but a course of understanding oneself, namely the course of improving oneself and developing independently through reflective practice. Therefore, to define specific objectives, education in China modifies the outdated lecture style system that emphasizes the special epistemology so as to encourage teachers to do practical studies and develop their own practical wisdom and teaching styles by solving problems in real educational situations. In other words, first, a teacher's identity is acknowledged after a long period of specialized intellectual training. Secondly, a teacher's identity is achieved on the basis of self-control and responsibilities, especially on the basis of common collective autonomy and organizations as well as common responsibilities. In a word, close attention should be paid to the formation of professional self-control of teachers. Thirdly, teacher professional development is in its essence an innovation of cultural background (ecological innovation) and the course of lifelong learning. Teacher professional development does not simply mean a course in which a teacher can directly apply their knowledge and experience in educational practice. Instead it is an interaction in which a teacher must combine their knowledge and experience with educational situations to form practical wisdom by solving real and complicated problems in educational practice with independent individual reflection as well as group cooperation and consideration. The three basic characteristics of teaching—recursion, uncertainty, boundlessness determine that teacher professional development is endowed with unaccomplishment.[20] Prospective teachers should form the habit of inquisitive learning and cooperative learning consciously which helps teachers to realize the integration of teaching and study as well as the integration of development and training. In this way, they can become lifelong learners and promoters of learning society.

It means the focus of the attention is changed to some extent, which highlights three key concepts. The first one is practical knowledge. The practical knowledge of a teacher is formed through case analysis, thematic exploration, experience sharing and behavior research. It is distinct from the theoretical knowledge of researchers in many respects. (1) Experiential knowledge is empirical knowledge, dependent on limited context. Therefore, it is not as logically rigorous and generally applicable as theoretical knowledge, but it is

---

20 Manabu Sato, *Curriculum and Teachers*, trans. Zhong Qiquan 钟启泉. Beijing: Educational Science Publishing House, 2003, 264–268.

rather functional and operative knowledge, diverse and flexible. (2) Experiential knowledge is generated by a particular teacher in a particular class with a particular textbook and a particular group of learners. It is accumulated and passed on as case knowledge. (3) Experiential knowledge is consciously generalized knowledge which does not necessarily explain phenomena in certain particular fields of research, and which aims to find and solve theoretically uncertain problems. (4) Experiential knowledge is not only conscious and explicit knowledge, but also includes the tacit knowledge that can be used unconsciously. 5) Experiential knowledge is personal knowledge in that it is generated on the basis of the personal experience and introspection of every individual teacher, and the inheritance of this experience is also based on the maturity of the receiver's practical experience. The second key concept is professional self-control. The key to understanding the professionalism of teachers' work lies in how to understand professional self-control. The professional self-control means that teachers as individuals and as a group can make independent judgments, decisions and implement them. Thus, the professional self-control in education refers to the teacher's autonomy in deciding what to teach and how to teach. However, it does not mean teachers can afford to be whimsical. On the contrary, it demands that teachers should scientifically study the logic and the teaching methods of the textbook based on academic studies before they teach. Educational practice is an academic practice. Teachers as a profession should work in compliance with the national education standards, and, at the same time, acknowledge the academic freedom in education practice. I once criticized four erroneous tendencies of teacher professionalization in China—engineering, administrativization, leisure and technicalization. These erroneous tendencies threaten to throttle the professional autonomy, professional dialogues, and professional ethics that serve as the basic elements or basic conditions of teacher professionalization, which then results in de-professionalization or anti-professionalization.[21] The third key concept is teachers as a group. Supportive places and teams are indispensable if teacher's qualities are expected to be brought into full play. It is not an uncommon phenomenon for excellent teachers to work in obscurity, completely unknown to the public. Therefore, discussion concerning the professionalism of teachers should not be confined strictly to the analysis at the level of individual teachers and their psychological features, but extended to the teachers as a collective group and institutional system. Namely, the discussion

---

21   Zhong Qiquan 钟启泉, Jiaoshi zhuanyehua de wuqu jiqi pipan 教师专业化的误区及其批判 [Misconceptions and criticism on professional development of teachers]. *Education Development Research*, 2003, (5), 119–123.

is required to study how teacher's self-innovation is formed and how a teacher's cooperative culture is formed, or what qualities are needed to make the professional teacher-team a group and how they are formed?

2.3 Curriculum Reform of Basic Education Calls for a Professional Image of Teachers

Since the implementation of the new curriculum in 2001, China has emphasized that the role teachers play in the development of curriculum is curriculum builder: Teachers are not passive mediators (a performer) of curricula but are responsible for choosing and organizing the learning experience of students, that is, their role should change from instruction to creativity; Teachers are not simply disciplinary teachers. Instead they need to develop a holistic vision of the curriculum. That is, their role needs to change from disciplinary vision to cross-disciplinary integrated vision; Teachers are not self-centered directors or dictators but are proponents and guides. That is, their role must change from dominators to supporters. Teachers are the driving force of the four key elements of curricula (teachers, contents, students and environment). The ideal of a curriculum is realized through teaching. Teachers are always the principal part of curriculum transformation and teaching practice in the teaching process where teachers transform the school's documentary curriculum to comprehensible curriculum interpreted by teachers and finally to operational curriculum implemented in classroom situations. Such being the case, teachers should be aware of current professional knowledge, teaching environments, and the presence of themselves. Only when teachers reflect introspectly from a new perspective and reexamine the practical value of curriculum and teaching practice can they awaken their curricular consciousness and pedagogical awareness, which will help to broaden the vision of teaching and promote the pace of reform. Curriculum standards should be specified into target areas. Specific targets and basic viewpoints analyze their respective basic contents, and sort out the logical relationship between the basic viewpoints. In terms of target areas, decomposing educational beliefs and responsibilities is to enable teachers to understand the basic concepts of education, be aware of their own responsibilities and form their own philosophy of education. Educational knowledge and skills aim to enable teachers to have a better understanding of the professional core knowledge and acquire necessary skills; educational practice and experience, in turn, aims to enable teachers to know themselves and their experience as well as feel and experience things and form practical wisdom. The framework has been inspired by the teacher professional standards of many countries including Schwab's common elements of curriculum.

The advantage of this framework lies in that it endeavors to approximate the core of professionalism of teachers from the perspective of awareness of pedagogical environment, awareness of pedagogical knowledge and self-awareness of teachers.

2.3.1 Awareness of Pedagogical Environment

The profession in which teachers are engaged is complex, diverse and constantly developing. Teaching activities are always influenced by external factors, from the space of the classroom, scale of classes, teaching equipment, school system, and community resources to cultural background, educational funds, and educational policies, all of which contribute to the formation of a unique logical relation of interaction. Only when teachers can quickly grasp this unique and interactive relationship can they react accordingly and shoulder their educational responsibilities.

2.3.2 Awareness of Pedagogical Knowledge

Teaching is the most interesting and complicated human problem-solving activity. Teachers must equip themselves with professional academic knowledge, teaching skills, sensitivity to students' reactions and emergency intelligence. As for students, teachers are role models who can provide new chances of learning. Alternatively, they can act as bad examples. The basic idea of all the teacher's work is to be child-oriented. If a teacher fails to understand the value of the school's educational life and does not show respect for the rights of students and the individual differences of each student, they will not really understand the occupational characteristics and professional spirit, let alone produce outstanding teaching. Early cognitive studies were focused on the relationship between disciplinary subject knowledge and pedagogical knowledge. Excellent teachers should also master the skills to transmit the above knowledge. L.S. Shulman put forward seven types of teaching knowledge—(1) Knowledge of educational contents, (2) Knowledge of general pedagogy, (3) Knowledge of curriculum, (4) Knowledge of teaching design, (5) Knowledge of learning and its characteristics, (6) Knowledge of educational background, (7) Knowledge of the value of educational results and purposes. Obviously, all these types of professional knowledge are diversified, practical, interdisciplinary, and integrated. This in fact criticizes the ability required by the narrow vision of education technology in the teacher hiring standard as it points out excellent teachers should distinguish themselves not only by their teaching techniques and decisions, but also by their proficiency in subject knowledge, teaching and learning theory, and educational psychology to qualify themselves with Pedagogical Content Knowledge (PCK for short), which is the knowledge central to teaching. This kind of knowledge is set up on the basis of case study.[22] It shows that the teaching knowledge needs to be centered on educational performance in order to achieve focal transfer from "factual knowledge" to "methodical knowledge".

2.3.3   Self-awareness of Teachers

Teachers' practical knowledge is based on deep practical understanding, practical experiences, and the educational study experience of individual teachers. Different teachers may have totally different teaching practices while facing the same groups of students in the same situations and with the same materials. Different professional education backgrounds, individual characters, beliefs, attitudes and values may produce decisive influences. In that case, a study on teachers' experiences should include the practical reflections not only based on themselves but also based on cooperations. The practical knowledge of teachers is distinct from the theoretical knowledge of researchers in many respects. (1) Practical knowledge is empirical knowledge, dependent on limited context. Therefore, it is not as logically rigorous and generally applicable as theoretical knowledge, but rather more functional, diverse and flexible. (2) Practical knowledge is generated by a particular teacher in a particular classroom with a particular textbook and a particular group of learners. It is accumulated and passed on as case knowledge. (3) Practical knowledge is consciously generalized knowledge which does not necessarily explain phenomena in certain particular fields of research, and which aims to find and solve theoretically uncertain problems. (4) Practical knowledge is not only conscious and explicit knowledge, but also includes tacit knowledge that can be unconsciously used. (5) Practical knowledge is personal knowledge in that it is generated on the basis of personal experience and introspection of every individual teacher, and the accumulation of this experience is also based on the maturity of the receiver's practical experience.[23]

---

22   Manabu Sato, *Curriculum and Teachers*, trans. Zhong Qiquan 钟启泉. Beijing: Educational Science Publishing House, 2003, 389.

23   Manabu Sato, *Curriculum and Teachers*, trans. Zhong Qiquan 钟启泉. Beijing: Educational Science Publishing House, 2003; Charles E. Silberman, *Crisis in the Classroom*, trans. Tadashi Yamamoto. Tokyo: Saimaru Shuppankai, 1973, 467. Charles E. Silberman, *Crisis in the Classroom*, trans. Tadashi Yamamoto. Tokyo: Saimaru Shuppankai, 1973, 416. Ibid, 460.

INNOVATION IN THE TEACHERS' EDUCATION SYSTEM IN CHINA

3　Re-Conceptualization: The Precondition of System Innovation of Teacher Education

3.1　*Learning Profession and Professional Learning*

Teaching is a learning profession which requires professional learning. J. Dewey has already suggested that it is a university's responsibility and mission to offer pedagogy that teaches educational discovery and experiment.[24] L. A. Cremin, an American education historian, emphasizes: "Education is a great cause with long-lasting vitality. Therefore, it cannot be entrusted to a purely technical worker."[25] C.E. Silberman also points out: "A teacher's general quality is necessary but not sufficient. A teacher must receive teachers' professional education."[26] From the perspective of international comparison, curriculum plans of teacher education vary from country to country, but according to J. Goodlad, there are the following similarities: (1) Prospective primary school teachers pay attention to quality education and general education while prospective secondary school teachers focus on the preparation of subject contents. (2) A series of foundation courses, such as philosophy of education, sociology of education, history of education, and psychology of education are offered. (3) One or more courses are offered on developmental psychology, learning psychology, and cognitive psychology. (4) Courses of teaching methodology and a series of learning courses based on on-site experience are provided. Therefore, the differences between courses lie in the priorities of the constituent elements, the purpose of the plan and course in the eyes of the mentor, and students' attitudes and beliefs towards the plan.[27] K. Zeichner and D. Liston maintain that the philosophical traditions that support the curriculum plan of teacher education in 20th century can be divided into four categories: (1) The tradition that emphasizes academic principles—which means that attention should be paid to teacher's knowledge on academic subjects and think that the function of a teacher is to help students understand the subjects. (2) The tradition that emphasizes social benefits—which focuses on the foundation of knowledge related to teaching that results from education and stresses teachers' practical ability to apply knowledge proficiently. (3) The tradition that emphasizes development—which stresses that teachers should

---

24　Ibid, 467.
25　Ibid, 416.
26　Ibid, 460.
27　American Research Promotion Association, *Transforming Teaching*, trans. Toshiaki Mori. Kyoto: Kitaojishobo, 2004, 209.

profoundly understand the developmental differences of students or in other words, understand students' psychological preparation for learning (due to developmental differences, students' learning abilities differ), so teachers can organize teaching activities based on the differences of students. (4) The tradition that emphasizes social reconstruction—which means that teachers should be equipped with the ability of accurately analyzing every condition of schools and society so that school education can help safeguard social equity and justice as well as improve people's living conditions.[28] Of course, this classification is only intended to help people understand the theoretical background of some curriculum plans of teacher education. Not all plans, however, can be divided into the above four categories. From the perspective of the philosophical tradition, *Curriculum Standards of Teacher Education* formulated by the Ministry of Education of China, obviously aims to reduce the influence of emphasizing academic tradition to leave room for tradition that emphasizes development, tradition that emphasizes social benefits and tradition that emphasizes social reform. Therefore, the curriculum design, conceptual framework and teaching methods in teacher education in China will be innovated so as to fully demonstrate the unique features and educational values of teacher education. First, the new curriculum will break down the strict division of disciplines and adopts the modular structure to highlight practice orientation and problem orientation, to provide guidance for the reform of educational schools and the implementation of educational subject curriculum. Second, the new curriculum will specifically stipulate the standards for the professional qualifications of kindergarten, primary school and middle school teachers, so as to offer a criterion for educational administration to regulate teacher education schools. Third, the new curriculum will advocates lifelong learning, which provides some basic clues for the course integration of pre-service training and in-service training.

Education in China is faced with many theoretical and practical issues that should be addressed in the system innovation of teacher education. First, China should develop a curriculum framework characterised by openness, selection and norms, which not only conforms to the requirements in the *Curriculum Standards of Teacher Education*, but also retains the distinctive characteristics of individual schools. In fact, this answers the question of how to strike a balance between the rigidity of standardized development and the flexibility of self-development of schools, or in other words, between individuality and generality. On this basis, China can establish the review and documentation

---

28   Ibid.

system of the curriculum plan of teacher education. Second, China should foster a teaching culture characterized by independence, dialogue and further research. This answers the question of how to achieve an integration of teaching and theoretical research and to strengthen the cooperation and communication among teachers by the reform of teaching methods, which is a process intertwined with the diversity and liberation of academic thoughts. In addition, on this basis, China can make full use of the rich curriculum resources to develop an educational probation system and educational practice system which focus on educational practical ability. Third, China should establish a life-learning oriented curriculum system, which integrates development and training. This answers the question of how to adapt to and satisfy the demand of professional growth for pre-service teachers and in-service teachers so as to achieve the integration of teacher education curriculum. Professional development is a lifelong pursuit of all professionals, which is equally important for both pre-service teachers and in-service teachers. Additionally, on this basis, China should design progressive education in accordance with the professional development stage of teachers.

The goal of teacher education reform is to establish the teacher's personal charisma and professional prestige and finally replace administrative authority with the help of teachers' professionalization. According to a survey by the Teacher Study Group of Japanese Educational Sociology, the group of teachers, as a professional team has the following characteristics: (1) Teachers are a group of people who are not extremely large in number with a high degree of informality. (2) Teachers are a professional group that needs professional liberty and subjectivity. (3) Teachers are a highly-educated group of male and female teachers. (4) Teachers' consciousness is a mixed sense of social mission and social inferiority. (5) Teachers are an obedient group whose possibility for promotion is limited, with a narrow circle of life. (6) Teachers are a group that is classified as the secular new middle class. (7) Teachers are a group still fettered by a hierarchical system in the transition of educational policies.[29] From this perspective, the first point indicates that the nature of the teacher group is semi-bureaucratic and from the second point it is assumed that teachers pursue professional freedom. The third point shows that this highly-educated group requires professionalism. However, education in China also notes something contradictory to professionalism: This can be seen from the social inferiority in the fourth point that teachers do not enjoy a mature sense of pride while developing their professionalism. The word obedient in the fifth point

---

29   Keiichi Takano, *On Modern Teachers*. Tokyo: Daiichihoki, 1984, 123–124.

and the statements in the sixth and seventh points are also at odds with the professionalism. The trait of the teacher group is closely related to the manner of educational leadership. First, since teachers are supposed to have a high degree of professionalism, they are required to develop their ability based on their in-service education. Second, the schools where teacher groups, together with the learning groups of students, conduct educational work should not be dominated by power and bureaucracy. For the control of school organizations, it is more effective to implement indirect control (control by regulation / norm) rather than direct control (top-down control by administrative power). That is to say, the teacher groups do not resemble groups in enterprises and bureaucratic organizations that obey powerful and rigid directions. Basically, the teacher groups form norms by self-discipline and take actions autonomously, so any external coercive specific behaviors do not apply to such a group. Third, teachers can only achieve when they conduct educational work by focusing on learners from multi-perspectives. The implication is that teachers train learners through the common effects and shared responsibilities that result from the autonomy of teachers as a group. Here, mutual trust in the group is a prerequisite because actions based on power cannot truly develop trust relationships in a group. Obviously, the top-down bureaucratic leadership that uses red tape to convey information adopted by the education administration in China as well as the quiet obedience of teacher groups are entirely incompatible with the formation of the teacher group in its real sense.

3.2 *Reconceptualization and System Innovation*

Reconstructing concepts and transforming the old mindsets are the prerequisites to realizing system innovation. When formulating the 11th Five-Year reform plan of teacher education, some provinces and municipalities had neither international vision nor experience summaries. As a result, such a plan is nothing but a dead letter. A number of problems cannot be avoided in the formulation of the *Reform Plan of Teacher Education*. First is defining the concept. Some may say that it is too demanding to train teachers as reflective education experts. However, such a view has erased the core elements—reflection and practice of teacher professionalization. Actually it is anti-professionalization, and the image of teachers in their mind is still a teaching-smith (*jiaoshujiang* 教书匠). It is a striking contrast that many experts voiced unprofessional opinions, and their professionalism is even not comparable to that of the front-line teachers in the education pilot areas. This phenomenon involves an essential key issue of formulating a reform plan—the definition of teacher's professional development, including two dimensions: an individual dimension and a collective dimension. That is to say, forming a teacher team should be regarded as a criterion to examine the professionalization of teachers, which is determined by the characteristics of teacher's work. The formulation of the *Reform Plan of Teacher Education* can never neglect the collective dimension. The construction of teacher teams cannot always be confined to the individual development of teachers, but great efforts should also be made to developing teacher teams in each school because the individual development of teachers is limited without the development of teacher teams. So it is time to change the conventional individualistic way of thinking on this issue. Second is understanding the current situation. It is necessary to have a general knowledge of the existing resources of teacher education in China to see whether teaching universities (adult education schools), and district education schools, as well as teaching and research offices are able to undertake the mission of teacher education in the new era. Plans should be made on the basis of a thorough investigation on this project to impress authoritative administrations in the above mentioned institutions. In particular, the mindset of both district education schools and teaching and research offices is seriously out-dated including their underdeveloped educational ideology, low educational level, obsolete curriculum designs, and so on, all of which are intolerable. How to change the organizational and personnel structures in these institutions should be the topic of top priority for the 11th Five-Year Plan. Otherwise, if these low level administrations lead the construction of teacher teams, the result will totally run counter to the purpose as they will produce more destructive than constructive effects of teacher professionalization. Therefore, in order to make the preparation of *Reform Plan of Teacher Education,* it is of the utmost urgency to fully understand the present situation of teacher education organizations especially that of district education schools and teaching and research offices. Third is supporting measures. Any plans will turn out to be inoperable if there is no funding support. Though phrases such as financial support at the level of municipality and financial support at the level of district are mentioned in the *Implementation Safeguard,* it seems that the issue has not been listed on the agenda for serious official consideration.

When thinking about curriculum reform of teacher education, it is of vital importance to set up a development mechanism where educational research, teacher training, and educational practice are closely intertwined with each other. Education in China hopes to advocate positive, reformatory and professional ideas in the process of promoting the *Reform Project of Teacher Education.* The process of reform can also be regarded as a process of constructive criticism or critical construction. All educators are entitled to present well-intentioned criticisms and rational appeals for the curriculum reform of teacher education, but criticisms and appeals must be based on academic studies or practical research. Any contemptuous or negative attitudes towards the reform are a manifestation of a lack of academic conscience and social responsibility. There will be different opinions which may even provoke heated ideological confrontation in the process of curriculum reform of teacher education. That is a good thing. However, the overall direction of reform cannot be denied. It is as good as abandoning reform if China continues to follow ideas and concepts of Kairov's Pedagogy and rigidly stick to the three old disciplines (laosanmen 老三门). China is undergoing a transitional period of social change, and education reform practice, especially curriculum reform practice of basic education, determined to dump educational disciplines like three old disciplines into the trash can. As educators, what should we do and where should we go? - This is the question that we all have to answer.

References

American Research Promotion Association. *Transforming Teaching*, trans. Toshiaki Mori. Kyoto: Kitaojishobo, 2004.

Charles E. Silberman. *Crisis in the Classroom*, trans. Tadashi Yamamoto. Tokyo: Saimaru Shuppankai, 1973.

Fang Mingsheng 方明生. Xinshiji Riben jiaoshi jiaoyu mianlin de keti yu daxue de yingdui 新世纪日本教师教育面临的课题与大学的应对 [Problems and strategies faced by Japanese teachers in the new era]. 2005, unpublished.

Hitoshi Yoshimoto. *Encyclopedia of Modern Pedagogy*. Tokyo: Meijitosho, 1987.

Keiichi Takano. *On Modern Teachers*. Tokyo: Daiichihoki, 1984.

Kojiro Imazu. *Teacher Education in Changing Society*. Nagoya: Nagoyadaigakushuppankai, 1996.

Li Qilong 李其龙 & Chen Yongming 陈永明. Jiaoshi jiaoyu kecheng de guoji bijiao 教师教育课程的国际比较 [*Global Comparison of Teacher Educational Courses*]. Beijing: Educational Science Publishing House, 2002.

Manabu Sato. *Curriculum and Teachers*, trans. Zhong Qiquan 钟启泉. Beijing: Educational Science Publishing House, 2003.

Seikichi Takaku. *Thoery of Education Practice*. Tokyo: Kyouikushuppan, 1990.

Tsukubadaigaku Pedagogical Research Association. *The Basics of Modern Pedagogy*, trans. Zhong Qiquan 钟启泉. Shanghai: Shanghai Educational Publishing House, 2003.

Wang Ling 汪凌. Faguo zhongxiaoxue shizi biaozhun he zhuanye peixun de yuanze yu kecheng moshi 法国中小学师资标准和专业培训的原则与课程模式 [French teachers' qualifications and professional training principle and curriculum]. 2005, unpublished.

Wu Gang 吴刚. Jiaoshi zhuanye fazhan: huhuan xingdong Jiaoshi zhuanye fazhan: Huhuan xingdong 教师专业发展：呼唤行动 [*Developing Teacher Education: Calling for Actions*]. *Shanghai Education Research*, 2005.

Yoshinobu Shoi. Development Aid of Finland Today. *Tokyo Education*, 2005, (6), 66.

Zhao Zhongjian 赵中建. Quanqiu jiaoyu fazhan de yanjiu redian 全球教育发展的研究热点 [*Popular Topics of Global Education*]. Beijing: Educational Science Publishing House, 2003.

Zhong Qiquan 钟启泉. Jiaoshi zhuanyehua de wuqu jiqi pipan 教师专业化的误区及其批判 [Misconceptions and criticism on professional development of teachers]. *Education Development Research*, 2003, (5), 119–123.

Zhong Qiquan钟启泉. Mianxiang xinshidai shizi peiyang de gaishan fangce—Jizi Riben de jiaoyu baogao (zhi san) 面向新时代师资培养的改善方策—寄自日本的教育报告（之三）[Innovation strategy of teacher training in the new era—Education Report from Japan]. *Education References*, 1998, (3), 40.

CHAPTER 8

Teaching Practices: Analytical Modes and Philosophies—Comments on the Assumption of Teaching Particularism

As a process of social cultural practice conducted by teachers and students, teaching practice represents the complex realization of political, economic, social, cultural and ethical values.[1] However, the study of teaching practice in international psychology has always been constrained to a simple form of applying the theories and conclusions gained from experiments directly into teaching, and regarding the pursuit of universal teaching methods as its basic study. With the development of cognitive science and qualitative research since the 1960s, fundamental changes have taken place in the entire teaching practice paradigm including methodology. This paper, using the recent studies on educational psychology as clues, systematizes the gradual progress of teaching practice mode, reviews the significance, features, and studies on teachers' practice thinking in social constructivism, and exposes the fallacy in Teaching Particularism limited by methodological behaviorism.

1 Development of Teaching Practice Mode: From Behaviorism to Constructivism

Classrooms over the world are quietly changing. As B.W. Wilson said, "Since the 1960s, the teaching practice mode has transferred from behaviorism to constructivism through information processing. This transformation, highlighting the importance of learners' self-realization that helps learners understand the objective world, discover its value and meaning, and then rebuild it, has brought an immense influence on education skills."[2] An era of classroom revolution has arrived.

---

1   Chapter title translated from *Educational Research*, 2012, (10), 108–114.
2   Brent G. Wilson & Peggy Cole, Cognitive teaching modes, in *Handbook of Research for Educational Communication and Technology*, ed. David H. Jonassen. New York: Macmillan, 1996, 601–621.

© KONINKLIJKE BRILL NV, LEIDEN, 2022 | DOI:10.1163/9789004473300_009

TEACHING PRACTICES 127

1.1 Behaviorist Mode of Teaching Practice: Making Class No Difference to Amphitheater

Since teaching serves as the core of school education, research on it has naturally become the focus of school education research. However, recent teaching research in China, even some scholars engaging in pedagogical research are still affected, consciously or involuntarily, by the traditional behaviorist paradigm, envisaging teaching as simple exercises. Hence, teaching is seen purely as an integration of teaching contents and teaching methods.

From the perspective of behaviorism, classroom teaching practice usually pursues teaching efficiency as the focus in accordance with teaching targets (mostly confined to behavior objectives reflected in actual behaviors). A representative example is the assumption of teaching particularism.[3] It defines children's study as merely a special cognitive process in terms of acquiring objective knowledge under the guidance of teachers. Thus, research on the assumption of teaching particularism is degraded to the level of only searching for skills of imparting knowledge, which, according to some scholars, is nothing but discussions about how to open the treasure chest of knowledge relying on teachers' teaching and students' listening. Both the memory mode of learning psychology study in early years and the well-known programmed teaching offer support for the assumption of teaching particularism to a certain extent. As G.R. Morrison addresses, "The behavioral learning theory regards the external conditions such as rewards and punishments as the determining factors for future behaviors."[4] B.F. Skinner deems children's learning process

---

3   N. A. Kaiipob addresses that "the feature of students' interpretation about reality is that they tend to learn the knowledge known and acquired by the human Beings. They are usually guided by experienced teachers. Teaching also involves developing children's intelligence, ethics and physical health step by step." See Kaiipob, *Pedagogy (volume one)*, trans. Shen Ying & Nan Zhishan. Beijing: People's Education Press, 1952, 60–61. Since 1980s, Kaiipob's theory was further refined, and he claimed that teaching in essence is "a special process of cognition" which led to the "Assumption of Teaching Particularism". Some representative interpretations are: "students mainly learn indirect experience, which gives rise to the special presentation of cognition process." See Zou Youhua, Epistomology of teaching. *Curriculum Teaching Material Method*, 1982, (1). qtd from Qu Baokui, *Collection of Pedagogy·Teaching (volume one)*. Beijing: People's Education Press. 1988, 273. "The subjects that students learn and their learning method are special. So indirect experience is important—learning indirect experience and applying it indirectly." See Wang Cesan, *Essays on Teaching*. Beijing: People's Education Press, 1985, 118. It is the same concept as L. Klingberg, a German scholar, who argues "Teaching is a special reminder of science truth and science knowledge" in *Contemporary Pedagogical Theory* (translated by Tadao Sato & Tokyo Meijitosho, 1978, 45).

4   Gary R. Morrison, *Designing Effective Instruction*, trans. Yan Yuping. Beijing: China Light Industry Press, 2007, 5.

being no more than cultivating "good homework habits". Based on this view, he created a "programmed learning" theory with concepts of stimulus, response and reinforcement, and then spared no effort on its promotion. Influenced by Skinner school's learning theory, high teaching efficiency thus becomes the most important subject in teaching research. From then on, the assumption of developing universal teaching methods enjoys great prevalence in teaching researches and teaching practice over a long period of time. Many people considered that adopting results on perception and memory from laboratory research as unquestionable and proper for subject teaching researches. People, therefore, followed the flow by employing these methodologies for doing experiments, even in actual classroom practices which stress strict control, before drawing general teaching methods, and demonstrating teaching effects based on the relevance of independent variables and dependent variables. In the 1950s, Cronbach initiated the concept of Aptitude Treatment Interaction (ATI) which sought a comparatively efficient research on teaching method from the perspective of teaching optimization.[5] However, this concept lacks verification in regards to its theoretical validity, having no adequate proof or research on whether or not teaching practice is restricted by the aptitude of the presumptive learners. Therefore, ATI and the relative research disclose the methodological weakness of the psychology of teaching as lacking analysis based on concrete social and cultural contexts, and disconnecting from teaching contents but being confined to the exclusive pursuit for teaching methods. Coincidentally in the 1970s, N.A. Flanders' interaction analysis, which commits to ameliorating teaching behaviors through real-life situation analysis on teaching, also goes no deeper than quantitative analysis. It fails to realize qualitative analysis in children's learning process.

Consequently, the training mode of behaviorism is just making the amphitheater as the ideal teaching mode wherein teachers propose questions and issue communiques while students take the role as a reactor responding mechanically in accordance with class rules. H. Mehan indicates that daily discourse begins with people who do not understand proposing questions and ends with expressions of gratitude toward reactors. The discourse basically

---

5   It was a concept addressed by L. J. Cronbach in his inauguration speech when appointed as the chairman of American Psychological Association in 1957. It infers that each child has his aptitude in learning, namely learning adaptability, which decides the treatment of teaching materials and methods as well as whether meaningful learning can be obtained in particular situations. Due to different aptitudes among different learners, different teaching outcomes will be achieved by different treatments. Cronbach names the variance the Aptitude Treatment Interaction (ATI for short), qtd by Kanji Hatano, *Book of Leaning Psychology*. Tokyo: Kaneko Shobo, 1968, 633–648.

TEACHING PRACTICES

consists of a question-answer-gratitude process. Whereas in class discourse it is the answer man (teacher) who proposes questions and comments on the answers by the people who do not understand (students), thus, the conversation consists of a question-answer-comment structure. Teachers are endowed with the right to propose questions and make comments.[6] Therefore, teachers should always be alert to avoid questioning that may potentially break the equal teacher-student relationship in the teaching process.

Defining the nature of teaching as a special learning process is bound to result in various malpractices. Firstly, teaching is arbitrarily attributed to a simple transfer of knowledge. "The primary task of teaching is to teach students how to arm themselves with knowledge and skills so as to develop their comprehensive capabilities, while other respects should be the byproducts during the transfer process."[7] Secondly, teaching is marked with separating subjects and objects. Teacher and student, respectively, serve as the subject in charge of shaping and the object being shaped. "Since teachers decide everything including teaching objectives, contents, methods, processes, results and quality, students do not have to make any decisions about their learning."[8] The binary opposition between subject and object determines the inequality between students and teachers, thus restricting students' subjectivity and creativity. Thirdly, the teaching process is treated as a closed, habitual system where everything goes in accordance with the syllabus. The teacher takes charge of explaining the knowledge in the treasure chest of knowledge and presents standard answers while the students' major obligation is to accept and deposit those given answers as knowledge. Confining teaching practice to micro-level skills is untenable. Like many other scholars, Brown criticized that "by participating in such ersatz activities, students are likely to misconceive entirely what practitioners actually do. As a result, students can be easily introduced to a formalistic, intimidating view of math that encourages a culture of math phobia rather than one of authentic math activities."[9] As early as the 1960s, the Polish researcher W. Okon contended with the substitution of "Memory Teaching" by "Thinking Teaching".[10] Some Chinese scholars are still

---

6 Mehan Hugh, Learning lessons, in *Curriculum and Teachers*, ed. Manabu Sato and trans. Zhong Qiquan 钟启泉. Beijing: Educational Science Publishing House, 2003, 349.

7 Qu Baokui 瞿葆奎, Jiaoyuxue wenji·jiaoxue (zhong ce) 教育学文集·教学（中册）[*Collection of Pedagogy: Teaching* (volume two)]. Beijing: People's Education Press, 1988, 657.

8 Wang Cesan 王策三, Jiaoxue lungao 教学论稿 [*Essays on Teaching*]. Beijing: People's Education Press, 1985, 123.

9 John Seely Brown, Allan Collins, & Paul Duguid, Situated cognition and the culture of learning. *Educational Researcher*, 1989, 18(1), 32–42 .

10 Wincenty Okon, On independence of thinking and behaviors, in *Overview of Teaching Theories*, ed. Toshio Hosoya. Tokyo: Meijitosho, 1981, 36.

talking proudly about the treasure chest of knowledge which is quite similar to the toolbox of knowledge criticized by Lave.

| 1.2 | *Teaching Practice Mode of Social Constructivism: Classroom for Social Interaction* |

In the late 1950s, cognitive psychology research in the laboratory began to make a shift from animal learning to human learning, from the past mechanical memorizing of null words to the memorizing of significant words and texts, suggesting that the learning process is information processing and knowledge acquisition where learners are information processors while teachers are information distributors. To put it in another way, cognitivism focused on exploring the interior psychological structure of knowledge acquisition instead of exterior and observable behaviors. Although cognitivism highlights the effect of environment and feedback exercises as much as behaviorism, the difference is that cognitivism puts its concern on learner's psychological activities and their learning initiative. It maintains that school classes ought to be a medium with dual functions for information process: firstly, teaching learners how to obtain information and master knowledge; secondly, helping them to discriminate noise and detect useful cues out of inadequate ones. However, both behavorism and cognitivism are developed on objectivism, worshiping the world existing beyond learners and the education aiming to match the structure of the world with that of learners. Behaviorism is concerned about overt, observable behaviors but avoiding covert interior factors, and interpreting the world by stimulus-response theory, while cognitivism, in contrast, goes much deeper to the diversity and complexity of mental structure, and develops formulated research with the aid of artificial intelligence. However, the cognition process, in a sense, is subconscious and thus subjective introspection is not possible. Consequently, a number of cognitive theorists began to question these basic objectivist assumptions.

By the mid-1980s, researches on information process had limits, which gave rise to some new research areas such as studies of mind and brain, studies of artificial intelligence, and studies of situated learning. In the late 1980s, situation theory based on a learning community probed into the culture of school and classroom teaching from a critical perspective, and proposed a framework for designing learning environment. Furthermore, the achievements of brain science research were connected with studies on efficiency of reading, writing, and calculating. After the 1990s, cognitive science began to be applied to learning science in education practice. And then learning science[11] demonstrated

---

11 Mayumi Takagaki, *The Forefront of Teaching Design: Intelligent Processes of Creative Theory and Practice*. Kyoto: Kitaojishobo, 2010, 3–20.

two research trends. The first trend was the cognitive research in the middle of the 20th century trying to clarify the brain activities—how cognitive changes and knowledge structure facilitate the changes of existing concepts established in children's mind. The second trend was the socio-cultural research formed in the second half of 20th century aiming at the dynamically interactive function of social awareness, and explicating children's knowledge construction. Both trends reached the same goal but by different routes. Cognitive research centered on individual knowledge construction, problem-solving competence, and committed efforts to concept reconstruction, equipping learners with intelligence for solving problems. Socio-cultural research focused on helping children to learn by community, cultivated their diverse and deep understandings on problem-solving, and assisted them shaping the responding knowledge structure by sharing social ideas and resolving conflicts.

People attempted to redefine learning in the light of constructivism and social constructivism. The former does not deny the existence of the real world but contends that we can know about the world because our personal experience helps make our unique interpretations. Humans create meaning as opposed to acquiring it.[12] Social constructivists argue that children and the object world, rather than being independent, are open to be united in classroom teaching for social interaction including tools and the other. In consequence, J. Lave and E. Wenger made studies on the process of knowledge acquisition. They proved the social constructiveness of knowledge in situated learning. In their explanation about community of practice and learning in schools, they emphasize that "the actor, the world, the activity, the meaning, the cognition, the learning and knowledge are inter-related and inter-dependent. In nature, meanings are the outcomes of social interactions, and personal knowledge and action involved in those activities are inseparable".[13] In other words, knowledge and action bind together initially. Basically, knowledge is fully immersed in the society and culture. Therefore, Dewey's "learning-is-practice" was re-evaluated by scholars. Meanwhile, Vygotsky's cultural-historical research attracted enormous attention in the society. That is to say, socio-cultural theory that was despised before has regained its popularity and importance in education research. By contrast, J. Piaget's cognitive development theory, centering on the interaction between objects and subjects rather than on the sociality, lost its long-standing influence. The American educational psychologist R. E. Mayer

---

12 Peggy A. Ertmer. Behaviorism, cognitivism, constructivism, trans. Sheng Qunli & Ma Lan, in *Contemporary Instructional Principles, Strategies and Design*. Hangzhou: Zhejiang Education Publishing House, 2006, 208.

13 Jean Lave & Etienne Wenger, *Situated Learning*, trans. Yutaka Saeki. Tokyo: Sangyotosho kabushikikaisha,1993, 26.

integrated behaviorism, cognitivism and constructivism with three significant assumptions—response intensification, knowledge acquisition and knowledge construction, and points out that "what we concern most is assumption of knowledge construction in that it has the greatest potential in improving education and conforms to the development of educational psychology. With the emphasis on knowledge construction, we by no means intend to reject the elementary learning skills. Rather, we argue that those skills ought to be acquired in broader learning tasks and situations instead of being taught independently".[14] The assumption of social contructivist teaching practice redefines teaching practice as the execution of sense and relation. To be specific, teaching and learning are realized by the following three discourses: discourse with the object world, discourse with the other in and outside the classroom, discourse with oneself. The three discourses are conducted in an intertwined manner in real-life teaching and learning.[15] Manabu Sato disputes about previous researches on teaching for being limited in the first category (cognitive process) while belittling the second (socialization process) and third category (introspection process), which topples and pungently attacks the assumption of teaching particularism.

2 Teacher's Practice Thinking in Social Constructivism: Significance, Features and Research Issues

For teachers, the process of teaching practice should be the settlement of realistic issues in complicated situations instead of the application of rational technology; it is a decision-making process involving higher level thinking, judging and choosing. Therefore, the teaching practice assumption in social constructivism requires the new professional teachers to go further than just evaluating ordinary axioms from the perspective of instrumental rationality, to involve a more complicated assessment—whether they are able to provide a framework of questions, to communicate with and reflect on various situations for solving problems. These requirements represent the two types of experts that D. Schon highlights. He believes that the integration of behavior

---

14   Richard Mayer, Learning and the science of instruction, trans. Sheng Qunli & Ma Lan. *Contemporary Instructional Principles, Strategies and Design*. Hangzhou: Zhejiang Education Publishing House. 2006, 177.

15   Manabu Sato, *Curriculum and Teachers*, trans. Zhong Qiquan 钟启泉. Beijing: Educational Science Publishing House, 2003, 154.

TEACHING PRACTICES

and reflection outweighs post-behavior retrospection.[16] He also distinguishes the differences between reflection on behavior and reflection in behavior, emphasizing the reflection on behavior while immersed in behaviors. Thus, Schon depicts teachers as "reflective practitioners" who are able to reflect on and cope effectively with complex situations.

2.1 Significance of Promoting Teacher's Practice Thinking

H. Jonassen makes it clear in his "Knowledge Syllogism"[17] that people acquire knowledge from learning at its primary level. Then, they move to the second level—highly structured study for high-level knowledge, before gaining professional knowledge and skills in the third level. The structural degree of knowledge acquisition and teacher's practice thinking are two important notions. Teaching skills derived of behaviorism emphasize that practice accommodates the learning of preliminary knowledge in further structured situations. The grand movement of Teacher's Teaching Skill Generalization in Japan, for example, was developed in accordance with behaviorism, proposing that teaching skills can be generalized in objective and transferable rules. In other words, leaners' behavioral goals are tacit in the way that the general rules of controlling learners' behaviors are accessible to all, which is especially proper for knowledge acquisition at the early stage. However, when more sophisticated and highly structured knowledge is demanded, it is imperative for learners to have a significant objective world. Theories, such as scaffolding instruction and cognitive apprenticeship, argue that learners interpret the meaning of the world through diversified relations in the objective world that they participate in.

Jonassen's syllogism shares similarities with martial arts learning in Japan: following—breaking through—surpassing. Following refers to the apprentice carrying out his or her teacher's instructions to the letter for the knowledge at this stage is merely a structured one. For more highly structured knowledge and advanced skills, the apprentice needs to learn from the master continuously, pursuing self-independence at the same time. Breaking through is the hard stage, equivalent to the transfer from the second to the third stage of knowledge learning mentioned above. Then the apprentice surpasses his or her master and develops a good command of individual skills, which is the surpassing stage. Differing from the educational school of thought that

---

16   Donald Schon, *Wisdom of Experts: Reflective Practioner in Action*, trans. Manabu Sato & Kiyomi Akita. Tokyo: Yumiru Shuppan, 2001,147.

17   David H. Jonassen, Objectivism versus constructivism: Do we need a new philosophical paradigm? *Educational Technology Research and Development*, 1991, (3), 5–13.

separates proposition education and skill education, Kumiko Ikuta[18] defines a developing process of a martial world with classical arts and craftsmanship, where learners engage in a craftsmanship world, and the real world for mastering martial arts, creating relations in meaning in an entire martial world. She does not perceive knowledge as a real-life notion that can be obtained but as a dynamic, cognitive and comprehensive judgment in interpreting the multiple phenomena in daily life and work contexts. This craftsmanship practice provides an essential viewpoint for teachers' practice thinking for which, martial art can be comprehended as the complex education process between teachers and students featured as dynamic, flexible, and with a high degree of freedom. This argument can be supported by the practice thinking and teaching skills of experienced teachers. Children's practice thinking, depending on their learning development, relies on the particularity shown in the process of growing up into adults. Information theory envisages the children's maturation process as the richness of their average information volume, which is crucial in the expanding of the children's world views through absorbing new information, thus making them different than before. Practice thinking that distinguishes constantly changing children as the subject, is a thinking for exploring the relations, cooperation and firmness of children, and has the potential for opening up a new world. Teachers correct their teaching skills and polish their thinking in experiencing the martial art practice.

2.2   *Features of Teacher's Practice Thinking*

Teaching is by no means simply repeating what the book says. The importance of teacher's practice thinking can be reflected from the fact that one third of the class time is dedicated to teaching strategies. So, what knowledge and skills scaffold teachers' practice thinking?

Shulman proposes that the knowledge of teaching practice covers at least seven categories of basic knowledge—content knowledge, general pedagogical knowledge, curriculum knowledge, pedagogical content knowledge (PCK), knowledge of learners and their characteristics, knowledge of educational contexts, knowledge of educational ends, purposes, and values, and their philosophical and historical grounds."[19] All of the above are explicitly clarified in the teacher's curriculum in teacher's universities in China. However, the knowledge that students from teacher's universities acquire serves as a stepping

---

18   Kumiko Ikuta, Teaching and learning in inheriting Craftsmanship, in *Composition of Practicing Ego*, ed. Yuji Moro. Tokyo: Kaneko Shobo, 2001, 230–246.

19   Lee S. Shulman, Knowledge and teaching: foundation of the new reform, *Harvard Educational Review*, 1987, 57(1), 1–22.

TEACHING PRACTICES 135

stone for their teaching practice. They gain direct or indirect knowledge from observing the classes of primary and middle schools, from the courses about subject knowledge and teaching principles that are in education programs offered in their universities, and from the internship or initial working experience as new teachers. By contrast, teaching in real-life situations always requires teachers to observe students' behaviors and facial expressions, and perceive and experience classroom surroundings as the critical foundations for their teaching. Teacher's practice knowledge entails complete commitment to the class mentally and physically. In this sense, first-hand teaching experience assists, usually as implicit knowledge, the mastery of practice knowledge. Explicit knowledge and implicit knowledge complement each other in teacher's practice knowledge.

Teacher's practice knowledge is based on specific education objectives, and specific teaching experience is gained through students in educational contexts, compatible with the 3Cs, namely content, context and cognition. Both this knowledge and experience are systematic in constant updates and refinement.[20] Teacher's knowledge structure is multilayered. (1) Empirical knowledge—knowledge depending on certain limited contexts. Compared with speculative knowledge, it is extremely concrete, versatile and dynamic although lacking preciseness and universality. (2) Case knowledge—knowledge recorded and inherited about individual child cognitive behaviors, individual teaching contents and individual class contexts. (3) Comprehensive knowledge—knowledge not stored as comprehensive knowledge about a certain academic field, rather, acquired through problem-solving and the integration of different types of multiple professional knowledge. Furthermore, it outgrows the bounds of existing academic knowledge to a deeper exploration of uncertainty; it probes into every possibility hidden behind the uncertainty and seeks for betterness. (4) Implicit knowledge—not just the teacher's explicit knowledge but also their implicit knowledge plays a role in teaching. In fact, in the decision making process, unconscious thinking, implicit knowledge and belief rather than conscious knowledge and thinking, make a huge difference in real teaching. (5) Individual knowledge—personalized knowledge based on each teacher's experience. Educationists in America and Japan have verified some fundamental features of experienced teacher's practice thinking through their comparisons with inexperienced teachers. Foremost, meditation takes place not only after teaching but also during teaching. Secondly, experienced teachers view teaching actively and sensitively in terms of reasoning students'

20　Manabu Sato, *Curriculum and Teachers*, trans. Zhong Qiquan 钟启泉. Beijing: Educational Science Publishing House, 2003, 386.

learning process, interpreting meanings in teaching and learning, and further, seeking more possibilities of teaching to solve practical problems in reality. Thirdly, practice thinking goes beyond unilateral teaching and, in retrospect, the teaching itself from dimensional aspects, taking students' viewpoint into account. Fourthly, they tend to judge and ponder on the relationship between teaching and textbooks, and between teaching and students' meditation according to the situation of teaching and learning. Fifthly, they can discover the complicated connections among different scenarios, thus rebuilding the existing framework for solving problems.[21] In addition, experienced teachers stand out not only for their adequate knowledge of cognition but also for their love and care for students due to a teacher's dedication and sense of duty. As H. Sockett explained: "In terms of teaching, virtue is in nature honesty, courage, care, love, fairness, practice and wisdom".[22]

2.3 *Cultivation of Teacher's Practice Thinking*

Theoretically speaking, the subject of the cultivation of teacher's practice thinking should be included in the agenda of teaching study. In reality, the study of teaching and teaching practice in China is still in the first phase of behaviorism, according to Jonassen. If teaching is viewed as a specialized profession still at the stage of behaviorism, or if the study of teacher's practice thinking moves away from cognitivisim and constructivism, we assert that the pattern of teaching practice founded on constructivism is rootless and unrealistic. On the contrary, if teaching is viewed as a process for the formation of education communication, teachers should pay full attention to research about the child's learning world and teacher's practice thinking in the process.

Teaching is the process of constant redesigning along with the formation of teacher's practice thinking as well. R.J. Shavelson and P. Stern,[23] who articulated the teaching process as that of practice thinking, reveal that, in a teaching course grounded in well-thought plans, the unexpected situations outside of the plans call for either immediate decisions or delayed responses. They also stated that teaching skills should include specific and observable behaviors such as questioning, blackboard-writing, and instructing that follow teacher's recognition and determination. These teaching skills feature in the

---

21 Manabu Sato, *Curriculum and Teachers*, trans. Zhong Qiquan钟启泉. Beijing: Educational Science Publishing House, 2003, 228–229.

22 Hugh Sockett, The moral base for teacher professionalism, in *Wisdom of Teaching*, ed. Masami Kjita.Tokyo: Yuhikaku, 2004, 190.

23 Richard J. Shavelson & Paula Stern, Research on teachers· pedagogical thoughts, judgment and behavior. *Review of Educational Research*, 1981, 51(4), 455–498.

judgment and decision-making for achieving the above behaviors. In addition, the decisions made by teachers should be characterized by a complex combination of simultaneous, instantaneous, continuous and pertinent due to the fact that they are made in pace with different classroom situations where the teacher influences children and dwells on his functions, and understands the children's responses. Therefore, teaching becomes a process in which teachers make instant reflections and decisions. Following D. Shon this is referred to as reflection in action and the practitioners of reflection in action are called reflective practitioners. Unlike logical thinking, the reflection is a way of thinking activated by explorations and judgments about the hesitations and confusions in actual teaching practice. Manabu Sato, as an advocator of reflective practitioner, redefines teacher's practice knowledge, thinking and cognition as latent knowledge that functions as potential knowledge in that it involves unconscious thinking, implicit knowledge, and belief based on the individual teacher's experience. The cognition of reflective practitioners includes recognizing the process, reflecting on the process, communicating with different situations, reflecting on the recognition and examination of the process, and conversing with the reflective situations.[24] The practice here is not confined to the simple application of theories and techniques.[25]

Teachers' practice thinking is not formed overnight. Knowledge obtained from textbooks can only be transferred to useful application through teaching practice. Knowledge and concepts deriving from sheer imitation is a more basic pedagogical knowledge than practice knowledge. In teachers' training, interpretations about content knowledge, specific teaching skills, and understandings about curriculum standards, or reports about teachers' life are not necessarily reliable. Therefore, what matters are the realistic and simulative experiences in real teaching. Hence, recommending experience-oriented learning and developing practice curriculum are of pressing urgency. However, the assumption of teaching particularism stands as the major obstacle in cultivating practice thinking among teachers. In his comparative research about inexperienced teachers and backbone teachers, Masami Kjita clarifies[26], that the subject of the former is to pinpoint teaching while the latter targets teaching quality including the relationship between group students and individual students, and ways of cultivating children's interest. Backbone teachers are more concerned with children's real development conditions in class

---

24   Manabu Sato, *Curriculum and Teachers*, trans. Zhong Qiquan 钟启泉. Beijing: Educational Science Publishing House, 2003, 242.

25   Ibid, 229.

26   Masami Kjita. *Wisdom of Teaching*. Tokyo: Yuhikaku, 2004, 164.

and coping with children's individuality, so as to further polish their skills in improving children's sense of involvement, and to widen their range of practice thinking in teaching. From the teacher's perspective, practice thinking as carried by experienced teachers features "simultaneous reflection on teaching practice", "active expert interference with teaching situations", "comprehensive cognition from multiple perspectives" and "strategies composed of discovering ability and reflective issues" and the like.[27] This practice thinking is realized in specific teaching practice and is deprived of realistic meaning if not examined in the practice context. Knowledge involved in practice thinking contributes to the reconstruction of learned knowledge, where implicit knowledge and unconscious belief play the crucial part.

Teacher's practice thinking is not so much achieved individually but in the sharing and formation of the school culture realized by teachers from the same schools. Outstanding teaching practice is supported by professional practice thinking that is not only personal and subjective but also, simultaneously, collaborative and inter-subjective.[28] A good example is class observation which serves as an excellent platform for teachers' training. The observers may produce their own subjectivity in comparison with that of their colleagues to explain the variance based on inter-subjectivity. An educational society expects teachers to bond not only with colleagues but also experts and parents into a learning network or community. Therefore, the teacher's role is more than just being a reflective practitioner, but to be an expert skilled in cooperation and community building.

A teacher's growth is ultimately determined by his development of practice thinking and intelligence practice. Only through appropriate training for practice thinking can teachers correctly understand the elements and origin of their teaching contents and the complexity of content knowledge so as to grow into a "reflective practitioner from a skillful worker."[29]

References

John Seely Brown, Allan Collins, & Paul Duguid. Situated cognition and the culture of learning. *Educational Researcher*, 1989, 18(1), 32–42.

Peggy A. Ertmer. Behaviorism, cognitivism, constructivism, trans. Sheng Qunli & Ma Lan, in *Contemporary Instructional Principles, Strategies and Design*. Hangzhou: Zhejiang Education Publishing House, 2006.

---

27   Ibid, 162–165.
28   Masami Kjita, *Wisdom of Teaching*. Tokyo:Yuhikaku, 2004, 175.
29   Manabu Sato, *Educational Methods*. Tokyo: sayūsha, 2010, 169.

TEACHING PRACTICES

David H. Jonassen. Objectivism versus constructism: Do we need a new philosophical paradigm?" *Educational Technology Research and Development*, 1991, (3), 5–13.

Kumiko Ikuta. Teaching and learning in inheriting Craftsmanship, in *Composition of Practicing Ego*, ed. Yuji Moro. Tokyo: Kaneko Shobo, 2001, 230–246.

Jean Lave & Etienne Wenger. *Situated Learning*, trans. Yutaka Saeki.Tokyo: Sangyotosho kabushikikaisha. 1993.

Manabu Sato. *Curriculum and Teachers*, trans. Zhong Qiquan 钟启泉. Beijing: Educational Science Publishing House, 2003.

Manabu Sato. *Educational Methods*. Tokyo: Sayūsha, 2010, 169.

Masami Kjita. *Wisdom of Teaching*. Tokyo: Yuhikaku, 2004.

Richard Mayer. Learning and the science of instruction, trans. Sheng Qunli & Ma Lan, in *Contemporary Instructional Principles, Strategies and Design*. Hangzhou: Zhejiang Education Publishing House. 2006.

Mayumi Takagaki. *The Forefront of Teaching Design: Intelligent Processes of Creative Theory and Practie*. Kyoto: Kitaojishobo, 2010.

Mehan Hugh. Learning lessons, in *Curriculum and Teachers*, ed. Manabu Sato and trans. Zhong Qiquan 钟启泉. Beijing: Educational Science Publishing House, 2003.

Gary R. Morrison *Designing Effective Instruction*, trans. Yan Yuping. Beijing: China Light Industry Press, 2007.

Wincenty Okon. On independence of thinking and behaviors, in *Overview of Teaching Theories*, ed. Toshio Hosoya. Tokyo: Meijitosho, 1981.

Qu Baokui 瞿葆奎. Jiaoyuxue wenji·jiaoxue (zhong ce) 教育学文集·教学（中册）[*Collection of Pedagogy: Teaching* (volume two)]. Beijing: People's Education Press, 1988.

Wang Cesan 王策三. Jiaoxue lungao 教学论稿 [*Essays on Teaching*]. Beijing: People's Education Press, 1985.

Brent G. Wilson & Peggy Cole. Cognitive teaching modes, in *Handbook of Research for Educational Communication and Technology*, ed. David H. Jonassen. New York: Macmillan, 1996.

Richard J. Shavelson & Paula Stern. Research on teachers' pedagogical thoughts, judgment and behavior. *Review of Educatiobal Research*, 1981, 51(4), 455–498.

Donald Schon. *Wisdom of Experts: Reflective Practioner in Action*, trans. Manabu Sato & Kiyomi Akita. Tokyo:Yumiru Shuppan 2001,147.

Lee S. Shulman. Knowledge and teaching: foundation of the new reform. *Harvard Educational Review*, 1987, 57(1), 1–22.

Hugh Sockett. The moral base for teacher professionalism, in *Wisdom of teaching*, ed. Masami Kjita. Tokyo: Yuhikaku, 2004, 190.

CHAPTER 9

New Challenges in Teachers' Training

1 Opportunities and Predicaments of Teacher-Training

1.1 Opportunities: Ideological Motivation and Knowledge Resources from New Curriculum Reform

1.1.1 Teacher Image

For a long time, the primary mission of a teacher has been to impart objective knowledge to students. The more knowledge imparted, the better the teacher, with a teacher's professional level is usually being indicated by his / her profound subject knowledge and proficient teaching skills. Under such circumstances, teaching practice is regarded as the application of some universally effective educational theory, and teaching process is seen as a technical process where teachers are no more than teaching technicians, who perform the work of this technical occupation. Thus, teachers' professionalism is equal to a definite and operational "technical practice". D. A. Schon criticized this teaching craftsman image dominated by technical rationality by putting forward the concept of "reflective practice",[1] encouraging teachers to be positive explorers and reflective practitioners whose professional practice is characterized by reflection in action and action in reflection. This means that the professional development of a teacher in effect is the development of his / her practical knowledge formed in problem-solving in various real-life situations. Teachers are not so much knowledge transmitters as supporters of children's learning. Teachers as well should play the role of researchers who do research on their own work. The new curriculum reform proposes that teachers should transform themselves from skilled teachers to reflective practitioners.

1.1.2 Public Induction

Many educational newspapers and periodicals have published a series of articles about domestic and international trends and typical experiences on teacher-training program. Forums and lectures as well as teachers training websites have been organized to make preparations for promotion of the program and to provide new information and reference materials for the front-line teachers. As a method of training, the first thing is to pay attention to practical

---

1 Manabu Sato, *Curriculum and Teachers*, trans Zhong Qiquan 钟启泉. Beijing: Educational Science Publishing House, 2003, 332.

© KONINKLIJKE BRILL NV, LEIDEN, 2022 | DOI:10.1163/9789004473300_010

knowledge or knowledge of methodology based on the great achievements of modern science including their universal applicability, logical property and objective features. The second thing is to emphasize cooperative research in that teachers training is not accomplished by the researcher's personal interest but the formation of the teaching teams, which requires cooperation across the subject areas. Cooperative research acquires positive significance from team work. It aims to enable the teachers to use their insights and critical judgments developed from their respective field of research to verify teaching practice and significance.

1.1.3 Official Institutional Framework

Compendium of Curriculum Reform for Elementary Education, Teacher Professional Standard, and *Teacher Education Curriculum Standard* published by the Ministry of Education form the general institutional framework for the teacher-training programs represented by academic training programs and non-academic training programs respectively. Academic training programs include educational background compensation training and professional degree training (Master of Education and Doctor of Education); non-academic training programs include job-entry or job-induction training, on-the-job training, elite backbone teacher training, head teacher training, and specialized field training. Since 2003, the Ministry of Education has implemented the "National Teacher Education Network Alliance Program", which has formed a huge teacher-training system composed of educational network of human resources, the satellite broadcast network Skynet and an Internet system participated in by many teachers' education institutions all over the country.

1.1.4 Practice Samples

Since the implementation of new curriculum reform, a large number of schools dedicated to the reform of practice research have emerged across the country. The practice research is an action research (research method) in order to solve the problems in school educational practice (research content), aiming at improving the school educational practice (research purpose). Teachers' practice research is an endless activity.[2] These practice samples are contributed by higher education teachers, teaching and research staff and front-line teachers.

---

2 Zhong Qiquan, Li Xuehong, & Xu Dingfang 钟启泉, 李学红, 徐淀芳, Zhuanxing zhong de ketang: Shanghai putuo qu tuijin youxiao jiaoxue liu nian xingdong yanjiu 转型中的课堂：上海市普陀区推进有效教学六年行动研究 [*Transforming Classroom: Research on the Six-Year Effective Teaching in Shanghai Putuo District*]. Shanghai: Shanghai Educational Publishing House, 2012, 2.

These samples have acted as a prelude to the education reform which serves as a classic example of classroom revolution throughout the world. Against this background of classroom revolution, the leaders of the Educational Bureau of Putuo District of Shanghai took the opportunity to work together with the Course and Teaching Research Center of East China Normal University and the Teaching and Research Office of Shanghai Municipal Commission of Education to organize professional teachers to form a team of researchers. Beginning from 2006, they launched a research campaign of effective teaching, resulting in a fanfare of classroom transformation symphony starting to make itself heard. They have not only created a lot of remarkable teaching cases, but also have prepared a rich lively practical knowledge waiting to be further explored. Teachers who used to be silent have started to express their opinions, conservativism has given way to liberalism, and communications between the teachers, disciplines and schools that used to be limited and passive have become active. All these changes have greatly enhanced the depth and extent of the participation of front-line teachers in classroom research. More and more higher education institutions in mainland China establish partnerships with primary and secondary schools. In the new curriculum reform, some universities have set up curriculum research centers and teacher education research centers to strengthen the system of cooperation in teacher-training between universities and elementary and middle schools and to encourage university teachers to participate in primary and secondary school teaching research. For example, partnership programs have been established in such areas as cooperation between some university research centers and teacher education research centers, construction of cooperative internship bases, extended employment of outstanding primary and secondary school teachers as part-time university teachers, demonstration classes for teacher university students, and cooperation mechanisms for classroom research.

1.1.5   Basic Consensus

Independence, self-discipline, diversity and cooperation of teacher professional development are reflected by the transformation of teachers education to school-based teachers training. According to the research of Gu Lingyuan and Zhang Feng,[3] many new forms of teaching and research group activities have appeared since the implementation of the new curriculum reform.

---

3   Zhang Feng 张丰, Xiaoben yanxiu de huodong cehua yu zhidu jianshe 校本研修的活动策略与制度建设 [*School-based Training Strategies and System Construction*]. Shanghai: East Normal University Publishing House, 2007, 81–92.

These forms include (1) teaching process management to ensure the smooth implementation of the teaching routines; (2) teaching design research - teaching analysis to improve teaching skills; (3) case study - practical reflection to solve practical difficulties in teaching; (4) action research - systematic study to overcome teaching difficulties in class; (5) resources construction to promote teaching efficiency and resource sharing; (6) seminars to promote the exchange of ideas and experiences; (7) network teaching and research to transfer resource exchange and development from offline to online; and (8) teaching competition to improve teachers' teaching ability. The teacher-training in the context of the new curriculum reform has experienced great changes in both quantity and quality while the communication and cooperation between teachers, disciplines, schools and even overseas counterparts has become common practice.

1.2 Predicament: Struggle between Exam-Oriented Education and Quality-Oriented Education

Today teacher-training is still being strongly affected by exam-oriented education. New curriculum reform stimulates different educational forces that compete with each other for dominance. One undeniable fact is that teacher-training has become an arena for the battle between old and new educational forces.

Force No. 1—The Renovative Force. By relying on the new curriculum reform, this force accelerates the transition from exam-oriented education to quality education among primary schools. It aims to turn primary and secondary schools into a learning community with the help of teacher professional development from school-based training.

Force No. 2—The Conservative Force. It calls the renovative force the radical force, and calls itself moderate one that represents the vast majority of front-line teachers, and criticize its rivals by using such exaggerated terms as mistaken trends of despising knowledge, general directional errors, dangerous, hard landing, disastrous adventure, Non-Marxism, in an attempt to have the new curriculum reform banned. In the face of the irreversible trend of the reform, they later modifed their claims by saying that their initial intention was not to oppose the New Curriculum Reform, but oppose the idealists' radical advocacy of the new curriculum reform. The basic characteristic of this conservative force is to oppose any ideas from the outside world, and to rectify every reform. For example, with reference to the three-dimensional goal they desperately have advocated the orthodoxical double basis, or insist on the organic combination of the double basis and three-dimensional goal. In their attempt to deny classroom teaching reform, they strive to stress the rationality of teacher-centered methodology.

Force No. 3 - The Middle Force. Advocates of this force maintain a neutral attitude claiming themselves to be neither radical nor conservative. Therefore, they are regarded as the wise party. Their basic idea is the organic combination of the exam-oriented education and quality education. The result of such an attitude is grand and spectacular campaign in quality education while down-to-earth movement in exam-oriented education. However, this organic combination of two opposing values is no more than an excuse to maintain the value of exam-oriented education.

Force No. 4—The Extreme Force. This force is essentially a modern version of the traditional conservative force. With the advantages and long experiences accumulated from exam-oriented education, it promotes its own elite education model, even advocating itself as the training base of exceptional innovative talents. Some people call it the second-generation of exam-oriented education or extreme exam-oriented education. The extreme force is the product of multiple factors. The first of these is the conceptual factor, which is in line with Kairov's educational belief whose influences in mainland China have not been eliminated. The second is the institutional factor, which holds that China's basic education school has experienced the construction process of key schools → model schools → special characteristics model school, forming a number of so-called prestigious high-quality schools. The third is the cultural factor, reflected in the superstitious belief that scores in high school entrance examination and college entrance examination are the only criterion for the evaluation of education quality. What is more, a symbiont circle and chain of mutual benefit exist between prestigious universities and key (demonstration) middle schools.

Different voices and conflicting views have come together to break the previous one way of thinking, and this should have been seen as a historical progress. However, the problem that comes along with it is that in the chaotic situation where values are misplaced, the exam-oriented education, having been proved absurd in history, is still popular and extensively practiced. A serious problem is that the education community in general still hails key schools as excellent models for future schools, assuming that they are inherently qualified to undertake the responsibility to train teachers, which in fact, continues to strengthen the culture of exam-oriented education. In the face of the exam-oriented education, China's educational administrations remain silent, and teachers' educational institutions remain silent, as have the teachers (including teachers in famous schools). Therefore, can such schools really become bases for teachers training? Can the model of exam-oriented education and its experience be the benchmark for teachers training?

NEW CHALLENGES IN TEACHERS' TRAINING

2   Prevention of the Regeneration Chain of Exam-Oriented Education

The dispute between quality-oriented education and exam-oriented education has lasted over 30 years. The new curriculum reform has also been implemented for more than 10 years. However, the reality is a paradoxical situation in which a grand and spectacular campaign in quality education coexists with a down-to-earth movement in exam-oriented education. It is hard to believe that a teacher-training characterised by misconceptions of values can lead teachers to successful professional growth. There are two drawbacks in China's modern school system. First, the school organization, order and relationship are unable to adapt to the development of a knowledge society. As a result of industrialization, the modern school system is formed and developed by undertaking the mission of standardizing people's language, behavior and values, and making people members of the country under the guidance of the government's forceful and yet thoughtful policies. out of which, the educational industry to supplement the school system came into being and developed. It is possible that a school system including the space, the organization of time, the order in which that knowledge transfer and acquisition of classroom teaching practice, and the order of behavior and relationship within the school are all under constraint may be in conflict with children's daily life. Second, the principle of performance selection, another function of the modern school, is entirely incompatible with the development of the new era. The task of teaching knowledge in school is reduced to the formation of basic learning ability (exam-oriented learning ability), and the students' ability to memorize and playback the essential, formalized and fragmentary knowledge in the process of large knowledge transfer is the top priority of teaching quality. The mastery of this exam-oriented learning ability dominates the learning objectives for students in today's society. Students can make personal and individual choices to engage themselves in learning activities and interpersonal relationships in classroom situations. Under the influence of the performance selection principle and meritocracy ideology, differences in life experiences and the inequality of opportunity are normalized in the expansion of regeneration of social structure (social structure of economy, culture, human resources and social inequality of opportunity) through the school system under the practice of school institution. The adverse consequences of the modern school system are maximized by the exam-oriented education in China's mainland and specifically manifested as follows:

First, the fundamental attributes of basic education schools are denied. For decades, no changes have been made in the traditional thought of elite education and the distinction between key schools and non-key schools in accordance with the development of times. Despite the invention of such new terms as key schools, model schools and model schools with special-features, the status of key schools has actually been all the more enhanced and strengthened. Basic education is the most essential part in the national education system for establishing proper citizen image of a country. The most essential characteristic of elementary education is its principle of public equality, which refers to the guarantee of educational opportunities and development for all children rather than for specific groups of them. This is determined by the requirement of a talented people and labor force that are necessary for social reproduction. The government makes a heavy investment in the construction of the key schools and their luxurious facilities, and leaves the majority of ordinary schools under-constructed. Consequently, children from rich families in rich regions have more access to better educational resources at better schools whereas children from lower social classes or in poor regions have to go to schools with poor conditions. This classification of people and educational resources will intensify exam-oriented competition and fundamentally destroy the principle of equal education opportunities for all. Key schools are often heard boasting of their excellent educational qualities. However, excellent education does not mean the benefit of the majority should be sacrificed by protecting the interest of a small group. The excellence in this context does not mean that one should over-ride others, but instead that no matter how difficult the conditions may be, each child has chances to excel in the pursuit and attainment of their highest goals.[4] Therefore, this should be the maxim of every school. Fundamentality is the second attribute of basic education. The difference between higher education and basic education is that higher education is the education of professional knowledge and basic education is the education of fundamental knowledge. Even the advanced placement courses offered by universities for high school students belong to the category of general educational courses, not specialized professional courses. Some of the primary and secondary schools in Beijing and Shanghai that are good at exam-oriented education have developed about 200 to 300 school-based courses, claiming that the more school-based courses are developed, the higher the level of the schoolmaster's leadership in curriculum management is. The higher the college enrollment rate is, the stronger the school principal's leadership is.[5] Today is an era in which one does not win by quantity, but by

---

4   Manabu Sato, *Challenges to Schools: Establishing Learning Community*. Shanghai: East Normal University Publishing House, 2010, 3.
5   Zhong Qiquan 钟启泉, Kecheng lingdaoli: shijian, fansi yu gaizhao 课程领导力: 实践、反思与改造 [Curriculum leadership: Allocation, reflection and transformation]. *Modern Educators—Pudong Education*, 2012, (10), 32.

quality. One elaborate high-quality course is better than a dozen low-quality courses put together. Some key schools are so enthralled by the so-called good performance in exam-oriented education and a few of them are so maniac about it that they indulge themselves in the top-notch innovative talent training base construction. However, they forget that they belong to the category of basic education for the purpose of public services and facilities. As a force in citizenship education, the key school mode is incompatible with the public mission that they are supposed to undertake. Some people might say, Chinese education is different from American education. American education is to cultivate socially qualified citizens, and it is more a mode of citizenship education. The notion of Chinese education, on the other hand, is more purposeful and utilitarian, because it encourages people to believe that the fate of students can be changed through education. Therefore they propose that the problem of Chinese education should be solved by the Chinese way of thinking.[6] According to them, the exam-oriented competition is perfectly justifiable, and the universal value of education and the citizenship education has no place at all in China.

Second, the target sequence of subject education is reversed. It is socially necessary for school education to cultivate students' academic thinking and technical mind. Therefore, the school curriculum should not only focus on academic courses, but abandon technical courses and art courses. However, in the context of exam-oriented education, the school curriculum tends to be subject biased, that is, the academic ability is of greater importance than interdisciplinary ability. Fundamental academic abilities that should be developed by basic education have been unfortunately marginalized. Moreover, different values have been misplaced on different subjects in that basic subjects are divided into key ones and non-key ones. Maths, physics and chemistry, for example, are considered as more honorable than those marginalized disciplines such as music, physical education and fine art. The theory of multiple wisdom contends that the nine intellectual elements of mankind are equivalent. However, in the context of examination-oriented education, they are categorized into more important and less important groups, i.e. wisdom related to science is placed in the first group while wisdom related to other aspects is placed in the second group. The escalating support for an exam-oriented education practice contradicts with the needs of society and the nature of human

---

6   Qin Chunhua 秦春华, Kan Meiguo jiaoyu yao you Zhongguo shijiao 看美国教育要有中国视角 [Viewing American Education from China's Perspective]. *Guangming Daily*, 2013, February 20, 14.

intelligence. The nature of exam-oriented education is in fact anti-education.[7] Last but not least, the sequence of subject education has been reversed. Subject teaching in the background of the exam-oriented education is centered on the teaching of knowledge points from the transmission of knowledge points to the consolidation of knowledge points then on to the evaluation of knowledge points. However, the correct sequence of subject education should begin with interest, motivation and attitude, and then thinking ability, judgment ability, expression ability, and then observation skills and experimental skills, and finally knowledge and comprehension.

Third, the boundary between real learning ability and exam-oriented learning ability is confused. Key schools have always advocated the value of exam-oriented learning ability, and they use this value to misguide public opinions and restrict education practice. However, theoretically speaking, exam-oriented learning ability and real learning ability are not opposing concepts, and there is significant overlap between them. Nevertheless, exam-oriented learning ability is, after all, a technique for coping with exams rather than true talent. Its basic characteristics are: (1) Learners' thinking ability is limited to the scope of test-maker's intention and they turn out to be passive receivers. Challenges, contradictions and originality are not acceptable or even forbidden. (2) The subject for learning is the training of students to quickly grasp the test-maker's intention. The outcome of such training is not the ability to find out real problems nor the comprehensive ability to analyze problems, but mechanical reaction or conditioned reflex like robots. (3) Exam-oriented learning is a violation of the nature of learning. It is the development of a cognitive ability by involving students in tons of the fixed types of questions usually designed in test papers.[8] In this way, education is alienated into a process of repeated training for high scores. In contrast, real learning ability is different from exam-oriented learning ability. It is a developmental learning ability, which is not the accumulation of fragmentary knowledge, but a solid grasp of knowledge and skills; it can be applied to real life; it can establish the co-relation and integration of knowledge, skill, thinking ability, judgment ability, and expression ability; it is a motivation and interest to explore the unknown world, a curiosity to seek the in-depth understanding of the world; it encourages children to think about lifestyle, and it cultivates their concept of labor and career development. In this sense, real learning ability, to some extent,

---

7 Zhong Qiquan 钟启泉, Yingshi jiaoyu benzhi shi fanjiaoyu 应试教育本质是反教育 [The essence of exam-oriented education is anti-education]. *Chinese Social Science Today*, 2012, July 16.

8 Ryosuke Kikuchi, *Framework of Learning Competence*. Tokyo: Minshusha, 1992, 95–96.

expresses the specific meaning of the real dynamic and initiative intellectuality.[9] Thus, it is self-deceiving to regard exam-oriented learning ability as the primary index of the students' development. Over the years, some of China's key schools have been proud of their exam-oriented learning ability achievements and have ignored the pursuit of real learning ability, while the mass media sensationalization about the college entrance examination top-scorers has further exacerbated the bias.

Fourth, the value expectation of exam-oriented education and that of quality-enhancement education are fundamentally different. For many years, some key schools have not produced sufficient valuable new pedagogical experiences, and their only strength is solidly promoting exam-oriented education. Moreover, they have obtained enormous financial resources that are far higher than those of general ordinary schools. Thus, they spared no efforts to recruit top students all over the country, along with taking measures to design all kinds of special classes such as Mathematical Olympiad classes, in order to cover their real intention to pursue exam-oriented education. They then use exam-oriented learning ability (usually the proportion of students who enter Tsinghua University and Peking University) as the topmost measure of their education success. However, exam-oriented competition seriously damages children's physical and mental health. Children's physical and mental problems such as net-love, autism, infirmity and bullying emerge, suicide one after another. The exam-oriented education, by essence, is anti-education. Even though some of the schools have been publicly criticized by the mass media for their extreme implementation of exam-oriented education, they still continue to do so and receive tribute from their admirers who travel great distances to learn from them. It is not hard to see that exam-oriented education is on solid ground to defend itself. In the face of the increasingly fierce exam-oriented competition, China's educational planning, educational policy, educational research and even daily educational practice show no signs of changing the situation. The national education development plan has not made institutional arrangements for the transformation from exam-oriented education to quality-oriented education. Virtually none of the key schools take the initiative in reflecting on their own exam-oriented education practice. Public opinions, however, do not venture to expose the problems of exam-oriented education to cut off vested interest chain of these key schools. A more serious fact is that the teacher-training is being affected by exam-oriented education. Shanghai educational administration is trying to terminate this chaotic

---

9 Humanity Education Research Association, New Instruction Highlights of Learning. Tokyo: Kaneko Shobo, 2008, 9–10.

situation by constructing new high-quality schools. The motivation behind it may be good, but objectively, this is no more than the protection of a small number of schools and a soothing gesture for the vast majority of schools. On the one hand, it in a way protects the vested interests of a handful of schools, because designating them as high-quality schools is like giving them official permission to do whatever they like to do. On the other hand, it requires other schools to strive to become the so-called new high-quality schools without giving them the privilege to enroll outstanding students, strive for high-ranking college entrance examinations nor obtain financial support. This is obviously a double standard. Only by adhering to the same standard of investment in accordance with the unified input - output scale to measure the achievements of school education, can the administrative policy be persuasive and credible to the public.

Teacher-training is a double-edged sword, which can be used either to intensify and exacerbate the exam-oriented education, or help to cut off and root out the regurgitation chain of exam-oriented education. The first challenge of teacher-training is to get rid of the impact of the exam-oriented education mode and its experience which is represented by extreme forces, and to cut off the regeneration chain of exam-oriented education.

3 Seeking Self-Discipline and Innovative Teacher-Training

3.1 Methodology of Teacher-Training from the Perspective of Teachers' Knowledge

The challenge of teacher-training is to seek a self-disciplined and innovative training system. For many years, most training projects only geared to excellent teachers and principals have not achieved the expected outcome, but rather caused a lot of unexpected problems. Abandoning traditional training styles and seeking a new style of self-disciplined and innovative training is necessary for the promotion of teacher's growth and the formation of a teacher's learning community. The educational belief established by most front-line teachers over the years was teachers' teaching equals students' learning and students learning well means teachers teaching well. Therefore, teacher-training was restricted in the study of teaching methods, especially the belief in the magical power of lecture methods. This kind of process-output model was a method of behavioral science developed in the 1950s which aims to achieve an optimal teaching effect. This serves as a method that uses the key constituents of the system process as the independent variable and the output of the process as the dependent variable for investigation and research. The new curriculum reform has brought a transformation of teaching research in a way that

NEW CHALLENGES IN TEACHERS' TRAINING

is different from this narrow version of teaching methods and techniques such as questions, illustrations and explanations. It chooses more teacher-inclusive activities as the research object. The new perspective of investigation has shifted its focus to the meaning and background of children's learning experiences rather than the reasonable control of teachers. The ideological basis of this transformation is that the classroom is not a place controlled by the management principles of a factory assembly line, but a place to realize interpersonal communication between teachers and children of diverse cultural backgrounds. The model of process to output teaching research lacks the 3Cs, i.e. content, cognition and context. However, behavioral science takes visible phenomenon as its research object in order to ensure a reasonable control over the object by helping students to understand the cause and effect relationship. Intangible events, such as teaching contents, the cognition of teachers and students, and the cause and effect that are unrelated to visible phenomena lie out of the range of the research. However, teaching research without inquiring into the value and significance of teaching contents, the cognition of teachers and children, and the relations between the classroom and the society, can hardly be considered as educational research. The transformation of teaching research is closely related to the study of teachers' knowledge. Internationally, teaching research after the criticism of the process-output model has been focused on teachers, characterized by teacher thinking research, teacher knowledge research and reflective practice research. The study of teacher thinking research, highlighting teachers as a decision-makers, became active after the middle of 1970s, while teacher knowledge research and reflective practice research began to be active after the 1980s. The study of teacher knowledge emerged as a result of two needs. First, teachers need professional education just as doctors and lawyers do. Therefore it is necessary to explore such essential factors of expert education as knowledge foundation in teacher education. Second, it is necessary to explore the essence and nature of practical knowledge to be applied in classroom situations. The concept of teacher knowledge proposed by L. Schulman in 1987 included 7 key factors. They are the subject content knowledge, teaching methodology knowledge, curriculum knowledge, pedagogical content knowledge, learner's characteristics knowledge, education development knowledge, and knowledge of educational aims, objectives and value and their philosophical foundation. In particular, pedagogical content knowledge, which is the compound of subject content knowledge and teaching methodology knowledge, is regarded as a teacher's unique knowledge.[10] Another study of teacher knowledge was conducted by D. Schon

---

10   Hikoyuki Yasuda, *Modern Education Reform and Teachers*. Tokyo: Tokyo Gakugeidaigaku, 2011, 155.

in his reflective practice study which promotes the study of reflective teaching. Reflective teaching refers to the situation where teachers and students work together to realize reflective thinking, namely the teaching practice of inquiry activities.[11] The idea of reflection which is stressed here, is based on dialogues between teachers and students to promote children inquiry activity. Through the reflection process, teachers enhance and reflect this inquiry to realize the development of reflective teaching. Due to the rampant influence of exam-oriented education, the study of the above-mentioned teacher knowledge and its related projects has been marginalized in China's mainland.

The study of teacher knowledge has raised many methodological issues for teacher-training programs and deserves more attention. In fact, case studies on reflective methods have also been initiated in teacher-training programs in the background of the new curriculum reform.

3.2 Teachers Training Supported by Government Policy, Theoretical Basis and Practical Experience

Teacher-training programs in China's mainland have received insufficient support from government policies, theoretical basis and practical experience which requires concerted efforts from all levels of educational administration, education researchers and educational practitioners.

The educational administration needs to dedicate itself to changing the mode of teacher-training from effective transmission model to cooperative construction model. The former model emphasizes a top-down transmission process, while the latter focuses on equal interaction process. The key to the teacher's learning process is the explicification of tacit knowledge, the sharing of practical knowledge by teaching observation, and the redesigning and implementation of explicit knowledge in one's own practice. Teacher-training cannot be separated from practice, reflection of educational experience, and grasp of educational theories. Teachers' development should be reform initiated and motivated by the teachers' own needs and experience. The three principles of teacher education (i.e. more effective teaching should be rooted in teachers' inner needs, fresh experience and reflections of practice, advocated by the pedagogy for international teachers) should attract due attention.[12] Teacher-training should enable teachers to find their own learning needs, discover effective experiences, and carefully reflect on their experiences. The results of teachers training are ultimately determined by teachers themselves.

---

11   Tadahiko Abiko, Introduction to Curriculum Study. Tokyo: Keiso Shobo, 2000, 169.
12   Fred A. Korthagen, *Linking Practice and Theory: The Pedagogy of Realistic Teacher Education*, trans. Nobuko Takeda. Tokyo: Gakubunsha, 2010, 65.

Only when teachers really cherish every in-service training opportunity, neither training because it is officially required nor training because they want to get a higher technical title, but training because they want their students to learn more, and training because they want to become professionally more qualified, can teachers change their own image, and change the entire teachers' culture.

The elimination of Kairov's negative pedagogical influences and the establishment of a new idea of learner-centeredness should be a key task for educational research. The study of children is the foundation of every educational and teaching activity. Due to the powerful influence of Kairov's ideas, child study in China has always been marginalized. However, from Ellen Kay's The Century of Children (1900) to the United Nations' Convention on the Rights of the Child (1990), child study in the world has never stopped. Child study in the twentieth century underwent a number of landmarking steps of development, i.e. child study from the scientific perspective; the study of family history of Western children under the influence of Aries's shock; the expanding child study under the theme of culture and science; and the study of children in the light of the Declaration on the Rights of the Child and Convention on the Rights of Children which exhibits a series of new research directions. Child study needs to be carried out from the perspectives of culture and sociology. Continuous interdisciplinary research and theoretical constructions should also be put on the agenda.

In the field of educational practice, efforts should be made to encourage the practical research of teachers to bridge the communication gap between theory and practice. School reform starts from the inside. If classroom practice remains unchanged, schools will not change. For more than 20 years, Manabu Sato from the University of Tokyo has observed more than 10 thousand classes in Japan, Europe and the United States as he has committed himself to school reform experimentation, and attempting to create a learning community.[13] He maintains that teachers should take class research as the starting point to enrich Pedagogical Content knowledge (PCK) knowledge and improve their teaching practice ability. The 1000 schools at the beginning of the reform failed, which shows how difficult classroom reform could be. However, the subsequent 3000 subsequent schools turned out to be successful. School-based teacher-training should begin with classroom reform. The first step is to establish the vision of the school community. The second step is to formulate an action plan with teaching research as its main orientation. The third step is to improve teacher's

---

13   Manabu Sato, *Curriculum and Teachers*, trans Zhong Qiquan 钟启泉. Beijing: Educational Science Publishing House, 2003, 1–2.

teaching practice ability through teacher's teaching research. Every teacher should leave the classroom door open and offer open classes to exchange views and to learn from each other.

Research and training are a teacher's base for growth. Teacher-training supported by self-discipline and creativity can enable teachers to transform themselves from teaching craftsmen to reflective practitioners.

References

Hikoyuki Yasuda. *Modern Education Reform and Teachers.* Tokyo: Tokyo Gakugeid-aigaku, 2011.

Humanity Education Research Association. *New Instruction Highlights of Learning.* Tokyo: Kaneko Shobo, 2008, 9–10.

Fred A. Korthagen. Linking Practice and Theory: The Pedagogy of Realistic Teacher Education, trans. Nobuko Takeda. Tokyo: Gakubunsha, 2010.

Manabu Sato. *Challenges to Schools: Establishing Learning Community.* Shanghai: East Normal University Publishing House, 2010.

Manabu Sato. *Curriculum and Teachers*, trans. Zhong Qiquan 钟启泉. Beijing: Educational Science Publishing House, 2003.

Qin Chunhua 秦春华. Kan Meiguo jiaoyu yao you Zhongguo shijiao 看美国教育要有中国视角 [Viewing American Education from China's Perspective]. *Guangming Daily*, 2013, February 20, 14.

Ryosuke Kikuchi. *Framework of Learning Competence.* Tokyo: Minshusha.1992, 95–96.

Tadahiko Abiko. *Introduction to Curriculum Study.* Tokyo: Keiso Shobo, 2000, 169.

Zhang Feng 张丰. Xiaoben yanxiu de huodong cehua yu zhidu jianshe 校本研修的活动策略与制度建设 [School-based training strategies and system construction]. Shanghai: East Normal University Publishing House, 2007.

Zhong Qiquan 钟启泉. Kecheng lingdaoli: Shijian, fansi yu gaizhao 课程领导力: 实践、反思与改造 [Curriculum Leadership: Allocation, Reflection and Transformation]. *Modern Educators——Pudong Education*, 2012, (10), 32.

Zhong Qiquan 钟启泉. Yingshi jiaoyu benzhi shi fanjiaoyu 应试教育本质是反教育 [The essence of exam-oriented education is anti-education]. *Chinese Social Science Today*, 2012, July 16.

Zhong Qiquan, Li Xuehong, & Xu Dingfang 钟启泉, 李学红, 徐淀芳. Zhuanxing zhong de ketang: Shanghai putuoqu tuijin youxiao jiaoxue liu nian xingdong yanjiu 转型中的课堂：上海市普陀区推进有效教学六年行动研究 [*Transforming Classroom: Research on the Six-Year Effective Teaching in Shanghai Putuo District*]. Shanghai: Shanghai Educational Publishing House, 2012.

CHAPTER 10

The Development of Future Educators

What teacher education in China faces as a project and a serious challenge in the new era is the training of future educators. We need to reflect on a series of essential issues about teacher education, such as how it should accommodate and guide the development of primary education; how it should root itself in local practice to improve educational standard; how it should interact and communicate with global teacher education, etc. We should be putting the curriculum reform of teacher education on the agenda in response to the challenges of our time.

1 Educator Development and TEC Innovation

In order to cultivate teachers who are morally as well as professionally qualified and bring up a whole generation of outstanding educators, Chinese educational government has launched the campaign for the innovation of China's teacher education by the Compendium of the National Medium-and-Long-Term Program for Education Reform and Development. In fact, early in 2004, Yuan Guiren, the PRC Minister of Education signed documents to initiate the drafting and development of the China's Teacher Education Curriculum Standard (TECS for short)[1] under the direct leadership of the Department of Teacher-Training. The Standard aims to establish a modern system of teacher education curriculum which can reflect the features of the time and accommodate and guide the development of China's primary education. The innovations strive to highlight the following two innovations:

Innovation one: The goal of TECS is to transform the educational mode from the training of teaching craftsmen (*jiaoshu jiang*) to the growth of educators so as to manifest the professional qualities of modern idealistic teachers as reflective practitioners. This means that it is necessary to transform teachers' roles and enhance their professional ethics, specifically as follows:

Firstly, we should turn from stereotyped teaching to situated teaching. The traditional stereotyped teaching emphasizes the preset knowledge and skills

---

1 TECS Experts Team 教师教育课程标准研制专家工作组, Jiaoshi jiaoyu kecheng biaozhun (cao'an) 教师教育课程标准（草案）[*Standards of Teachers Educational Courses (Protocol)*]. Research Institute of Curriculum and Teaching of East China Normal University, 2010.

© KONINKLIJKE BRILL NV, LEIDEN, 2022 | DOI: 10.1163/9789004473300_011

to be taught in accordance with established procedures. Teachers always concentrate on the accomplishment of every teaching process and teaching goal. Teachers, dominated by such technological rationality, pay more attention to their teaching rather than students' learning. This stereotyped teaching runs counter to the current Chinese social core values and the main-stream education theories. Modern teachers should focus on the shift from knowledge teaching to methods of learning or as the Chinese proverb says, we should teach a man how to fish to feed him for a lifetime rather than give him a fish to feed him for a day. It is more important to master the methods of learning than knowledge itself. Teachers are more obliged to create proper teaching situations for students, motivate their interest in learning, promote positive learning habits and offer appropriate help. In situated teaching teachers must think and make choices constantly according to the on-line situation without any established patterns or procedures to follow. In the context of situated teaching, prescriptive teaching plan is no more than a proposed action program. Teachers should listen to students' voices and understand their thoughts so as to develop new teaching methods and explore new curriculum resources.

Secondly, we should turn from technological practice to reflective practice. In China, teachers are usually regarded as teaching craftsmen, which indicates that the teachers' role is to only use certain techniques to process the information in textbooks written by others and impart the textbook knowledge to students. In this technical practice, the teachers' work is usually considered as a process of applying scientific principles and imposing external control on teaching activities, while teachers' potential value as an integral part of teaching practice becomes less and less significant. Teaching has degenerated into a skill-oriented job, and it has lost, eventually, the dynamic creativity of professional development. However, in the mode of reflective practice, teachers' teaching behavior is not decided by some fixed educational theories or technologies but by the practical wisdom accumulated from their daily teaching experiences and their reflections on these experiences. Practical wisdom is usually something implicit, founded on a teacher's individual experience and personality. It is embedded in a teacher's daily work and varies from situation to situation. The practical wisdom of a teacher can not only originate from their reflection on their teaching experience, but also develop on the basis of their re-interpretation of education theories in practical situations.

Thirdly, we should turn from application of theories to theorization of practice. Practice is not just simply a domain where theories can be applied, but it is also a domain where practical theories can arise and develop. For teachers in general, it is of course important to apply theories in practice, but practical theories or theorization of practice is even more important. When they play the role of teaching craftsmen, teachers usually concentrate on pursuing maximization of knowledge transfer while ignoring their life experience and significance. Teachers, responsible for the mission of knowledge imparting, can hardly analyze or reflect on the rationality of their teaching practice. They usually hope to reach the expected goal by using the coursebooks designed by others and abandon the role of their own experiences, understandings, and reflections on the effect of teaching. Teachers, as reflective practitioners though, are facing the problems of various situations. Such teachers will consider and solve problems by consciously using theories. Moreover, they will form and construct their own teaching theories according to practice. Under such circumstances, teachers will become the reflectors, researchers and creators of practical theories" rather than teaching craftsmen.

Innovation two: The construction of TEC demands the realization of both conceptual innovation and institutional innovation to manifest the three major principles in today's teacher education reform. Drawing on the domestic achievements following China's implementation of opening to the outside world and international successful experiences in teacher education, TECS highlights three reform principles by addressing the specific problems of Chinese TEC.

Firstly, child-centered principle should echo with the content and value orientation of teachers' learning, which is the specific embodiment of people orientedness in education. Teachers nurture the development of children aged from zero to eight, and the development of children is both the starting point and the destination of teachers' work. Child-centered principle means to discover children's characteristics and respect them. This means: (1) children are human beings; (2) children are children who should not be treated as young adults; (3) children are dynamic, and grow and develop in both biological and socialization processes.[2] To respect children to guarantee their fundamental human rights means ensuring every child's right of learning.

Secondly, practical orientation is the practical character of teacher learning. Teachers are reflective practitioners. Teachers work under the guidance of educational theories while they form their own practical wisdom and teaching styles by solving practical problems and reflecting on their practical experiences in complex and changeable situations. This educational practice ability is the core of teachers' professional development. Therefore, TEC should attach great importance to personal experiences, strengthen the sense of practice, pay close attention to real problems, and combine theories with practical

---

2 Kiyomi Akita & Manabu Sato, *Rudiments of Teachers in New Era*, Tokyo: Yuhikaku, 2006, 91–92.

reflections. Teachers need to develop professionally based on their own specific experiences.

Thirdly, lifelong learning should be viewed as the constant and sustained development of teachers' learning ability. UNESCO has stressed that teachers' work is a profession, a learning profession and a lifelong learning profession. A learning profession requires professional learning. There are three fundamental principles for teachers' professional learning: (1) the more the learners' internal needs are satisfied, the better the learning effect becomes; (2) the more deeply-rooted in the learners' real-life experience, the better the learning effect becomes; and (3) the more reflective a learning activity is of the learners' own experience, the better the learning effect becomes. Therefore, teachers' development requires lifelong learning.[3] Teachers who are determined to cultivate lifelong learners should first of all be lifelong learners themselves.

2 Laying Foundations for China's TEC Innovation

Teaching consists of three important factors: children, teachers and teaching materials according to "triangle model of pedagogy"[4] that form an interactive and integrated whole. However, the problem is that for many years this has turned out to be the weakest point in Chinese educational research. Without the support of studies on children, teachers and teaching materials, it is impossible for teachers' universities to boast of their advantages.

2.1 *Study of Children*

Children, as defined by UNSECO, refer to people aged from 0 to 18 who are old enough for preschool and school education. Studies on children are the basis of all types of education and teaching activities. Kairov's Pedagogy stressed the class character of education and regarded paedology as a pseudoscience. His theory has been criticized and was abandoned in late 1950s as it was anti-education or an education against children. Even Kairov self-criticised in the great debate on education in the Soviet Union, admitting that his pedagogy was a theory that lacked consideration on the education of children. In fact, Kairov became known because of his anti-paedology. Kairov's pedagogy, however, still exerts a negative influence on China's education system. There is no making without breaking. It is time for us to eliminate these out-dated beliefs.

---

3   Fred A. Korthagen, *Teaching and Teacher Education*, trans. Nobuko Takeda. Tokyo: Gakubunsha, 2006, 65.

4   Hitoshi Yoshimoto, *Encyclopedia of Modern Education*. Tokyo: Meijitosho, 1987, 55–56.

THE DEVELOPMENT OF FUTURE EDUCATORS   159

It was not until the 18th century that a clear, straight forward definition of children was put forward in western educational circles, to become a main topic of discussion in modern humanistic pedagogy represented by such scholars as J. J. Rousseau, J. Pestalozzi, and F. W. Frobel, who began to explore ways to respect children's personality and initiative. From the middle of the 18th century, the ideological trend of The Discovery of Children represented by J. J. Rousseau came into popularity in the global educational circle. In the late 19th century, G. S. Hall initiated studies on children with emerging scientific psychology. Since then, the Children Research Movement, started to rise in the United States of America with the help of scientific psychological methods such as observation, questionnaires and so on. O. Chrisman was an example who advocated studies on children by following this movement in 1896. In the 1920s, the studies on children became popular not only in Europe and America but also in the education reform led by the Soviet regime in 1920s.[5] Unfortunately, the Soviet Union of the 1930s was under the dictatorship of Stalin, and studies on children represented by Lev Vygotsky (Л.С.Выготсий) were labelled as pseudo-science. Moreover, the studies on education, especially studies on children, were replaced by educational thoughts represented by Kairov's Pedagogy, which was politically accepted as the authoritative pedagogy by Party's decisions. As a result, studies ignoring and rejecting children gradually formed the foundation of Kairov's Pedagogy. More seriously, studies ignoring and rejecting children came raging into China's educational circle just like the spread of SARS and Influenza A. It is surprising that 30 years after China's reform and opening-up, some Kairov followers are still enthusiastic about learning from Kairov's Pedagogy. They still regard exam-oriented education based on the rote-learning model as the law of education development, and this is truly the tragedy of the Chinese educational discipline.

Problems related to children that emerge one after another in the contemporary society make it necessary for the world to take a multidisciplinary and interdisciplinary view in the research on children. Throughout history, an endless supply of thoughts of children studies are presented to the world. *The Child and Family Life in the Ancien Régime* (*L'enfant et la vie familiale sous l'Ancien Régime*)[6] written by Philippe Ariès, a French historian, is a classic contemporary study on children for its pioneering research on families and children. Ariès showed, from the perspective of social and cultural history, that there is no such thing as universal and hypostatic children. The form of childhood which is considered to be self-evident today is but a historical product

---

5   Hisashi Hirai, *Development Theory*. Tokyo: Keirinshobo, 1983, 293–294.
6   Michio Ogasawara, *Evolving Pedagogy*. Tokyo: Fukumura shuppan, 2009, 14.

of a special time. That is to say, whether the pedagogical thoughts represented by views on children or what is believed to be biological features of children are no more than products of a deeper and more potential attitude and explanations of children in that historical time. This interdisciplinary research on children can help to obtain a clear view on the formation and mechanism of childhood in modern society so as to solve problems in contemporary education system. *The Child and Family Life in the Ancien Régime* (the English version was published in 1962, and the Japanese version was published in 1980) brought about a Copernican shift of views on children and education for children, and it opened a new era for worldwide research on children. In a similar vein is *The Disappearance of Childhood* written by N. Postman[7] in which the author raised an amazing point on a civilization shift: it was the printed word that had created the concept of children, and it is the modern media that is making childhood disappear. The point concerning the birth of the concept of children and its subsequent disappearance demonstrates some basic information about world research on children in the view of social culture.

Today, world research on children and paedology and the specialty development of child studies in universities have reached an apex. Interdisciplinary research on educational neuroscience based on brain science in America, Japan and European countries deserve attention. The mission of the Japanese Children's Society founded in 2003 is to offer relevant information and opinions to solve problems related to child-rearing and various other problems in education and to provide a favorable environment for children's growth, by using the research achievements of the society. The Society aims to conduct interdisciplinary research on children, both mentally and physiologically, by comprehensively using biological views in natural science and cultural views in humanistic and social science, so as to have a re-recognition on children and establish a system for science of children. Universities in developed countries such as America and Japan have built research networks or network alliance of universities. A considerable number of universities have set up the discipline of paedology. By March 2008, 105 Japanese universities had established schools and disciplines of paedology. Japanese curricula of paedology covers research areas in paedological medicine, paedological sociology and paedological culture to form a multi-dimensional system of modular curricula, such as children and adults, children and welfare, children and society, children and families, children and customs, children and musical instruments, children and singing, children and styling, children and games, children and sports,

---

7 Neil Postman, *Disappearance of Childhood*, trans. Wu Yanting. Nanning: Guangxi Normal University Press, 2004.

children and languages, children and expression, children and media, and so on. In 2007, Harvard University along with 28 other US universities jointly organized the University-based Children and Family Policy Consortium. What this research on children aims to achieve is an exploration of the real children's world rather than the abstract children's world, which is the fundamental demand in Chinese TEC reform.

Advocacy of child-centeredness is a perfectly justifiable principle in school education. The educational belief of the American educational circle is that there would be no top-quality school education without research on children or without teachers' immediate research on children in classroom situations. During the past few years, the Japanese educational circle has been dedicated to ideas and practice of the new TEC—curriculum on understanding of children. These curricula consist of four levels: (1) To put forward the idea of clinical pedagogy centered on the understanding of children to promote future teachers' awareness of problems, (2) To accumulate experiential learning and researches on the understanding of children by engaging future teachers in participating the training course centered on practical understanding of children, (3) To implement theoretical learning and research on the basic conceptions and methods of the understanding of children through literature reading in class discussion, and (4) To generalize the problems of concern into research topics so as to write academic papers.[8] This new Japanese TEC is entirely different from and stands in sharp contrast with the Chinese education disciplines (pedagogy, psychology and methodolgy) which are detached from social reality, children's reality and teachers' practice.

2.2 *Study on Teachers*

Teaching is a professional discipline based on the public mission to realize the right for every child to learn and to provide every child with a chance to strive for a high level of learning.[9] The quality of a teacher determines the quality of a course. Where there is a good teacher, there is a good course. Without a good teacher, it would be empty talk about striving for the best course. Teachers should make efforts to process, improving, transform and create if they wish to move from a text-based curriculum to a practice-based curriculum, then to an acquisition-based curriculum. It is natural to pay close attention to studies on teachers in China.

---

8   Takahiko Tanaka & Hideo Teraoka, Exploring the pedagogy of inservice teachers. *Pedagogy*, 2010, (3): 41.

9   Manabu Sato, *Challenges to Schools: Establishing Learning Community*. Shanghai: East Normal University Publishing House, 2010, Introduction 1.

There are various thoughts of studies on teachers in world education circles including research on academia, development, social efficiency doctrine, social reform and so on. All studies on teachers, though, cover various domains and are developed on the reflection of specific angles of teachers' practice. Here, we will take the educational thoughts of American teachers as an example to have a better understanding of the features of the educational thoughts in accordance with the historical changes of teacher education.

2.2.1 Academic Study Paradigm

The academic study paradigm takes the position of essentialism which attaches great importance to academic studies and acquisition of classic knowledge. Teachers having been criticized by researchers and educators for lack of understanding of subject contents. thus Lee. S. Shulman then conducted research to investigate the interactive effects between teachers' understanding of subject contents and their education subject knowledge. The result was that proper knowledge of subject contents in teacher education should be considered as the "foundational knowledge" for teachers, and included: (1) subject content knowledge; (2) general pedagogical knowledge about principles and methodologies of class management and organization; (3) curriculum knowledge about teaching materials and teaching plans; (4) teaching design knowledge or PCK (pedagogical content knowledge); (5) knowledge about learning and its characteristics; (6) education background knowledge; and (7) knowledge about goals, purposes, values of education and historical background of philosophy.[10] There are quite a number of research papers related to the knowledge base and the most significant is to seek conceptual understanding. This research on subject teaching program in Michigan State University was conducted from the perspective of cognitive psychology. Similar research was the cognitive induction teaching introduced from the teacher teaching plan in the University of Wisconsin at Madison. This research aims to build the general principle of cognitive teaching for children through a study of children's mathematic cognition.

2.2.2 Social Efficiency Paradigm

The social efficiency paradigm was the second major educational reform in the 20th century that started with the development of scientific courses. In the face of the unclear definition of teacher education's goals and plans in the early 20th century, this paradigm conducted research on the construction of a

---

10   Manabu Sato, *Courses and Teachers*, trans. Zhong Qiquan. Beijing: Educational Science Publishing House, 2003, 389.

THE DEVELOPMENT OF FUTURE EDUCATORS   163

necessary foundation to specify the contents of teacher education. From the 1960s to 1970s, teacher education based on ability and performance emerged with the accumulation of data from this research. This teacher education, with its aim to enable participants to obtain specific and observable skills that would facilitate the teaching of children's learning, had a great influence not only in the United States, but also in other western countries. However, there is no general agreement about whether it is appropriate to put the teaching ability acquired by means of this method into practice. One of the main features of teacher education based on ability and performance is that it clearly stipulated the range of knowledge and skills teachers were supposed to acquire and clarified the criteria to evaluate the teachers' acquisition of the knowledge and skills. On this basis, the corresponding teaching system and evaluation system were also developed. The micro-teaching developed by Stanford University, for example, is a means with which the participants could systematically grasp the specific teaching skills. Micro-teaching has been incorporated into the mini-course, a more comprehensive program of teacher education. In relation with the development of these studies, digital teaching materials and simulation materials have been developed, and a school observation system and skill training model came onto the scene. By the 1980s, the social efficiency paradigm had drawn more extensive attention in the educational debate of teacher education based on studies. In the past ten years, study on teaching had formed a knowledge base -- the basis for the curriculum of teacher education according to the Holmes group's proposal of teacher education. Then, a general cognitive study of reflective teaching and skill training plan based on micro-computer simulation came into being. In this way, studies based on the social efficiency paradigm, though various in research directions, have one thing in common, that is, providing a scientific research basis for teaching.

2.2.3   Developmental Paradigm

The developmental paradigm, originating from studies on children represented by G. S. Hall and others, featured the notion that the learner's stage of development is the basis for the determination of teaching contents at the school. Children's developmental stage depends on the study of observations and description of children's behaviors. This is especially true when the advocates of developmental paradigm in the early 20th century started to scientifically study children's behavior in consideration of children's developmental stages and plans of school environment. On the basis of this scientific evidence, progressives advocated creative and imaginative teacher education. Thus, advocates of the new children-centered teacher education criticized those mechanical teaching methods. According to V. Perrone's study,[11] the developmental paradigm divides prospective teachers into three possible roles: the naturalists' role, the artists' role and the researchers' role. Teachers, playing the role of the naturalists, usually lay stress on observing children's behavior and the importance of children's abilities and skills. Teachers, playing the role artists, attach importance to inspiring children's learning initiative based on children developmental psychology, and teachers, playing the role of researchers, concentrate on their own experimental studies about educational practice. Therefore, study on children has become the basis of teachers' teaching research.

2.2.4   Social Reform Spectrum

The social reform paradigm maintained that the American intellectual social transformation plan, accelerated by the economic crisis and social instability, had enhanced the role of schools. With social reformation, it is possible to make a fair distribution of national wealth, and public interests can take precedence over individual interests. G. S. Counts,[12] representative of social reform, proposed that nationalist education should be promoted to popularize the value and idea of social transformation in education. M. Holmes, for example, openly opposed the contemporary education practice by emphasizing the cultivation of the ability to think critically about social order. William Kilpatrick and J. Dewey also criticized the teacher education tradition for its deviation from the target and for its focus on technology. In addition, they called on teachers to study the philosophy of social education and improve the goal of public civilization. William Kilpatrick was the best-known representative of American teacher education reform in the 20th century. Towards the 1940s, the views of William Stanley, Kenneth Benne and other educators converged to form the core of the social fundamental group. Landon Beyer, representative of social reformism in modern teacher education, proposed the concept of teacher education as a practice.[13] That is to say, Beyer, based on the ideas of democracy, equality and principle of autonomy, applied the derivative study of the laying-foundation into teacher education. Based on this position, teacher education implies its contribution to schools and society. The core or the basic position of social reform is to ensure the settlement of social instability and

---

11   Yasushi Mizoue, *Study on Qualities of Professional Teachers and Implication of School Education*, Exchange material with Hyogokyoikudaigaku, 2005, 17.

12   Manabu Sato, *Courses and Teachers*, trans. Zhong Qiquan. Beijing: Educational Science Publishing House, 2003, 361.

13   Yasushi Mizoue, *Study on Qualities of Professional Teachers and Implication of School Education*, Exchange material with Hyogokyoikudaigaku, 2005, 17.

THE DEVELOPMENT OF FUTURE EDUCATORS   165

injustice. However, Beyer's view did not become the mainstream in teacher education. Due to attacks from both the left as well as the right of politics, it had little influence on school education.

2.2.5   Study on Reflective Teaching

Reflective teaching, first proposed by D. Schon, is the teaching practice that involves both teachers and students in reflective thinking or inquiry activities. In D. Schon's view, future teachers should train themselves from technique-qualified people to become reflective practitioners[14] because, compared with the skilled teachers, introspective and reflective practitioners possess more complicated knowledge of language structures and functions with which they can build a realistic and equal relationship with children to seek for the construction of cultural meaning and creation of more valuable experience.[15] Since the mid-1980s, a huge amount of research has been carried out and produced concerning reflective teaching practice in the following two aspects: teacher education and teaching research. For example, in Japan, with the help of empirical studies on teachers' practical thinking, Manabu Sato and Kiyomi Akita expounded the five basic characteristics of teachers' practical thinking mode. These are (1) improvisational thinking in practice; (2) sensitivity to uncertainty, laying great importance on the participation of the students and probing deeply into problems; (3) comprehensive ability to solve practical problems from multi-dimensional perspectives; (4) ability to think about clinical construction of linguistic strategies to solve problems and their relations arising in practice; and (5) strategic thinking to constantly represent problems based on teaching[16] In recent years, the study on teachers' thinking has become popular and the study on reflective teaching in teacher education has attracted great public attention. Along with this, exploration-directed teacher education came into being. This teacher education has something in common with the teachers as researchers in the developmental paradigm above.

The five paradigms, as educational thoughts, respectively focus on the special areas of educational practice, such as teaching materials, children's thinking and social background, specific teaching methods, and reflective teaching research. Moreover, all of these are explored in the context of specific

---

14   Donald Schon, *Reflective Practioners: How Professionals Think in Action*, trans. Manabu Sato & Kiyomi Akita. Tokyo:Yumiru Shuppan, 2001, 7.
15   Shinjo Okuda, *Encyclopedia of Modern School Education*. Tokyo: Gyosei kabushikikaisha, 1993, 312.
16   Manabu Sato, *Courses and Teachers*, trans Zhong Qiquan. Beijing: Educational Science Publishing House, 2003, 228–229.

education activities. The extensive scale of study today on reflective teaching commissions teachers to the development of new professional qualities that they should improve themselves as reflective practitioners. Japanese educators propose that the concept of teachers' profession should be rebuilt from the following aspects: (1) Teachers as coordinators should be able to support children's practical ability of learning and growth; (2) Teachers should be able to manage to organize cooperative learning and reform; (3) Teachers should be able to constantly improve the quality of educational practice and research capabilities; and (4) Teachers should have the correct notion and responsibility as professional school teachers of public education. Japanese educators propose to develop this professional TEC design on the basis of qualities mentioned above.[17]

We should pay close attention to the focal points of international studies on teachers. First, it focuses on the study of the individual teachers' personal improvement. The improvement, from a novice teacher to an experienced mainstream teacher and then to an expert teacher, is a challenging but rewarding process of constant reflection, and gradual professional maturation. Second, it focuses on the study of teachers as a team (a teachers learning community). This is because it is the whole school rather than a classroom, just as it is the whole teachers team rather than the individual, that undertakes the responsibility for students' learning and development. The teachers learning community is a concept that transcends the boundaries between disciplines, classrooms, and schools and is interrelated with the whole society, and even with the whole world. Third, it focuses on the study of educational relations. International studies on teachers emphasize that education, primarily concerned with the teachers' understanding of students means that teachers should influence and instruct students. Teachers need to know students' individual differences and their respective needs so that they can teach students according to their aptitude. At the same time, teachers should realize that the students' understanding of teachers is vital to the success of education. In this sense, education is constructed on the basis of the mutual understanding between teachers and students.[18] In recent years, Japan has been working hard on clinical pedagogy, a brand new discipline which aims at listening to

---

17   Takahiko Tanaka & Hideo Teraoka, Exploring the pedagogy of inservice teachers. *Pedagogy*, 2010), (3): 41.

18   Keiko Toki, *Rudiments of Teachers*. Tokyo: Mikunishuppan, 2010, 20.

THE DEVELOPMENT OF FUTURE EDUCATORS

the voice of children and seeking educational relations to support children's survival and growth.[19]

The role of Chinese teachers is changing along with the new curriculum reform. First, there is a shift from knowledge imparting to creativity in teachers' ability. Second, there is a shift from subjects to curricula in teachers' visions. Third, there is a shift from controllers to guides in the roles of teachers. A number of schools have already constructed some embryonic form of teachers learning community, providing a wide space for every individual teacher in their professional improvement. This is a significant advance in educational reform. There is an urgent need to study and sum up the transformation of teachers' role, the formation of teachers team, and the strategy of class-revolution and creation of schools with special characteristics.

2.3   *Study on Teaching Materials*

Teaching material is fundamental to teaching. A broad definition of teaching material offered by contemporary pedagogical theory contains three components. First, teaching material refers to the facts, concepts, rules and theories arranged as part of the students' knowledge system. Second, teaching material is closely related with knowledge, which can help teachers to proficiently command all types of abilities and teaching systems, various procedures of mental operations and practical tasks as well as working mechanisms and skills. Third, teaching material, is closely related with the knowledge system and ability system, laying the foundation of world outlook, and manifesting itself in such forms as cognition, concepts and norms in beliefs, politics, world outlook and morality. This broad definition shows that not only does teaching material express the value of education as a medium for activities, but it also includes the specification of contents, quality of activities, methods of activities and steps of activities which aim to cover all the necessary conditions for the realization of various features of students' initiatives. This is the definition of teaching material in its broadest sense. Textbooks for compulsory education, in the final analysis, should serve as a carrier that can reflect the dominant mainstream value, and as the epitome that can represent an idealistic image of a citizen. An excellent textbook requires textbook editors to put in elaborate and meticulous efforts and professionalism.

The development of teaching material has undergone a long history into various modern shapes and forms. The teaching materials, including the three traditional Chinese classics (The Three Word Primer, Hundred Family

---

19   Takahiko Tanaka, *Understanding Children: Attempts to Clinical Education.* Tokyo: Iwana-mishoten, 2000, 185.

Surnames and Thousand Character Classic) have enjoyed a history of 700 years as textbooks for beginners learning Chinese characters since the southern Song Dynasty. Orbis Pictus (Visible World in Pictures), the first widely used textbook for children written by J. A. Comenius, has existed for over 350 years. The role and function of textbooks in school education change along with the changes of social and education systems and the improvement of academic culture and education research. Pre-modern schools used the original versions of classics such as the Christian Bible, The Four Books (The Great Learning, The Doctrine of the Mean, The Confucian Analects, and The Works of Mencius) and The Five Classics (The Book of Songs, The Book of History, The Book of Changes, The Book of Rites and The Spring and Autumn Annals) as textbooks. Of course, early schools took it as their mission to indoctrinate and civilize people so that they could understand sacramental contents in textbooks such as the six arts including music, archery, mathematics, ritual, chariot-riding and calligraphy in accordance with Confucian doctrine, but on the part of the students, they were first and foremost required to memorize these textbooks by rote learning. J. A. Comenius, initiator of modern teaching theory, believed that it made learning a drudgery and painful experience to use unadapted classics, which are hard even for adults to understand, and to force children to learn by rote. He devoted himself to the study on the whole art of teaching all things to all men which aimed at enabling children to have a quick, happy and thorough understanding of science, to purify themselves in moral behaviors, and to acquire knowledge in pious respect. Contemporary teaching materials, more or less, have echoed these requirements that teachers should impart knowledge to students in a way that they can accept happily.

From the old traditional paper textbooks to the new present-day electronic textbooks, textbooks may have changed the way they present themselves, or the way they are read and written, but the basic functions of textbooks such as transmitting knowledge, guiding learners to engage in exploring, having dialogues and accomplishing themselves to develop their competence and inherit values do not change.[20] Traditional textbooks made of paper are a type of printed matter and an intentionally structured tool which intervenes with learning to improve their effects.[21] This kind of textbook, such as programmed teaching material, is an integrated and self-sufficient whole which contains all the necessary elements in learning including information, methods, exercise and evaluation. However, it fails to take students' real learning

---

20   Francois Mary Gerard, *Teaching Materials for Learning*, trans. Wang Lin. Shanghai: East China Normal University Press, 2009, 70–78.

21   Ibid, 2.

THE DEVELOPMENT OF FUTURE EDUCATORS   169

process and interest into account. Of course, it is a closed type of textbook with the implicit function of carrying socio-cultural values. Recently, some educators have proposed the notion of open type textbooks, a tool which can be improved according to specific situations and in different ways. Some of these textbooks, for example, provide blank pages for students to write so that they can record their preliminary cognition about the concepts or structure they are going to learn. Some invite students to contribute their own supplementary information and improvement for the contents. Others may open up the reference functions, such as grammar books, atlases for students, literature collections and so on.[22] These open textbooks can meet many new demands, such as cultivating students' learning habits, recommending learning strategies and combining knowledge acquisition with daily life. Teaching material is not only the carrier of cultural heritage and knowledge, but also a dynamic open system of generating meaning. We can draw inspirations from the teaching material developed by our predecessors to develop the technology for the editing of modern teaching material. Studies on modern teaching material have summarized three basic functions of textbooks. First, it can serve as a source of information for selecting and supplying valuable and true materials for students. Second, it can serve as a means to structurize information to help students to build their own knowledge structures. Third, it can serve as a direction to guide students to learn how to know, and to learn to do things and behave themselves properly.[23]

Teaching materials evolve along with the development of times. However, it is over-simplistic to forecast that multimedia will replace the traditional textbooks made of paper, which are still the most popular and most effective learning tools in our era. Compared with multimedia, they possess greater potential to accommodate a more flexible function of utility in different situations.[24] On the other hand, NTIC(Network Technology for Information and Communication), nevertheless, can provide us with possibilities to learn online. Based on the interpersonal interactive function of NTIC, learners can interact with others rather than learn alone from textbooks in the classroom so as to broaden the space of online learning. This online learning can provide more social chances for cognitive and cooperative learning. Therefore, there is a broad space in which we can study the development of teaching material.

---

22   Ibid, 83.

23   Zhong Qiquan 钟启泉, Kecheng de luoji 课程的逻辑 [*Logics of Curriculum*]. Shanghai: East China Normal University Press, 2008, 303.

24   Francois Mary Gerard, *Teaching Materials for Learning*, trans. Wang Lin. Shanghai: East China Normal University Press, 2009, 1.

Research on teaching materials is the prerequisite for developing textbooks in the new era. We are confronted with numerous challenges in the development of textbooks now. From the global perspective on textbook policy, modern teachers must possess the quality and ability to study and develop teaching materials whether they are teaching in the mode of many textbooks under the guideline of one syllabus, or many textbooks under the guideline of many syllabi for the same course, or even no textbooks under the guideline of one syllabus. Compared with international teaching materials, we can reasonably say that Chinese science textbooks are more difficult, while those for liberal arts are of a lower level of difficulty. However, we still have not solved the inherent problem of textbooks, which is the unification of disciplinary logic and psychological logic. Teaching materials self-styled as those for the new curriculum are not necessarily new due to the insufficient support of research. Ordinary and average publishing enterprises are unable to undertake the mission for the study of teaching material in sociology, informatics, psychology, pedagogy and, even international comparative studies. The main forces are normal universities with the advantage of multidisciplines and interdisciplines.

To ensure the growth of a new generation of educators, it is necessary to implement Chinese Teacher Education Curriculum reform. We look forward to the day when we shall be able to establish national research centers of study on children, teachers, and teaching materials in normal universities so as to develop paedology, the scientific study of teachers, and the scientific study of textbooks as core subjects. It is high time that we lay the foundation for our Teacher Education Curriculum focusing on the three studies mentioned above.

References

Francois Mary Gerard. *Teaching Materials for Learning*, trans. Wang Lin. Shanghai: East China Normal University Press, 2009.

Hisashi Hirai. *Development Theory*. Tokyo: Keirinshobo, 1983.

Hitoshi Yoshimoto. *Encyclopedia of Modern Education*. Tokyo: Meijitosho, 1987.

Keiko Toki. *Rudiments of Teachers*. Tokyo: Mikunishuppan, 2010.

Kiyomi Akita & Manabu Sato. *Rudiments of Teachers in New Era*. Tokyo: Yuhikaku, 2006.

Fred A. Korthagen. *Teaching and Teacher Education*, trans Nobuko Takeda. Tokyo: Akubunsha, 2006.

Manabu Sato. *Challenges to Schools: Establishing Learning Community*. Shanghai: East Normal University Publishing House, 2010, Introduction 1.

Manabu Sato. *Courses and Teachers*, trans. Zhong Qiquan. Beijing: Educational Science Publishing House, 2003.

Michio Ogasawara. *Evolving Pedagogy*. Tokyo: Fukumura shuppan, 2009.

Neil Postman. *Disappearance of Childhood*, trans. Wu Yanting. Nanning: Guangxi Normal University Press, 2004.

Donald Schon. *Reflective Practioners: How Professionals Think in Action*, trans. Manabu Sato & Kiyomi Akita. Tokyo: Yumiru Shuppan, 2001.

Shinjo Okuda. *Encyclopedia of Modern School Education*. Tokyo: Gyosei kabushikikaisha, 1993.

Takahiko Tanaka. *Understanding Children: Attempts to Clinical Education*. Tokyo: Iwanamishoten, 2000.

Takahiko Tanaka & Hideo Teraoka. Exploring the pedagogy of inservice teachers. *Pedagogy*, 2010, (3), 41.

TECS Experts Team 教师教育课程标准研制专家工作组. Jiaoshi jiaoyu kecheng biaozhun (cao'an) 教师教育课程标准（草案）[*Standards of Teachers Educational Courses (Protocol)*]. Research Institute of Curriculum and Teaching of East China Normal University, 2010.

Yasushi Mizoue. *Study on Qualities of Professional Teachers and Implication of School Education*. Exchange material with Hyogokyoikudaigaku, 2005.

Zhong Qiquan 钟启泉. Kecheng de luoji 课程的逻辑 [*Logics of Curriculum*]. Shanghai: East China Normal University Press, 2008.

CHAPTER 11

Critical Comments on Kairov's Pedagogy

Early in the late 1950s, the theoretical development in the education circle of the former Soviet Union had thoroughly transcended Kairov's Pedagogy. But in China's education circle today, there are still some people who are indulged in the "complex of Kairov Pedagogy" and unable to extricate themselves from it. Some of them even think highly of Kairov's Pedagogy as a comprehensive expression of the modern educational thought, saying that China's education is doomed to fail without it.[1] But we need to be cautious in our verification of the important role of Kairov's Pedagogy in modern education discipline, because it is far from enough to just base our judgment on a succession of bold assumptions.[2] The author of this paper believes that we should resort to

---

1 Wang Cesan 王策三, "Xinkecheng linian," "Gainian chongjian yundong" yu xuexi Kairov jiaoyuxue "新课程理念""概念重建运动"与学习凯洛夫教育学 [The New Curriculum rationale, Reconceptualization Movement and learning Kairov's Pedagogy]. *Curriculum, Teaching Material and Method*, 2008, (7), 10.

2 Wang Cesan published an article entitled "The New Curriculum rationale, Reconceptualization Movement and learning Kairov's Pedagogy" (hereinafter referred to as "Wang's Article") in the journal of *Curriculum, Teaching Material and Methodology*, expressing his "pity" for China's failure to "reprint and republish" (p. 4) Kairov's Pedagogy. He was surprisingly partial and perverse in his defence of Kairov's pedagogy. "Wang's Article" totally repudiated the progressive educational theory of Dewey, regarding it as a typical example of "educational failure" on the one hand, and eulogized "Kairov's Pedagogy for its substantive contribution to traditional modern pedagogy founded by Comenius and Herbart" (p. 11) on the other hand. Wang also coined his so-called "technical terms" of "Comenius, Herbart, Kairov's Pedagogy and Essentalism Education," for his frequent use (p. 11, p. 15, p. 18, p. 20). He exaggerated the role of Kairov's Pedagogy by saying that it has "laid the cornerstone to educational theory of modern schools" (p. 14) and it has "occupied a leading position in modern pedagogy" (p. 20). Wang claimed that "in the past several decades, Kairov's Pedagogy has existed and developed extensively across the world, and it continues to exert its influence." (p. 9) "Kairov's Pedagogy will remain significant in the long future," (p. 14) "Kairov's Pedagogy has not been and will not be discarded" and "it cannot be defeated and will not be defeated" (p. 16). How preposterous these claims are! According to the logic of "Wang's Article," the world pedagogical development "from Comenius, Herbart and Essentalism Education to Kairov's Pedagogy," (p. 18) came to a complete stop at Kairov's Pedagogy. How illogical and ridiculous it is! But if it were true, how is it that the name "Kairov" cannot be found in the entry of the authoritative *"World Educational Dictionary"* in Europe, America and Japan, while we can easily find access to such names as "Vygotsky," "Leontiev" and "Zankov"? "Collection of Soviet Pedagogies in Modern Times" (12 volumes in total) published in Mexico and Tokyo concurrently in 1983, was designed and edited by Soviet educationists and Japanese educationists, which aimed to systematically describe the full picture of Soviet pedagogies in modern times, giving

CRITICAL COMMENTS ON KAIROV'S PEDAGOGY 173

the facts themselves and clear definitions of concepts, if we wish to evaluate Kairov's Pedagogy in the context of the world education discipline and development. In other words, we should clarify two basic and fundamental issues. First, we should not comment on the value of Kairov's Pedagogy in isolation without considering its social historical background. Second, we should not confuse Kairov's Pedagogy with "Soviet Pedagogy." And these are two issues that the author has in mind. More specifically, this paper aims at reviewing some of the basic historical facts in the history of the Soviet education, so as to reveal the role that Kairov's Pedagogy played in the educational development of Soviet schools. It also discusses what it means to restart "the study of Kairov's Pedagogy" counterbalance or resist "the new curriculum rationale" and "reconceptualization movement" in China today where new curriculum reform is being vigorously implemented.

1

What are the distinctive features of Soviet educational theories? We can view Soviet educational theories from the perspective of the purpose, contents, methods and other aspects of the Soviet school education. However, the principle of "combining education with life" is deemed as the fundamental principle of utmost importance that represents the features of Soviet educational theories.[3] The important role of this principle in Soviet education theories can be easily concluded whether from the angle of historical development of Soviet education researches since the October Revolution (1917), or from that of the law that prescribed "the basic principles of Soviet national education"[4]

---

lengthy introductions to and descriptions about the "Pedagogy" of Baranov, "Teaching and Development" of Zankov and "Analects of Psychology" of Petrovsky, without a single word of Kairov's Pedagogy. "Selections of Modern Educational Thoughts" (8 volumes in total) (Gyosei kabushikikaisha, 1981) which was co-edited by Hitoshi Matsushima and Satoshi Kawanobe devoted Volume Six to the description of life stories and important educational contributions of people in Soviet Russia, with separate chapters on Lenin, Krupskaya, Luna Chalsky (А. В. Луначарский), Shatsky, Brunsky (П. П. Блонский), Marylianke (А. С. Макаренко) and Suhomlinski (В. А. Сухомлинский), without mentioning Kairov's Pedagogy. This is the truth. Therefore, it sounds just as ridiculous to flatter Kairov to the sky, as "to attempt to fly to the sky by pulling up one's hair" satirized by Lu Xun, a famous Chinese writer, in his work "The Third Group."

3 Yoshimatsu Shibata, *Russian Teaching Theories*. Tokyo: Meijitoshi, 1982, 9.

4 "The basic principles of Soviet national education" in Article IV of the *Basic Law of National Education* (July, 1973) consists of 12 clauses, and it is stipulated in Clause Eight that, "the education of the young generation should be combined with practical life and the practice

listed as the article IV in the *Basic Law of National Education*[5] enacted by the Soviet Union in 1973. Actually, soon after the October Revolution, the Soviet educational circle was engaged in a series of debates on this principle, which touched upon the reform of the whole educational system. Meanwhile, from a worldwide horizon, the above principle is also a fundamental principle of universal significance in modern education theories. We shall devote our discussions below to the arguments and controversies surrounding this principle of "combining education with life" among different educational forces in the Soviet educational circle in the 1920s and 1930s, and outline the essential characteristics and background of Kairov's Pedagogy.

1.1 *Ideological Basis of Soviet School Construction and Aberration of "Deschooling"*

It is generally known that education should take place at school, but school education is originated from and developed out of social life—which is required by the development social life. Therefore, it is proper to say that school education which comes from and is based on social life should be closely related to it. The question is, however, that modern school education is usually detached from the social life. The principle of "combining education with life" is also an issue of great importance in modern teaching theories. How to combine school education with life, however, is not always self-evident. And the definitions of "education" and "life" can vary from person to person. So what did this combination mean in the Soviet educational circle at that time? What debates among different educational thoughts were staged? If we work out answers to these questions, the background and the real meaning of Kairov's Pedagogy will be disclosed.

In "The Tasks of the Youth Leagues," Lenin said, "the separation of books and living practice is one of the greatest evils that the capitalist society has left to us."[6] The concept of "books" here can be interpreted as "school education." Likewise, his wife, Krupskaya also criticized "schools that depend too much on textbooks and implement rote-leaning" in her article "National Education and Democracy." She pointed out in no unambiguous terms that, "In such kind of schools, students are required to behave themselves by sitting quietly at their desks only to learn booklore (which bears little relationship with real life)

---

   of communist construction." See Haruyoshi Ebihara, *Information about Education Reform in Modern Times*. Tokyo: Sanseido, 1983, 444.

5 Haruyoshi Ebihara, *Materials of Global Educational Reforms*. Tokyo: Sanseido, 1983, 444.
6 Lenin, The tasks of the Youth Leagues, in *Lenin's View on Education*, trans and ed. Department of education of East China Normal University. Beijing: People's Education Press, 1990, 241.

CRITICAL COMMENTS ON KAIROV'S PEDAGOGY   175

from their teachers, with no additional information from the realistic practical world. This is disastrous to students' personality development and the apparent strict discipline, and the endless mechanical knowledge imparting have turned our students into machines."[7] What deserves our consideration is that they were criticizing the isolation of school from real life in old society in two senses. That is to say, on the one hand, the knowledge imparted at school is useless and cannot reflect our real life. In other words, it raises the question of the authenticity of knowledge, i.e. how knowledge and practical life can be combined. On the other hand, it touches upon the class issue of school education. That is to say schools are allowed to impart useless knowledge to serve interest of the ruling class, because the ruling class is afraid to share the practical knowledge with the mass for the sake of their own benefit. Lenin pointed out that, "in old backward schools, students are forced to learn a heap of futile, verbose and dead knowledge which crams their head."[8] And those schools should be abolished.

Lenin was not always consistent in his comments about the old school system. Although he severely criticized the old backward schools, yet he was against the attitude of total negation and irrevocable repudiation of the old schools. He said, "when we hear young people or those who advocate the new education system blaming the old backward schools as institutions that implement rote-leaning, we tell them that there is still something acceptable in them. We are not ready to accept such a way of teaching practice that fills the young brains with indefinite, useless and distorted knowledge, which should be discarded...Only when we enrich our brains with all the wealth created by human beings, can we become communists."[9] Thus, he criticized the old backward schools for their wrong class spirit orientation and puppet's role of capitalism on the one hand; and he also said that we must adopt something valuable from those schools. On the surface, this seemed to be contradictory. However, it is exactly this seemingly contradictory thought that implied an extremely significant meaning for the construction of Soviet new-style schools. We can say this thought was brought about by the incisive insight of Lenin into the contradictions in class society, and those in schools and culture. The knowledge that benefits the bourgeoisie may bring profits to laborers as well.

---

7 Krupskaya, National education and democracy, in *Literary Selections of Krupskaya* (Volume one), ed. Li Yuezhang and trans. Wei Daozhi. Beijing: People's Education Press, 1987, 153.
8 Lenin, The Tasks of the Youth Leagues, in *Lenin's View on Education*, ed. and trans. Department of education of East China Normal University. Beijing: People's Education Press, 1990, 242.
9 Ibid, 244

Although the type of knowledge for both classes may be essentially different, yet it is not completely opposed to each other. Denying and blaming bourgeois culture and the old backward schools is not hard, and the same is true with throwing away the textbooks separated from practice. What is difficult is how to compile new textbooks and construct new-style schools. In his consideration of the complexity of this situation, Lenin said, "the proletarian culture rightfully developed out of the oppression by capitalist society, feudal society and bureaucrat society, not created out of nothing."[10] That means, the new proletarian culture is established on the basis of its opposition and struggle with the bourgeois culture. The conflict and struggle inside this culture is correlated with the conflict and struggle in life. Therefore, when he proposed combination of school education with real life, Lenin stressed that, "We have no trust in the training, cultivation and education only restricted to school campuses and separated from dynamic real life. What we want is to develop people who can participate in the struggle against exploitation and who are determined to eradicate exploiters while they are learning at school."[11]

Under the guidance of the thought of Lenin, Krupskaya was committed to the construction of soviet new-style schools and education from the perspective of both theory and practice, which contributed a great deal to the establishment of Marxist-Leninist pedagogy and laid a solid foundation for the Soviet educational thought.

Krupskaya explicated Marxist education theory about the overall development and put forward the idea that the goal of Soviet education was to cultivate well-rounded whole persons.[12] She discussed her view of children that supported this educational goal in the article "What are the Problems in Free Schools." That is, to give children due respect in their personality development. From her point of view, three steps are contained in children's personality development.[13] In the first step, children are considered as observers, who acquire "impression," "emotion" and "questions" from their observation, which is deemed as an activity that will lead to the formation of children's world outlook. In this connection, the first step serves as a cognitive process that enables children to embrace subjectivity and self-education. The second step is a process in which children are expected to develop strong willing to share their

---

10   Ibid, 243–244.
11   Ibid, 251.
12   Hitoshi Matsushima & Satoshi Kawanobe, *The Selected Works of Modern Educational Thoughts* (Volume six, Soviet Russia). Tokyo: Gyosei kabushikikaisha, 1981, 228.
13   Krupskaya, What are the problems in free schools, in *Literary Selections of Krupskaya* (Volume one), ed. Li Yuezhang and trans. Wei Daozhi. Beijing: People's Education Press, 1987, 229–230.

CRITICAL COMMENTS ON KAIROV'S PEDAGOGY

knowledge with others, and based on their need for activities, children are considered as beings who are able to initiate their practical and creative activities. This is a joyous practice in which children can work to gain confidence and achieve improvement by self-evaluation and self-recognition. In the third step, children are urged to be persons who can work to benefit themselves as well as others. Practical activity should therefore proceed under the guideline of altruism. This is the process of children's social development, or a process in which children can happily achieve self-realization of accomplishment as individual beings and social beings. In this way, Krupskaya expounded the self-development of children by analyzing the process of personality development based on the inner life. And it is the inherent quality of children as human beings that forms the very core of overall development. Therefore, she insisted on awakening children's sense of self-activity to cater to their spiritual pursuit and develop their personality. This view on children and their development was the foundation of her educational theory about labor schools and collectivism. At the same time, she also conducted research on children from the perspective of biology and held the view that heredity, cerebrum and nervous system are of great importance in revealing the law of child's personality development.

Having said that, how did she combine education with life in the construction of Soviet new-style schools then? After the October Revolution, Krupskaya defined those schools that could help children to realize overall development as "unified labor schools" and then she committed herself to the implementation of polytechnic education. She used "labor schools" to replace the backward schools in the old society. She grasped the educational thought of Marx, and sought for the historical inevitability of school revolution. According to Marx, the combination of education and productive labor allows social productivity to be improved, and contributes to the overall development of human beings and reformation of modern society. Krupskaya believed that this was the fundamental principle with which the working class organized the new-style schools. It was on the basis of the educational thought of Marx and Krupskaya that the Soviet Union immediately plunged into the campaign of constructing "labor schools" after the October Revolution. *The Regulations of Unified Labor Schools of Union of Soviet Socialist Republics (USSR)* enacted on September 30 in 1918 stipulated that "the fundamental principle of school life is not the necessary tuition from children or the renovation of teaching methodology, but the productive labor—the productive labor that is socially necessary. And the productive labor should be closely and organically combined with teaching that can explain everything in the surrounding world with enlightening knowledge," under the title of "Fundamental Principle of School

178   CHAPTER 11

Education" listed in Article Twelve.[14] Together with polytechnic education, the combination of productive labor with teaching constituted the fundamental principle of labor schools. But Krupskaya's proposal of "combining school education with life" in the 1920s did not consist of the double meanings. Life is different from productive labor. Encouraged by John Dewey's "life as education," she stresses the importance of "combing child's productive labor with vibrant life" and emphasized that schools should closely combine education with socialist construction and life of workers and peasants. The changing life educated people in an unprecedented way, and the educators should be educated as well. She also paid close attention to the movement launched by communist youth league and young pioneers, which was conducive to the direct communication between students and workers and peasants. Undoubtedly, backward schools were negated in the stormy socialist revolution, and schools and teachers should be educated in this turbulent life.

However, Krupskaya's idea about education from life is not one-sided. At the same time she also proposed that schools should play a positive role in the construction of new life—the important role of "educationalization of environment." Especially in the 1930s, there was an increasing demand for the transformation of subject knowledge teaching in school education. Even in the initial stages after the enactment of resolution *On Primary and Secondary Schools*[15] by the Communist Party of the Soviet Union (CPSU) (Bolshevik), "polytechnic education and combination with productive labor" was adopted as the fundamental principle in Soviet schools. But the problem was there was a serious shortage of students from secondary vocational schools and colleges that socialist industrialization needed due to the four-year compulsory education program of the time. Therefore, the focus of school work at this time was shifted from striving to be closely related to life to using school resources to enrich life. Krupskaya made the following comments in 1932, saying that the Central Committee of the CPSU (Bolshevik) was committed to improving the quality of teaching and the standard of general pedagogical knowledge in the whole year of 1931, which, of course, did not mean that the Communist Party had ignored the polytechnic education.[16] Nevertheless, shortly afterwards, this trend led to the separation of teaching and life again." From the late 1930s, the problem that "theories were isolated from practice" and "schools were separated from productive labor" became prominent. And in a letter sent to the

---

14   Tsuguo Iwasaki, *Hisotory of Western Educational Thoughts*. Tokyo: Meijitosho, 1987, 160–161.

15   Yoshimatsu Shibata, *The Teaching Theory in Soviet*. Tokyo: Meijitoshi, 1982, 15.

16   Ibid.

CRITICAL COMMENTS ON KAIROV'S PEDAGOGY

general secretary of the Central Committee of CPSU (Bolshevik) in February, 1937, Krupskaya showed her anxiety, in which she wrote, "it is a regret to see that labor education classes in schools have disappeared completely in recent years...They have disappeared not as a result of recombination of labor subjects, but they have been canceled."[17] However, not long after, on the pretext of "over-reliance on handicraft industry," the People's Committee on Education abolished the labor course as an independent subject, with the result that "many labor studios in school are closed, and labor education and polytechnic activities are laid aside."[18] This trend was going from bad to worse with the advance of socialist industrialization and secondary education, and the spread of Stalin's cult of personality and bureaucracy in the Second World War. Although polytechnic activities were still being mentioned, actually schools had already been deviated from productive labor into the old way of rote-learning.

The topic of discussion "to combine education with life" came back into popularity in the late 1950s, when Scarlett emphasized that "teaching is a subject of study that relies on science which reflects the natural and social life. And school curricula should have been closely related to life" in his book *The Combination of Teaching and Life in Eight-Year Program* (1962).[19] From his point of view, the most important way to combine education with life was to further develop the quality of subject contents, which did not mean merely imbuing predesigned teaching materials, but combining teaching of knowledge with familiar everyday life. The "life," however, was a multivalent concept in his view, and Scarlett further explained the seven basic ways[20] to realize the combination of education with life. In this connection, the principle of "combining education with life" proposed by Krupskaya was originally connected with undifferentiated living environment (revolutionary struggle), and then gradually came to be combined with some fundamental aspects in life in a differentiated way. In the only thesis entitled "The Combination of Schools and Surrounding Social Life" (1924) in which Krupskaya directly discussed her

---

17   Ibid, 16.
18   Ibid, 16.
19   Ibid, 17.
20   The seven basic ways of combination are: (1) to be combined with struggles that serve the purposes of politics and communist construction; (2) to be combined with national and regional economy, production and life and neighboring enterprises; (3) to be combined with scientific methods and achievements; (4) to be combined with literature and art; (5) to be combined with rural life; (6) to be combined with students' own life, experience and practice; (7) to be combined with students' voluntary social work and productive activities. See Yoshimatsu Shibata, *The Teaching Theory in Soviet*. Tokyo: Meijitoshi, 1982, 17.

view of combination,[21] she warned the educational circle against the isolation of schools and called on students to involve themselves in the life and activities of workers and peasants and to interact with the grassroots of Communist Youth League, and encouraged factories to be united with farms. Although she did not give further explanations of the specific ways to combine teaching contents with social life after breaking down the barriers between schools and life outside, she clearly insisted that school education should follow Lenin's thought on education, i.e. schools should be involved with dynamic social life.

In our discussion above, we have sketched a general outline about the basic principles of Leninist education thoughts represented by Krupskaya. These basic principles became the dominant ideas for the construction of Soviet schools at that time.

In the late 1920s, an educational reform at the Soviet historical turning point dramatically swept the country. And on October 1, 1928, the Soviet Union began its implementation of its socialist construction with the first Five-Year Plan, after its economic condition rapidly recovered to its prewar level in 1926. Under such circumstances, the educational circle in Soviet Union was also extremely active with burning passion. Shulgin, Krupenina and other educators from the School Activity Research Institute criticized the People's Committee on Education for its inability to provide research projects concerning cultural revolution in this special period of socialist construction. A heated argument was launched among well-known educators such as Pinkevich and Kalashnikov. They vehemently proposed "Deschooling" with its basic idea in that "people begin to learn on the basis of their practical experience in factories, farms and class struggle rather than in schools. This is true with children's learning. It is real social life and socialist construction sites that accommodate education."[22] They predicted that "schools will eventually disappear along with the disappearance of countries in a communist society."[23] It is unnecessary for us to demonize these predictions and assumptions. The problem that arises with it is the destructive effect that can be brought about by this either-or thinking and polarized behavior: to blindly cannonize the "design method of teaching" imported from the United States and totally negate classes, teaching plan, subject teaching, and textbooks in school educational practices, was out of line with educational thought of Leninism and the demand for talent in socialist construction. Supporters of "Deschooling" condemned Shatsky, a

---

21   Yoshimatsu Shibata, *The Teaching Theory in Soviet*. Tokyo: Meijitoshi, 1982, 18.

22   Hitoshi Matsushima & Satoshi Kawanobe, *The Selected Works of Modern Educational Thoughts* (Volume six, Soviet Russia). Tokyo: Gyosei kabushikikaisha, 1981, 299.

23   Ibid.

CRITICAL COMMENTS ON KAIROV'S PEDAGOGY

famous educator, as a "right" deviationist due to his approval of schools' influence. Shatsky's educational ideology, however, was enthusiastically defended by Krupskaya. From the late 1920s to the 1930s, Shatsky, out of his favorable position for the combination of education and real life, held a positive attitude to the Dalton Plan and the Design Method of Teaching from America. But soon these methods, together with the "teaching plan" in unified labor schools sponsored mainly by Soviet National Academic Conference of People's Committee on Education were harshly criticized by the Central Committee of the CPSU (Bolshevik).

Soviet education in the 1920's after the October Revolution was poles apart from that in the post-1930's period. That was an era of exploration that addressed to such issues as children's personality, and probed deeply into such themes as "labor" and "life." Shatsky was the person that has left important influences on the Soviet education in the 1920s. A whole generation of educators headed by Shatsky made outstanding achievements in the hard times after the October Revolution. Although generally ignored in the 1930s, their contributions were rehabilitated after the downfall of Stalin. Even though entangled in the ideological trend of "Deschooling" and repudiated by CPSU (Bolshevik), Shatsky still presided over "The Central Pedagogy Department" as a member of People's Committee on Education. And from February 1932, he devoted himself to the education reform as the president of Moscow National Conservatory. A Japanese educator commentated that "In the 1930s, the old backward schools that were characterized by their deviation from life, inclination to theory and implementation of rote-learning revived, because of the dedicated efforts made by Shatsky and other educators in the 1920s in the Soviet Union." "It is not theoretically difficult to discuss science but the history of real education seems to evolve around the anxiety and bitter struggle of these two issues"; "The educational thought that developed out of Shatsky's experience and practice still seems to be a heart-shocking tocsin to our current education."[24]

1.2   *School Policies in 1931 and Vicissitudes of Kairov's Pedagogy*

In the 1930s, the CPSU (Bolshevik) began to criticize the thoughts of "Deschooling" and "the 'left' deviation of anti-Leninism," which, to some extent, changed the situation of Soviet education and paved the way for Stalin's ideology to spread. With the enactment of the *Resolution for Primary and Secondary Schools* the most spectacular educational document in the Soviet educational

---

24   Ibid, 331–335.

history enacted by the Central Committee of the CPSU (Bolshevik) in 1931, "the school policies in 1931" began to be put into effect step by step. The keynote of this resolution was "systematical mastery of subject knowledge" and "enhancement of the consciousness of class struggle at the ideological level." In accordance with this, a series of steps were taken.[25]

Firstly, to develop a syllabus for each subject and course, which was required to be done before January 1, 1932 according to the resolution of 1931. And in November 1931, the People's Committee on Education proposed that all the new syllabi should be based on the principle of departmental system in order to systematically pass on "cardinal direction" of basic knowledge.

Secondly, to reconstruct teaching methodology suitable for systematic imparting of knowledge and the organizational structure for the implementation of learning activities. The resolution *On the Syllabus and Teaching System of Primary and Secondary Schools* enacted by the Central Committee of CPSU (Bolshevik) in August, 1932, stressed the universal significance of systematic instruction of subject knowledge by means of lectures and presentation. Students' autonomous, initiative and exploratory learning could be discussed only under the precondition that the teachers' role of instruction had been guaranteed. The basic way of learning activities for primary and secondary schools should be collective learning with strictly scheduled timetables and the fixed size of classes.

Thirdly, to reedit textbooks. According to the resolution *On Textbooks of Primary and Secondary Schools* enacted by the Central Committee of CPSU (Bolshevik) in February 1932, specific textbooks were required for each subject, and "alternative textbooks" such as loose-sheet textbooks or textbooks adapted from magazines which were associated with extracurricular activities should be strictly banned from publication.

Fourthly, to develop a system of students' learning assessments" (a system consisting of grading, testing and rewards and penalties). All testing systems which were abolished by *The Decree of Unified Labor School* in 1918 restored. The two-level (or three-level) grading system was replaced by the five-level grading system. In spring of 1933, the national entrance examination was initiated, and then examination became a common practice in school life.

Lastly, to launch a critique on pedology. According to the resolution *On Misinterpretation of Pedology from the People's Committee on Education* (July, 1936), pedagogy and teachers' rights were fully recovered, and a series of measures

---

25 Konstantinov, *Soviet Educational History*, trans. Wu Shiying. Beijing: The Commercial Press, 1996, 445–461.

CRITICAL COMMENTS ON KAIROV'S PEDAGOGY

were taken concerning the revocation of teaching and research groups of pedologists and their related textbooks in schools.

From the resolution *On Primary and Secondary Schools* (September, 1931) to the resolution *On Misinterpretation of Pedology from the People's Committee on Education* (July, 1936) enacted by the Central Committee of CPSU (Bolshevik), the "school policies in 1931" came to a tentative end in the history of education in the Soviet Union. However, what was the specific time for pedology to disseminate and how it made its way into the educational theory and practice in this country was unclear. Nonetheless, we know that the earliest time for the problem of "misinterpretation of pedology" to emerge was after the 1930s, although the idea of pedology appeared in the early 1920s. From the official direction initiated by the People's Committee on Education, the above-mentioned problem arose in around 1933. Such being the case, what is "pedology"? According to the research of Petrovsky,[26] an expert on psychological history in the Soviet Union, there were two different schools of pedology: One was "biology-oriented school," the other was "sociology-oriented school." The first group maintained that human (including children) psychological development was determined by biological factors and they proposed the notion of "spontaneity of child's psychological development" or the idea of "development independent from education." Education for them was no more than an external factor which could deter or promote a certain psychology property constrained by congenital heredity. For the second school called themselves "group of sociological development," which just the opposite of the "biology-oriented group." They advocated the decisive role of social environment in the determination of children's growth, and regarded children as passive receivers or devices of external stimulus. In compliance with the official direction of the People's Committee on Education, these pedologists constructed classes, set up regulations in schools, and were responsible for instructing children and even expulsing academically retarded students from the perspective of pedology. These two groups analyzed the causes that lead to poor-performing students from the standpoints of hereditary constraint and sociological constraint respectively, and attributed the academical disadvantage to heredity or environment, without considering the responsibility of teachers. Both groups underestimated the impact of education and teaching on children's development. It was claimed in the resolution that the theorical and practical assumptions of pedology were based on pseudoscience and anti-Marxism. And the main principle of pedology, namely, the "principle" of fatalism which ascribed

---

26   Petrovsky., *Developmental and educational Psychology*, trans. Yoshimatsu Shibata. Tokyo: Shindokushosha, 1977, 6–9.

learning effects to genetical or biological factors and invariable environments, was incompatible with everything concerning socialist construction. However, in "Several Issues on the Reconstruction of Educational Science" (1989), Petrovsky pointed out that, " the last textbooks about pedology (*Pedology* compiled by Chalgin in 1934; *Pedology* compiled by Sokolov in 1936) published around the time when pedology was being criticized did not contain the development view of fatalism. That means fatalism had been discarded before 1933 at least, and the criticism of pedology had no theoretical basis. Even the issues concerning the questionnaire tests at the practical level and the mechanical application of psychological tests did not exist, for the development diagnostics constructed by Vygotsky viewed learning activities in the zone of proximal development."[27]

We should say that the permeation of "the school policies in 1931" was intermingled with various internal conflicts in the Soviet society. It was an extremely formidable task to figure out the process and consequences of debates that went on among different educational thoughts. However, during the promotion of this policy, especially after the mid-1930s, "the school policies in 1931" was entangled with the reinforcement of Stalin's regime, and lots of new drawbacks started to emerge in Soviet education theory and practice. Here, we would like to summarize two pedagogical results brought about by this policy.

First, the "Verbalist Schools" resurged. "The school policy of 1931" indeed brought some positive effects such as eliminating the distraction of "Deschooling." But there arose two problems on school education. The first was the resurgence of the teaching methods dominated by formalism and verbalism. The second was that teachers no longer showed any concern for students' interest and autonomous thinking but just implemented rote-learning, with the consequence of the ascendancy of learner-marginalizedness. And there was no more the pursuit for polytechnic education and combination of production with education under the guidance of Marxism. Therefore, in her twilight years, Krupskaya expressed her strong discontent and severely criticized the trend for "Verbalist Schools"—where education was divorced from real life, students' autonomous activities were ignored and the quality of knowledge-learning was replaced by the quantity of rote-learning.[28]

Second, it marked the end of the era of experiment and exploration. From the perspective of educational research, the problems of educational science, teaching theories and psychological problems were decided by the resolutions

---

27   Vygotsky, *The Theory of "Zone of Proximal Development"—Child's Development during Teaching (postscripts)*, trans. Shozo Doi. Otsu: Sangaku shuppan, 2003, 225–226.

28   Kunio Komabayashi, *Modern Soviet Teaching Theories*. Tokyo: Meijitosho, 1975, 59.

CRITICAL COMMENTS ON KAIROV'S PEDAGOGY

of the Central Committee of CPSU (Bolshvik) instead of scientific research, which led to the "arteriosclerosis" in the scientific work of educators in the Soviet Union.[29] Even though the resolution of 1936 claimed that "we should take the educational purpose of systematically grasping basic scientific knowledge as our starting point, and emphasize the important role of teachers," it also concluded that "the pedology that lays emphasis on heredity in children's psychological development is an anti-Marxist heresy," which in fact criticized the traditional thoughts that attribute children's development to biological or the invariable social factors. It should be acknowledged that the endeavor to change children by means of education had indeed some historical significance.[30] However, the resolution of the Communist Party trammeled the research work of pedologists. This resolution prohibited the experimental exploration in learning and teaching processes. The autonomous research activities of educators were replaced by the Party's political doctrine. After the criticism of "the deviation of pedology" and the prohibition of the research on hereditary and environmental factors in children's development, "Education Omnipotence" was widely spread. In other words, "the principle inherent in children's natural development was ignored, and children did not take the initiative to learn but were regarded as the receptacles that passively receive knowledge. When pedology was criticized as pseudoscience, children research which was established on the basis of true science was abandoned as well."[31] "After the criticism of pedology, Krupskaya showed her deep concern that the developmental issue of age would lose significance in pedagogical and psychological research."[32] And her concern turned into reality. The problem of overlooking children in pedology became all the more conspicuous. And the pursuit for respecting and studying child's development in the 1920s disappeared. So the era of experiment and exploration during which various schools of educational science could explore freely came to a natural end,[33] which was an inevitable result of cultural autocracy of Stalinism.[34]

---

29   Ibid, 60.

30   Zhong Qiquan 钟启泉, Xiandai kechenglun 现代课程论 [*The Study of Modern Curriculum*]. Shanghai: Shanghai Educational Publishing House, 1989, 422.

31   Ibid, 422.

32   Vygotsky, *The Theory of "Zone of Proximal Development"—Child's Development during Teaching (postscripts)*, trans. Shozo Doi. Otsu: Sangaku shuppan, 2003, 226.

33   Kunio Komabayashi, *Modern Soviet Teaching Theories*. Tokyo: Meijitosho, 1975, 59.

34   We can look into one aspect of the cultural autocracy of Stalinism from Vygotsky's cases. Vygotsky (1896–1934) had broad interests and superior talent. He was admitted by the Moscow State University in 1913, majoring in medicine. But he left medicine for law owing to his interest. In the meanwhile, he studied psychology and philosophy in Shenivsky University and was deeply versed in the humanities. He finished the paper "Hamlet: The

186   CHAPTER 11

Kairov's Pedagogy (1939, 1948, 1956) appeared in such a social and historical background. It is reasonable to say that Kairov's Pedagogy systematically
summarized the working experience of rectifying educational activities in
primary and secondary schools from the 1930s to the 1940s, which had some
positive influence and significance. However, because the deep-rooted negative influence of the political resolution of the Communist Party taking the
place of scientific research, what teachers had to do was to implement the
standardized rote-learning in their teaching process. Furthermore, research on
children, research on curricula and research on teachers had no place at all
in Kairov's Pedagogy. It is, therefore, considered rational and appropriate to

---

Tragedy" during his school years and loved the works of Spinoza throughout his life. From
1924, he worked at the Institute of Psychology and the Institute of Defectology successively,
worked as the director of the Educational Department for Mentally and Physically Hand-
icapped Children in the People's Commissariat of Education and taught in Krupskaya
Communist Normal School and Leningrad Normal School. He was appointed as the head
of Division of Psychology in the Experimental Medical Academy not long before he died.
He dedicated himself to psychological experiments since he was a university student and
had collected lots of materials about children's development. It was not until 1928 when
the first issue of the journal of *Pedology* came out that he began to publish articles, which
laid a foundation for the construction of the development theory of advanced mental
functions—the soul of Vygotsky's theories. Although he died at a young age of 38, he
published nearly 200 academic papers and left many unfinished manuscripts. His major
publications include *Awareness: the Question of Behavior Psychology* (1925), *Educational
Psychology* (1926), "Development of Voluntary Attention in Childhood" (1929), *Thought
and Language* (1934), *Proceedings of Psychological Research* (1956), *The Development of
Advanced Mental Functions* (1960) and *Psychology of Art* (1965). Vygotsky died of tuber-
culosis in June 1934, when Stalin started the Great Purge in December of the same year.
In 1936, pedology began to be criticized, and some relevant curricula were banned and
books about pedology were destroyed. At that time, Vygotsky was labeled as an "eclectic,"
and his works and were ruined and his academic contributions were denied. Because of
the supplementary relations between the theory of "zone of proximal development" and
pedology, his works about pedology were generally ignored, and scholars who used to
follow Vygotsky's school closely retreated to avoid potential problems, even during the
period when Stalin's cult of personality was being criticized. Western scholars, such as
Bruner (J. S. Bruner), however, showed interest in the concept of "zone of proximal development." They got to know Vygotsky's thoughts through Loria and began to explore the
multivalent meanings and values of "the zone of proximal development" in dealing with
issues in relation to education and psychology and in relation to social and philosophical
problems. Furthermore, the collapse of the Soviet Union in 1991 brought the works of
Vygotsky to light again. The development of cognitive science in America generated a
wave of "Vygotsky Fever" and Vygotsky's status as an international renowned scholar was
re-established. See Levitin, *Vygotsky School—The Formation and Development of Soviet
Psychology*, trans. Yoshimatsu Shibata, 1984, 23–24; Vygotsky, *The Theory of "Zone of Proximal Development"—Children's Development in the Course of Teaching*, trans. Shozo Doi.
Otsu: Sangaku shuppan, 2003, 219–227.

CRITICAL COMMENTS ON KAIROV'S PEDAGOGY

accept Kairov's Pedagogy as a handbook for many educators. The three basic concepts of Kairov's Pedagogy were "education," "upbringing" and "teaching." Although these concepts contained some brilliant views of Comenius, Herbart and other pioneers in education circle to some extent, many topics of discussion concerning outlooks on children and epistemology were outdated due to the time limitation and the ideological deviation. And the three concepts also had many drawbacks that could not be supported on solid ground: "The class nature of education" was misconstrued as an exaggerated statement of tool in class struggle in the definition of education; the definition of "upbringing" was ambiguous owing to the lack of necessary curriculum concept; and the definition of "teaching" was fragmentary for its undue emphasis on special epistemology and so on and so forth. In conclusion, Kairov's Pedagogy was the product of cultural autocracy of Stalinism from the perspective of educational ideologies.

Two articles entitled "Calling for Deep and Comprehensive Research on Children" (August, 1956) and "Avoiding the Consequences of Personality Cult in Pedology" (September, 1956) were anonymously published in the *Journal of Russian Academy of Education* soon after the 20th Congress of the Communist Party of the Soviet Union.[35] Based on the criticism on personality cult and dogmatism, both essays aimed to highlight the necessity of research on children. These articles pointed out that, "of all the causes of educational drawbacks in Soviet education, the excessive personality cult of Stalin was top on the list. Lots of educationists put dogmatism in the most prominent place and overlooked educational experiment, independent thinking and free self-expression." The articles went on saying that, it was intolerable even today for us to accept the attitude of many educationists for their "dogmatism's position" in misinterpretation of pedology in the 1930s when the resolution of the Party Central Committee was dominant. Because of the educationists' absence in and even refuse of research on children, "the pedagogy overlooking children" became a fatal problem. And the drawbacks in primary and secondary schools such as rote-learning, mechanical training, and replacing intelligence development by knowledge infusion became the target of public criticism. The articles emphasized that we could not get rid of the constraint of the pedagogy that "overlooks children" unless we regard children as "active rational agents who possess the innate potential of development." Because of its intrinsic negligence of children and its inherent cultural autocracy, Kairov's Pedagogy was criticized and conspued in the ice-breaking period of ideas in the late 1950s.

---

35   Zhong Qiquan 钟启泉, Xiandai kechenglun 现代课程论 [*The Study of Modern Curriculum*]. Shanghai: Shanghai Educational Publishing House, 1989, 421–424.

Accurately speaking, it was in 1956 that the education circle in China began to criticize Kairov's Pedagogy and proposed to initiate China's own educational science.[36] However, today, more than thirty years after China's reform and opening up to the outside world, there are still a group of people who attempt to deify Kairov's Pedagogy and seek to restart the study of Kairov's Pedagogy in China. They assert, "Kairov's Pedagogy has not been discarded, but inherited and developed well."[37] They even intentionally obscure the difference between "Kairov's Pedagogy" and "Soviet Pedagogy," using the scientific research of Ville-ju's school, Zankov, Davydov and other scholars on educational development as evidence for the development of Kairov's Pedagogy.[38] The following descriptions are some of the phrases that can be used to account for their complex mixed mentalities: stuck in the old dogmas, intimidated by the new theories and disdaining innovative practice. Losing themselves in historical muddledness and perverting logic, they tried to bring back the good old sentiment for Kairov's Pedagogy. These are the typical symptoms of "the complex of Kairov's Pedagogy" (or "Kairov-affection complex"). And it is not surprising that these people think this way because they are stranded by their professional bias and constraint of their time. But we should not follow their steps and hold fast to the obsolete "complex of Kairov's Pedagogy." What we need is new horizons and transcendence. Such being the case, it has been repeatedly stressed that, "If we had not engaged ourselves in the large-scale movement of learning Soviet Pedagogy and the huge amount of investment in education in the early

---

36   In the early years after the founding of the People's Republic of China, when all things needed to be rebuilt, Kairov's Pedagogy summarized some specific educational strategies from the perspective of educational system and education methods initiated in the Soviet Union during the 1930s had some positive effects in rectifying China's school education. But the development of school education and science of education in China could not exclusively rely on the total and uncritical acceptance of Kairov's Pedagogy. Criticism of Kairov's Pedagogy in China can be traced back to 1956 when Mao Zedong indicated that, "we should analytically and critically learn from others rather than blindly and mechanically copy them" in "On the Ten Major Relationships" and "A Talk with Musical Workers." See Mao Zedong, *Mao Zedong's View on Education*. Beijing: People's Education Press, 1999, 230. Mao also pointed out, "China should develop and create its own culture by learning from the outside world." Ibid, 241. It was not until 1958, when Chairman Mao directly criticized the general practice of "mechanically applying the experience of the Soviet Union" in China's education circle at a Chengdu meeting that China started to rebuild its own science of education.

37   Wang Cesan 王策三, "Xinkecheng linian," "Gainian chongjian yundong" yu xuexi Kairov jiaoyuxue "新课程理念""概念重建运动"与学习凯洛夫教育学 [The New Curriculum rationale, Reconceptualization Movement and learning Kairov's Pedagogy]. *Curriculum, Teaching Material and Method*, 2008, (7), 16.

38   Ibid, 11.

CRITICAL COMMENTS ON KAIROV'S PEDAGOGY

years after the founding of People's Republic of China, there would not have been the early construction of China's education. It would be inconceivable, then, for us to launch the eighth (it should be the second from the perspective of transformation of educational thoughts and curriculum standards) national-scale curriculum reform, without the corresponding preparations in public opinions, the new round of reconceptualization movement and the necessary supporting funds contributed to education."[39] The reconceptualization movement is essential to the development of China's educational science and a criticism of Kairov's Pedagogy is an inevitable and yet grave issue in China's educational development.

2

What we need is to carry on with serious academic discussions by presenting the truth rather than talking recklessly. In our assessment of Kairov's Pedagogy, we should not obscure the difference between Kairov's Pedagogy and Soviet Pedagogy, and mistake the achievements of subsequent educationists and psychologists in Soviet for the development of Kairov's Pedagogy, because they bear diverse educational ideologies. Especially after the ice-breaking period of educational thought in Soviet, many educationists and psychologists raked up Leninism and Krupskaya's educational ideologies, criticized Kairov's Pedagogy and made a differentiation between them. For this reason, prating that the developmental research on teaching developed from Kairov's Pedagogy is against the truth.[40] To be accurate, the latter is criticized by the former. Let's look at several significant historical facts in the history of Soviet educational science.

---

39   Zhong Qiquan 钟启泉, Kecheng gaige: Tiaozhan yu fansi 课程改革：挑战与反思 [Curriculum reform: Challenges and introspection], in Kecheng de luoji 课程的逻辑 [*The Logic of Curriculum*], ed. Zhong Qiquan,. Shanghai: East China Normal University Press, 2008, 36.

40   After citing the three basic concepts of Kairov's Pedagogy, Wang's Article suggested that, "later Villeju's school transcended and developed Kairov's Pedagogy," which misled readers to think that these two thoughts had the legitimate relationship of inheritance. It was ahistorical. In fact, the so-called Villeju's school, to be accurate, refers to the cultural-historical school engaged in the research of human psychology. The theoretical basis of this school is that "psychology and advanced intellectual functions are the products of culture and history in human society," which can be commanded only through the research on the nature and origin of social experiences by individuals and their mentalities." If we apply this assumption to children's psychological development, we can say: "Children's cognitive activity is a fundamental stage and characteristic in the historical and social process, and it is constrained by the social experiences accepted by individuals, the orga-

190   CHAPTER 11

2.1   *Criticism of Pedagogy "Overlooking Children" and Significance of "Argument about Development"*

Let's first of all review how educationists and psychologists started the vigorous argument about development surrounding the topic of development and education while adhering to Krupskaya's view on children and her proposition concerning children study in the ice-breaking period of educational thought in the late 1950s Soviet Union, in allusion to the disastrous effects of criticizing pedology in the 1930s and especially to the drawback of overlooking children in Kairov's Pedagogy. Just as a Japanese scholar put it, "the argument about development and education in Soviet Union was so magnificent that it was a rare phenomenon in the world. The origin of this debate can be traced back to the 'Critique on Pedology in 1936' from a historical perspective."[41] In this argument, Kostyuk's self-development theory, Menchinskaya's theory of variability concerning age characteristics, and Leontiev's developmental view of materialism added radiance to each other to demonstrate their own educational thoughts and brand-new theoretical visions that varied from Kairov's Pedagogy.

It is noteworthy that the journal *Soviet Pedagogy* (Issue 12 of 1956) published an article entitled "The Relationship between Children Education and Development" written by Kostyuk, a Ukrainian psychologist, which initiated the heated argument about development.[42] Kostyuk emphasized the importance of deep inquiries into the relationship of education and development in view of the common problems in textbooks that gave abstract and even mechanical interpretations to the leading role of education. By exploring into the conditions

---

nization system of social culture and its methods." This thought came from "the development theory of culture and history" put forward by Vygotsky from the 1920s to the 1930s. So cultural-historical school is also referred to as the Vygotsky school, which includes not only the Vygotsky school represented by the research group that consisted of Vygotsky's colleagues and his students, but also the Vygotsky school represented by the new arising team of psychologists that advocate the development and command theory. In other words, the former is the Vygotsky school in its broad sense while the latter is that in its narrow sense. It is represented by Leontiev, Loria, Zankov, Halperin (П. Я.Г альперин), Zaporozhets (А. В. Запорожец), Elkonin, Davydov and Talyzin (Н. Талызина). The academic achievements made by the Vygotsky school are universally acknowledged, and Vygotsky engaged his research activities earlier than Kairov. It is unreasonable to put Kairov's Pedagogy above the Vygotsky school. It is groundless to put them on a par with each other. By the way, the so-called the developmental research on teaching is an international phenomenon, because educators in Germany and Japan have published relevant books as well. So, it would be illogical to claim that all these Western studies are developed from Kairov's Pedagogy. See Levitin, *Vygotsky School—The Formation and Development of Soviet Psychology*, trans. Yoshimatsu Shibata. 1984, 9–119.

41   Hisashi Hirai, *Children Development Theory*. Tokyo: Keirinshobo, 1982, 319, 319, 305–308, 323.

42   Ibid, 319.

CRITICAL COMMENTS ON KAIROV'S PEDAGOGY

under which the development (or factors that trigger children's development) can take place, he strove to answer the theoretical question "how education can play a guiding role in development" so as to provide a theoretical basis for the discussion of the relationship of education and development. In his article, he expounded the following well-known points of argumentation.

Firstly, he believed in social restriction on children's development. He indicated that, "children's psychological development takes place in their interaction with the surrounding environments. However, this interaction and children's recognition of the objective world obtained from this process is based on their communication with adults and social experience with the help of language." Hence, it is wrong to regard the innate psychological activities as the premise for children's intellectual development. But external factors including education do not exert direct influence on children. They take effect indirectly because of children's attitudes, and activities that influence their inclinations and intentions in their experience.

Secondly, he believed in mutual dependence between teaching and development and variations. He pointed out that, "teaching is an important but not the only factor that contributes to children's cognitive and spiritual developments, which depend not only on teaching, but also on the surrounding environment and other activities, and still on the maturation of their physical faculties and nervous system."

Thirdly, he believed in the immanent contradictions in the motivation of children's development. The development of all things comes from their own unique inherent contradiction. He insisted that this basic principle of materialistic dialectics could be applied to children's development and their psychological development as well. Children's immanent contradictions may be manifested in a number of ways. For example, their new demands, interests and ambitions may be in contradiction with their potential level of development. The requirements of the social environment may be in contradiction with their skills and proficiency necessary for the acceptance and practice of these requirements; the new school subjects may be in contradiction with their previously familiar ways of thinking and behavior; their subjective wishes may be in contradiction with their objective environments; and all these contradictions may be in further contraction with their status in their family and community. Besides, many new contradictions can be derived from the above-mentioned ones. An accurate understanding of these immanent contradictions is right way to understand children's psychological development. He stressed, personality development should be understood as a dynamic process of "self-movement" in the form of spontaneity, rather than as an inertance caused by external forces.

Fourthly, he believed that self-movement of children and the leading role of teaching are not in conflict. In relation to this basic issue of Soviet educational science, Kostyuk explained that, "the developmental process as a self-movement and the leading role of teaching in children's psychological development are not an issue of contradiction. They are by no means in contradiction." "Many people believe that it seems contradictory to acknowledge the spontaneity of personality development and to acknowledge at the same time the social restrictions of this process and the leading role of education. This belief arises from 'the mentalistic explanation of spontaneous development on the one hand, and simplified and mechanical interpretation of restraints in development on the other hand.' Actually, spontaneous development is not entirely free from any constraint. On the contrary, it comes into being under certain conditions. The 'self-movement' and 'self-development' of all existence are restricted by 'the sum total of multiple relations' with their surrounding realities."

Fifthly, he believed in the possibilities of education and the inner principle of development. Kostyuk believed, if children's spontaneous development is repudiated, the instruction in the course of development would be over-simplified, and if spontaneous development is negated, the infinite possibilities of the seemingly omnipotent education would be in fact restricted since primary and secondary school teachers would lose their ways. He said, "the possibilities of education would increase, if education does take control of children's life as a whole, and educators have a deep understanding of essence and principle of children's development and tactfully put it into practice."

Lastly, he stressed the superb skills of teachers. He said, "all education and teaching may not result in children's development. It is flexible, skillful and tactful education and teaching that will make it." The components of this accomplishment are (1) taking hold of children's life as a whole, who are regarded as both subjects and objects of education; (2) fully understanding age characteristics and personal traits in children's development; (3) continually observing children's life, and paying close attention to how they change and what they think, experience and pursue after being influenced by education.

Kostyuk's paper stroke a chord among many psychologists such as Bogoyavlensky, Menchinskaya and Leontiev. Menchinskaya's understanding, however, was unique in that she put forward a theory of changeability of age characteristics, in which she advocated: (1) "division of children's developmental stages must be in line with that of school educational stages." In her opinion, it is groundless to doubt that the changes in education and teaching conditions can play a decisive role in children's mental and especially cognitive activities; (2) emphasis should be given to the training of thinking and autonomy. Only when the initiative of children's learning is cherished, can teaching really play

CRITICAL COMMENTS ON KAIROV'S PEDAGOGY

a "leading role" in their intellectual progress. Conditions for children's independent thinking must be created, while, at the same time, autonomous thinking activities, such as analyzing, synthesizing, comparing, summarizing, classifying, analogizing, deducting, inducting and reasoning must be designed for children to train them systematically. Intellectual training and independent thinking lay at the core of Menchinskaya's development and teaching theory. Leontiev, however, put forward the materialist development theory.[43] He believed that metaphysical assumption on development attributes children's development to external forces and influence of external factors, while dialectical materialist theory on development sees development as a form of self-movement, which means that we should acknowledge the existence of spontaneity of development, that is, to acknowledge the existence of the implicit immanent principle in the process of development. However, metaphysical assumption does not always insist that external factors have automatic impact on children. They also admit external effects must be realized by relying on children's present conditions (such as their previous experience and current development level). Therefore, the indirect effect of external factors on children alone is not a concept that could be used to distinguish these two opposing theories. Moreover, to use contradictions or not as a motive power for development is not a distinctive feature between these two claims, either. The problem is the metaphysical assumption only sees this motive power merely as external contradiction. Such being the case, what is the essential distinctive feature of these two theories? According to Leontiev, the key lies in whether or not the concept of development is understood or acknowledged to be a self-movement or spontaneity caused by the internal contradictions of the developing subject that makes the difference between the two thoughts. Kostyuk's view is in line with Mao Zedong's principle that external causes become operative through internal causes in Mao's "On Contradictions." However, Leontiev stressed the role of activities on the developing subjects (children), and brought forward the idea of educational control of activity.

The argument about development from the late 1950s to the 1960s broke the ice of dogmatism and experientialism of Kairov's Pedagogy, and initiated an era of emancipation for educational thought in the Soviet Union. Supported by the editorial department of the journal of *Soviet Pedagogy*, Zankov summarized this argument and generalized the following two points: First, it stressed that children was not only the objects to accept education, but also the subjects to learn and self-develop. He also affirmed that the research on

---

43   Ibid, 305–308.

children's development played an essential role in rectifying all textbooks of pedagogy including Kairov's Pedagogy that overlooked children. Second, it clearly pointed out that, pedagogy had ignored the resource collection about children's psychological development, including their age characteristics and personalities. In the meanwhile, this argument emphasized the necessity of researching on children's psychological development.[44]

In a word, the argument about development that strove to overcome various defects in Soviet pedagogy had greatly emancipated the practice and creativity of Soviet educationalists and psychologists, promoted the diversity of educational theories and marked a new stage for Soviet science of education in its modern sense.

2.2 The Confrontation between Zankov's New Teaching System and Kairov's Teaching Principles

If we regard argument about development as a clarification of Kairov's education thought at the theoretical level, the active research centralized on elementary education on the basis of this argument in the 1960s was a criticism of Kairov's teaching principles at the practical level. The experiment on Zankov's new teaching system was an example.[45] The central topic of this research was to excogitate a teaching system (teaching contents and teaching methods) that can be optimally used for junior students (grade one to four) to facilitate their overall development, and to reveal the co-relationship between teaching system and children's development by experimental data.

As such, what methodology did Zankov depend on to design a new teaching system? Three characteristics could be summarized for his methodology.

First, the influence of teaching should be highlighted in children's general development. Zankov, discovered that there was a scissors difference between the command of knowledge and skills and the development of children. That is, children who had a good command of knowledge and skills did not make corresponding progress in their overall development. How did this come about and why? That was because the sole aim of teaching was pitched to impart knowledge and skills. Teaching that was highly focused on knowledge and skills would not contribute to the overall development of children. Therefore, teaching should be designed to have special orientation or special directionality to show concern to children's overall development.

---

44   Kunio Komabayashi, *Modern Soviet Teaching Theories.* Tokyo: Meijitosho, 1975, 112–114.

45   Zankov, Experiment on new teaching system in primary school (1964), in *Construction of Teaching and Learning*, trans. Kikuzo Hoshino and ed. Shuichi Katsuta. Tokyo: Meijitosho, 1968, 141–185.

CRITICAL COMMENTS ON KAIROV'S PEDAGOGY

Second, close attention should be paid to the autonomy of children's intellectual activities. Zankov gave high praise to Vygotsky's theory of zone of proximal development. He thought the two levels of children's intellectual development put forward by Vygotsky had great significance for the design and organization of teaching activities. The core of his theoretical standpoint was that children's psychological activity had social features. That is to say, teaching played a decisive role in it. But children's development did not simply equalize mastery of knowledge and skills. In the course of teaching, their psychological functions could be reconstructed and new personalities could be obtained. His theory had important implications for educational science and its practice, and promoted the creation and application of efficient teaching methods that could encourage children's psychological development. Zankov pointed out that, in the research we came to understand that the zone of proximal development was not the one and only teaching method influencing children's development. The specific effect of teaching did not only manifest itself in the form of adults helping children to engage in cognitive activities and to imitate adults by using cues and examples, for instance, teachers could organize children in a way to help them deal with data and materials. On such occasions, children could advance independently in some psychological domains without imitation and teachers' help. For this reason, the organization of autonomous activities was the focus of teaching designs.

Third, it was remarkably different from the existing educational system in terms of teaching contents. Age characteristics are reflected in specific and complex ways when we talk about the relationship between teaching and development. Undoubtedly, age characteristics should be considered when we organize the teaching process. But according to Zankov, information about general characteristics at a certain age could not be collected unless we put students in a specific teaching condition.

In order to formulate the teaching principles that had the above three characteristics, Zankov proposed three principles of new teaching system (not one-to-one correspondence with the above three characteristics). The first one was the principle of high degree of difficulty in opposition to the principle of working within one's capability in Kairov's Pedagogy. The traditional principle of working within one's capability oversimplified teaching process and could not evoke children's creative intelligence. According to Zankov, the new teaching system must be organized with a principle which should be in direct opposition to the traditional principle. This was the principle of high degree of difficulty. "High degree" in this context was a relative concept which should be understood as moderately high degree. Only by exposing children systematically to intense intellectual activities and abundant and useful teaching processes could we bring about rapid progress in children. The second one was the principle of high speed, which was in organic relation to the first one. In the new teaching system, apart from the textbooks for the present academic year, children were also required to learn the prescribed textbooks for the next academic year. The rapid acquisition of knowledge and skills was, of course, not the purpose. The research of Zankov revealed that, the optimal speed of knowledge acquisition was determined by the teaching procedures that teachers used to enhance the overall development of children. From this point of observation, he disapproved of the contemporary teaching method in school, because repeated teaching of the knowledge already familiar to the students by "chewing" the textbooks would lead to intellectual laziness and retardation and impede students' development. The third was to use textbooks that laid particular stress on theories. Zankov stressed, no hesitation should be made in exploring the effect of theoretical knowledge in the textbooks of elementary education. The command of theoretical knowledge should be organically integrated with skill acquisition.

The heated argument, especially about the above three principles, triggered by Zankov's experimental research further expanded the mind of education reformers. As a result of this theoretical argument, it was generally affirmed that Zankov's experimental research had partly improved the current teaching system. Davydov, nonetheless, thought that teaching contents should be the basic consideration of elementary education, and all other issues are derived from this basis. He indicated that the problem with Zankov's new teaching system was that it had just redistributed the ratio between theoretical contents and practical contents or laid stress on a deeper understanding of the principles and laws. It did not construct a really new system applicable to new teaching contents.[46] He also warned that "over-estimating the possibility of children's learning is not acceptable."[47] In spite of this, the characteristics of

---

46 Kunio Komabayashi, *Modern Soviet Teaching Theories*. Tokyo: Meijitosho, 1975, 158.

47 It is interesting to note that Davydov, director of the Department of Psychology in Soviet Institute of Educational Science, participated in the criticism of Kairov's teaching principles. He proposed that there should be a fundamental change concerning traditional teaching theories and principles of curriculum development through his experiment of intelligence accelerator program. He put forward some new principles in direct opposition to the traditional teaching principles. The cohesive principle, the principle of working within one's capability, the scientific principle and so on are some example of these principles. In terms of cohesive principle, he emphasized that primary education must be linked with preschool education and secondary education, insisting that we should give qualitative considerations to different subject curricula according to different teaching stages. And with regard to the principle of working within one's capability, he suggested the developmental teaching principle, which means development of children's intelligence follows a natural route and must be guided by teaching. That is to say, teaching

CRITICAL COMMENTS ON KAIROV'S PEDAGOGY

"view on children development" upheld in Zankov's research had the following characteristics: (1) It supported Vygotsky's theory of "zone of proximal development"; (2) It stressed the autonomy of child's cognitive activities. These ideas deserve our attention.[48]

Both education and teaching have both scientific and artistic qualities. On this issue, Zankov criticized not only Kairov's teaching principles with results from his teaching experiments, but also two pedagogical textbooks in his monograph entitled *"The Target and Method of Teaching Theory"* (1962), one was *Pedagogical Textbook* (1956) edited by Kairov, in which he said, "pedagogy should be a theory to help educators and parents to mastery of teaching principles and it should provide practical guidelines for adolescent's education and teaching activities."[49] The other was the pedagogical textbook (1950) co-edited by Esipov and Goncharov. in which they said, "We must command educational technology and skills related to educational work by relying on the 'scientific' knowledge of education."[50] Zankov indicated, "throughout these propositions, there is such a belief that educational technology is realized on the basis of 'science of education', which is diametrically different from Ushinsky's idea of pedagogy because he believes that pedagogy is not a science as it contains not rules. The rules of educational theory are supported on the basis of anthropology."[51] Zankov also criticized that the pedagogical textbooks didn't clearly define the corresponding relationship between educational science and educational art. However, as long as this relationship is not clear, people would feel skeptical whether there are factors irrelevant to science in the work of teachers and irrational things that did not follow the objective laws; and whether the creativity and art in teacher's work should be deemed as objects of analysis."[52] Zankov exclaimed, "we have not really established an educational domain in the pedagogy so far, even though we have done comparative studies on the efficiency of various teaching methods."[53]

---

should take place ahead of students' development rather than after it. In addition, although scientific principle is part of the traditional teaching theory as well as the new, scientific principle in its new sense should aim at changing children's thinking pattern. He also insisted, creative attitude should be developed from stage in primary schools, which serves as the basis of transition from experiential thinking to rational thinking. See Zhong Qiquan ed., Xiandai jiaoxuelun fazhan 现代教学论发展 [*Development of Modern Teaching Theory*]. Beijing: Educational Science Publishing House, 1992, 370–372.

48   Hisashi Hirai, *Children Development Theory*. Tokyo: Keirinshobo, 1982, 323.

49   Zankov, *The Target and Method of Teaching Theory,* trans. Masahiro Misawa. Tokyo: Meijitosho, 1964, 29.

50   Ibid.

51   Ibid, 29.

52   Ibid, 30.

53   Ibid, 32.

2.3 Divergence between "Development-education Theory" of Cultural-historical School and Kairov's Pedagogy

In the eyes of some people, "development-education theory" inside the cultural-historical school represented by Vygotsky became the heritage and development of Kairov's Pedagogy. But the absurdity of this opinion can be easily detected if only we understand the theoretical assumption and explanation framework of the cultural-historical school.

It is generally assumed that Vygotsky's "development-education theory" relies on two theoretical pillars: "cultural-historical theory of psychological development" and "theory of zone of proximal development." Vygotsky criticized the biological perspective of human mind and its development, and put forward "cultural-historical theory" to counter against it. The central idea of the theory was "human development is a reformation of psychological and natural mechanisms in the course of historical development and individual development" and "a result of individual's acquaintance with human cultural products in the process of interpersonal communications based on this reformation."[54] Vygotsky pointed out, "the general occurrence law of cultural development (development of advanced mental functions) can be explained as follows: 'all functions in children's cultural development will make their appearances in two places, first in the place of the society, then in the place of their heart. In other words, they first take place as mental activities among individuals, followed by activities in children's inner world.'[55] That is to say, 'any advanced mental function is demonstrated as two rounds in children's development: the first round is psychological function of the communal and social activity among individuals, and the second round is demonstrated as the individual activity i.e. thinking activities inside children's mind"[56] This basic law of "cultural development" is essential for us to understand "the relationship between teaching and development." From Vygotsky's perspective, it goes without saying that teaching should, to some extent, be adapted to children's levels of development. It is important to note that there were two levels: one was the current level of development, and the other was the zone of proximal development. The real purpose of teaching was not to train the existing inner mental function that had already been formed. A good teaching was conducted

---

54 Takehisa Takizawa, The role of teaching played in child's development—The comment on developmental theory by Vygotskian School, in *Xiandai jiaoxuelun fazhan* 现代教学论发展 [*Development of Modern Teaching Theory*], ed. Zhong Qiquan. Beijing: Educational Science Publishing House, 1992, 298.

55 Lev Vygotsky, *Theories of Intellectual Development*, trans. Yoshimatsu Shibata. Tokyo: Meijitosho, 1970, 212.

56 Ibid.

CRITICAL COMMENTS ON KAIROV'S PEDAGOGY

in advance of development."[57] From this point of view, we can deduce such a proposition that in children's intellectual development, the predominant role of teaching is to create the zone of proximal development for the psychological process. Actually, after the ice-breaking period of Soviet educational thought, the developmental teaching researches of Zankov, Elkonin, Davydov and many other psychologists were all based on Vygotsky's "development-education theory."

The concept of "mastery" (присвоение) advocated by the cultural-historical school plays a fundamental and pivotal role in understanding human psychological development. It can be said that they unfolded their developmental theory by centering around the concept of "mastery." Leontiev said, "the experiences specific and peculiar to human beings do not exist in man's genetic structure, not inside but outside, i.e. external objective world, and in the surrounding objects and phenomena in human society."[58] Mastery of this social hisotrical experience in the external world by individuals will result in development. The "development and mastery theory" is the central thought of the cultural-historical school. There are subtle differences between "development and mastery theory" and "development and self-movement theory." Although it did not explicitly negate the intrinsic process (self-movement process) of refining and transformation by relying on internal logic and law, they took a cautious attitude towards the interpretation of "development of self-movement." Therefore it lost the ground held by the concepts of "spontaneity of development" and "inner logic and law of development." In their discussions of "the relationship between teaching and intellectual development," the cultural-historical school was obsessed with the external influence on the intrinsic process of "generating," "awakening" and "driving" development. And teaching was the main external driving force for school-age children's psychological development. Although it held the same proposition in "leading role of teaching" for children's psychological development, it was different from Kostyuk and Zankov in basic theoretical assumptions and interpretations.

In the preface to *Activity, Consciousness, Personality*, Leontiev stated, "the author suggests that his task is to seek the methods to obtain the principles of human nature, human activities, consciousness and personality in accordance with historical materialism, rather than confirming some specific principles of

---

57 Takehisa Takizawa, The role of teaching played in child's development—The comment on developmental theory by Vygotskian School, in *Xiandai jiaoxuelun fazhan* 现代教学论 发展 [*Development of Modern Teaching Theory*], ed. Zhong Qiquan. Beijing: Educational Science Publishing House, 1992, 298, 302.

58 Kunio Komabayashi, *Modern Soviet Teaching Theories*, Tokyo: Meijitosho, 1975, 176.

psychology."[59] We would like to use *The Historical View of Human Psychological Research*,"[60] the representative work of Leontiev, as a central topic to present some basic contentions and key concepts of psychological development theory from cultural-historical school.

(1)   In the development of human phylogeny, its progress was subject to the constraint of social and historical conditions rather than that of the biological law. And this social and historical law restricted the development of individual's phylogeny as well. This was the basic contention of Leontiev in his discussion of "the biological and social factors in the historical development of human society."

(2)   Congenital qualities were a necessary condition for human psychological development. But this natural premise, especially the peculiar quality as the quality of an individual's anatomical physiology could by no means be regarded as his or her ability. Personal quality could not be manifested in the form of ability nor would it grow into ability. It was less possible that the development of human ability would be constrained by fatalism just because of the natural premise. Leontiev suggested, human abilities should be divided into natural ability (essentially belonging to the domain of biology, such as the quick response ability) and specific human ability (the peculiar ability owned by human beings) which had its origin in human social history.

(3)   The "source" of psychological development was the environment unique to human beings: the objective world of human beings. For children's development, "The environment does not appear as the platform or condition of development, but as the source of development."[61] The "source" in this context differed from Kostyuk's motive power in that it was equivalent to "external factors." This environment was the social environment, or the objective world of human beings. Therefore, the environment used in the sense of source of human development was fundamentally different from that of animals.

(4)   Children forged a relationship with the external objective world of human beings in which they lived, but this was an interactive relationship. On the one hand, children would not be adapted to the objective

---

59   Leontiev, *Activity, Awareness, Personality*, trans. Li Yi 李沂. Shanghai: Shanghai Translation Publishing House, 1980, 11.

60   Leontiev, The historical view of human psychological research, in *Soviet Psychological Science* (Volume one), ed. Leontiev, trans. Sun Ye 孙晔. Beijing: Educational Science Publishing House, 1962, 1–31.

61   Elkonin, *Soviet Children Psychology*, trans. Kunio Komabayashi. Tokyo: Meijitosho, 1960, 236.

CRITICAL COMMENTS ON KAIROV'S PEDAGOGY

world, but actively command, obtain and "acquire" knowledge of the world, the result of which was progress. On the other hand, children came to command the world by communicating with the adults who organized and guided this command. The "communication" used here also referred to "social interaction," which implied contact, cooperation and integration. Communication was first carried out in an external form and as one aspect of the common activities of human beings, or that was a communication with the characteristics of the "immediate groups," and then conducted in an internal or internalized way, which was a necessary condition unique for human beings as far as the individual's command of the process of human historical development and achievements was concerned. He lay special emphasis on the "enormous and undeniably decisive role" of language as a communication means of high-degree modality in children's psychological development. In the meanwhile, he also pointed out the irreplaceable role of linguistic communication in the process of "commanding" the knowledge of the world.

(5)   The motive power of children's psychological development was to command how to take initiatives in activities. It was realized through communication with adults with social-historical experiences accumulated by mankind as specific carriers. It was a kind of reproductive activity of the unique human capability externalized by various existence in objective world. This activity, however, must be carried out on the basis of communication between children and adults. We could say, teaching was essentially a social historical phenomenon and a special form of communication, in which, teachers were not merely the organizers of children's experiences, nor were they mediators of their own experiences, but representatives of science and facilitators of children's new knowledge in their communication with children. Leontiev stressed that, "knowledge should not be understood as the command of knowledge within certain domains. In the process of learning, we should strive for the development of learners' intellectual ability, independent personality and many other noble characters, we should seek to realize learners' overall development."[62]

As one of the theoretical foundations for social constructivism, the academic achievements of the Soviet cultural-historical school, especially the theory of Vygotsky enjoy special prestige in the academic circle in the world.

---

62   Leontiev, The historical view of human psychological research, in Soviet Psychological Science (Volume one), ed. Leontiev, trans. Sun Ye 孙晔. Beijing: Educational Science Publishing House, 1962, 1–31.

Under the leadership of Vygotsky, the cultural-historical school is a treasure accumulated from the history of pedagogy in the Soviet Union. We can predict the future by reviewing the past. When we retrospect the development of education thought in the world, it is not hard to find almost all theoretical discussions concerning children's psychological development by regarding children as normal human beings keep focus on such propositions and topics as "teaching is a special form of communication," "teaching contributes to the development of children's personalities," "the process of teaching is also a social process of collective organization" and "from teaching to adapt to development to teaching to promote development." And these discussions never fail to take notice of the definitions and applications of concepts about "activity theory" such as "communication," "autonomy," "activity," "experience" and "personality." This is true with the thoughts of Western educational progressivism, postmodern education and social constructivism. It is also true with the Soviet cultural-historical school. This is exactly where they differ from Kairov's Pedagogy.[63] It also explains why Kairov's Pedagogy was discarded by Soviet educational circle in the 1950's. Leontiev pointed out, "Marx offered a strict materialistic definition for the concept of activity when he introduced it into epistemology. He thought the inceptive and primary form of activity was actually perceptual. In this activity, when people made actual contact with their surrounding objects, they realized their resistances and exerted influence on them according to their objective attributes. This is the fundamental difference between Marxist theory of activity and its mentalistic counterpart which just acknowledges abstract and speculative activities. But in modern times some people who distort Marxism and intend to abuse this theory by saying that the

---

63   "Wang's Article" indicated, "in its (Kairov's Pedagogy's) hometown, all of its successors such as Zankov and Suhomlinski, no matter who they are, stick to the educational theory in modern schools (in opposition to 'Deschooling'). They have the same standpoint with Kairov's Pedagogy and have the identical strain." (16). This is another confounded judgment. It is known to all that Suhomlinski is honored as "Makarenko II." According to a Japanese educator, Suhomlinski's education thought and educational practice are full of "love and trust for children." On this point it differs from Kairov's Pedagogy. "Overlooking people" is the fatal weakness of Kairov's Pedagogy. So how can we say that they "have the identical strain"? Besides, "children's rights and their development cannot be put aside, as long as people are the target of education. Children are prerequisites of teachers. And then we can discuss school system and education methods." See Hitoshi Matsushima & Satoshi Kawanobe, *The Selection of Modern Education Thoughts* (Volume six, Soviet Russia). Tokyo: Gyosei kabushikikaisha, 1981, 387, 419. With this mind, we can say that "the basic standpoint" of sticking to the education theory in modern school upheld in "Wang's Article" forgot "children" as the foundation of education.

CRITICAL COMMENTS ON KAIROV'S PEDAGOGY

principle of Marxism is the expression and demonstration of pragmatism."[64] The words that Leontiev said more than three decades ago still have practical and realistic significance. We can say, they are a stern warning for those who have "Kairov-affection complex" and favor "pragmatism" in China.

•••

The three decades since China's reform and opening up have seen the liberation of educational thought and reconceptualization. And the eight years of new curriculum reform have seen a series of criticism of Kairov's Pedagogy by innovative teachers through their practical experiences. Therefore, it is unrealistic to reject the vibrant "new curriculum rationale" and "reconceptualization movement" by returning to Kairov's Pedagogy put forward 50 years ago.[65] Undoubtedly, we should absorb the essence of Soviet educational science represented by Vygotsky school, and follow the belief "to give the childhood back to children"[66] in our educational reform. But it is no good and even a historical

---

64   Leontiev, *Activity, Awareness, Personality*, trans. Li Yi 李沂. Shanghai: Shanghai Translation Publishing House, 1980, 3.

65   "The new curriculum rationale" can be generally expressed as "for the rejuvenation of the Chinese nation, and the development of each student." It is the demand of the times that no one can deny and the "reconceptualization movement" based on this theoretical assumption inevitable and irresistible. But "Wang's Article" devoted more than 30,000 words to dwarf and vilify this movement by contending that this movement "could not be equated" or "put a par with" "Kairov's Pedagogy." It is "Kairov-affection complex"! Undoubtedly, there are indeed some problems in the practice of the new curriculum. But theoretical problems should not be confused with practical problems. Besides, theoretical development takes place along with practical development. For example, the policy of replacing "one guideline, one textbook" by "on one guideline, more textbooks" in China, was a result of China's educational transformation from exam-oriented education into quality education in the new century. Chaos did occur during the implementation process. But this was due to the deep-rooted weakness in exam-oriented education, the nonfeasance of some educational administrations, the incomplete fulfillment of reform measures, the refractoriness of old liners (represented by "theory of mainstream textbook") and many other complex elements rather than "the new curriculum rationale" and "reconceptualization movement."

66   "To give childhood back to children," which was the banner of reformation held by some Soviet educators represented by Shatsky in the 1920s and was the essence of Shatsky's education thoughts extracted from years of educational practices. Shatsky insisted, the idea to simply view children "as preparations for future life" "is a prejudice that will constrain, humiliate and harm children's life." To avoid the defect that "the disciplines taught in schools will deprive children of their spirit of inquiries and self-consciousness" in "Verbalist Schools," he advocated, "school should teach children how to acquire knowledge by active activities." "The 'school' should be a place where children can process and

regression to restore "the study of Kairov's Pedagogy"! This is because Kairov's Pedagogy that "overlooks children," lacks academic foundation and bears close relationship to the cultural autocracy of Stalinism is incompatible with China's construction of a harmonious society and overall development of quality education. In his summary of "the reconstruction and development of China's science of education since its reform and opening up," Professor Gu Mingyuan said, "after the founding of the People's Republic of China, our country once adopted a Pro-Soviet policy and used the Soviet educational science as our blueprint, and criticized and discarded all western education thoughts. From then on, Soviet pedagogy ruled the whole country"[67]. Let bygones be bygones. We have already turned over this page in history. Today, our academic world is active with diverse thoughts and is much better than that in the past when Kairov's Pedagogy was eulogized and prevailed. We should not be closed-minded and refuse to make progress. We should not return to the old track. In fact, the achievements in China since its reform and opening up are obtained because of our implementation of the policy that stresses "broad international perspective" and "reform practice that takes root in China." We have confidence and competence in "terminating outmoded conventions, and learning from the world," and we are determined to reconstruct and develop China's own science of education despite all kinds of challenges in our educational practice.

References

Elkonin. *Soviet Children Psychology*, trans. Kunio Komabayashi. Tokyo: Meijitosho, 1960.

Gu Mingyuan 顾明远. "Gaige kaifang yilai woguo jiaoyu kexue de chongjian yu fazhan 改革开放以来我国教育科学的重建与发展 [The Reconstruction and Development of China's Educational Science since Its Reform and Opening up. *Educational Research*, 2008, (9), 3.

Haruyoshi Ebihara. *Information about Education Reform in Modern Times*. Tokyo: Sanseido, 1983.

Hisashi Hirai. *Children Development Theory*. Tokyo: Keirinshobo, 1982.

---

systematize their own experiences and share others' achievements." See Hitoshi Matsushima & Satoshi Kawanobe, *The Selection of Modern Education Thoughts* (Volume six, Soviet Russia). Tokyo: Gyosei kabushikikaisha, 1981, 307.

67　Gu Mingyuan 顾明远. "Gaige kaifang yilai woguo jiaoyu kexue de chongjian yu fazhan 改革开放以来我国教育科学的重建与发展 [The Reconstruction and Development of China's Educational Science since Its Reform and Opening up. 教育研究 [*Educational Research*], 2008, (9), 3.

CRITICAL COMMENTS ON KAIROV'S PEDAGOGY

Hitoshi Matsushima & Satoshi Kawanobe. *The Selected Works of Modern educational Thoughts* (Volume six, Soviet Russia). Tokyo: Gyosei kabushikikaisha, 1981.

Konstantinov. *Soviet Educational History*, trans. Wu Shiying. Beijing: The Commercial Press, 1996.

Krupskaya. National education and democracy, in *Literary Selections of Krupskaya* (Volume one), ed. Li Yuezhang and trans. Wei Daozhi. Beijing: People's Education Press, 1987.

Kunio Komabayashi. *Modern Soviet Teaching Theories*. Tokyo: Meijitosho, 1975.

Lenin. The tasks of the Youth Leagues, in *Lenin's View on Education*, trans and ed. 华东师范大学教育系 [Department of education of East China Normal University]. Beijing: People's Education Press, 1990.

Leontiev. *Activity, Awareness, Personality*, trans. Li Yi 李沂. Shanghai: Shanghai Translation Publishing House, 1980.

Leontiev. The historical view of human psychological research, in *Soviet Psychological Science* (Volume one), ed. Leontiev, trans. Sun Ye 孙晔. Beijing: Educational Science Publishing House, 1962.

Lev Vygotsky. *Theories of Intellectual Development*, trans. Yoshimatsu Shibata. Tokyo: Meijitosho, 1970.

Levitin. *Vygotsky School—The Formation and Development of Soviet Psychology*, trans. Yoshimatsu Shibata. 1984, 23–24.

Petrovsky. *Developmental and educational Psychology*, trans. Yoshimatsu Shibata. Tokyo: Shindokushosha, 1977.

Takehisa Takizawa. The role of teaching played in child's development—The comment on developmental theory by Vygotskian School, in *Xiandai jiaoxuelun fazhan* 现代教学论发展 [*Development of Modern Teaching Theory*], ed. 钟启泉 Zhong Qiquan. Beijing: Educational Science Publishing House, 1992.

Tsuguo Iwasaki. *Hisotory of Western Educational Thoughts*. Tokyo: Meijitosho, 1987.

Vygotsky. *The Theory of "Zone of Proximal Development"—Child's Development during Teaching* (*postscripts*), trans. Shozo Doi. Otsu: Sangaku shuppan, 2003.

Wang Cesan 王策三. "Xinkecheng linian," "Gainian chongjian yundong" yu xuexi Kairov jiaoyuxue "新课程理念""概念重建运动"与学习凯洛夫教育学 ["The New Curriculum Rationale," "Reconceptualization Movement" and Kairov's Pedagogy]. *Curriculum, Teaching Material and Method*, 2008, (7), 5–23.

Yoshimatsu Shibata. Russian Teaching Theories. Tokyo: Meijitoshi, 1982.

Yoshimatsu Shibata. *The Teaching Theory in Soviet*. Tokyo: Meijitoshi, 1982.

Zankov. Experiment on new teaching system in primary school (1964), in *Construction of Teaching and Learning*, trans. Kikuzo Hoshino and ed. Shuichi Katsuta. Tokyo: Meijitosho, 1968.

Zankov. *The Target and Method of Teaching Theory*, trans. Masahiro Misawa. Tokyo: Meijitosho, 1964.

Zhong Qiquan 钟启泉. Kecheng gaige: Tiaozhan yu fansi 课程改革：挑战与反思 [Curriculum reform: Challenges and introspection], in *Kecheng de luoji* 课程的逻辑 [*The Logic of Curriculum*], ed. Zhong Qiquan 钟启泉. Shanghai: East China Normal University Press, 2008.

Zhong Qiquan 钟启泉ed., Xiandai jiaoxuelun fazhan 现代教学论发展 [*Development of Modern Teaching Theory*]. Beijing: Educational Science Publishing House, 1992.

Zhong Qiquan 钟启泉. Xiandai kechenglun 现代课程论 [*The Study of Modern Curriculum*]. Shanghai: Shanghai Educational Publishing House, 1989.

CHAPTER 12

A Review of the Paedological Research of the Vygotskian School

Lev Vygotsky (1896–1934) was a famous psychologist in Soviet Russia who was committed to establishing Marxist psychology after the October Revolution (1917). He emphasized Karl Marx who said in *Das Kapital* that the general principle of dialectics is realized by such mediations as value, class, commodity, and land price. Guided by Marxism, all kinds of academic research should take *Das Kapital* as a model. Therefore, in psychology, there must be a representative work of psychology comparable to *Das Kapital*.[1] As a faithful follower of Marxism, Vygotsky upheld this practice and was devoted to carrying out theoretical researches and empirical researches for 10 years in a wide variety of fields, such as paedological methodology, the relationship between thoughts and languages, children's conceptual development, developmental education theory, and even art psychology and psychopathology. His far-reaching insights on all these boosted the rise of the Vygotskian School. He was a true pioneer and guide of Soviet psychology.

However, the history of the paedological research of the Vygotskian School was not always smooth. In the 1930s, with the rise of Stalin's cultural autocracy, the pedagogy thoughts represented by Kairov Ivan Andreevich replaced those of Vygotsky, whose research was criticized as "the pseudo-science of bourgcoisic". In his illustration of the development of Soviet Russian psychology, Leonardo Gligolievich Petrovsky pointed out four trends of developmental psychology and educational psychology in the 1920–1930 Soviet Russia: (1) a thorough criticism of the three well-established theories of paedological research, namely the biologic genetic theory that regarded genetic influences as decisive factors in the development of psychology which was constructed on the basis of the combination of reflexology and mechanical behaviorism, the social developmental theory that regarded immediate environments as decisive factors of behaviors and emphasized the adaption to and counter-balance against environments, and the eclectic composite theory of both the genetic theory and the environmental theory with their disadvantages; (2) a large scale of research on developmental and educational psychology to

---

1 Lev Vygotsky, *Vygotskian School—Formation and Development of Russian Psychology*, trans. Yoshimatsu Shibata, Moscow, 1984, 66.

© KONINKLIJKE BRILL NV, LEIDEN, 2022 | DOI: 10.1163/9789004473300_013

208   CHAPTER 12

collect rich research resources in accordance with the social needs and the
rapid development of national education; (3) the theoretical system of personality research on children, and the children-as-a-group research established by
Makarenko Anton Semiohovich, a famous educator; (4) the early indication
of the scientific developmental view, not yet necessarily a perfect system, but
a development theory of advanced psychological functioning that provided a
methodological framework for modern psychology today.[2] In 1936, the paedology criticism movement[3] not only concentrated on the first trend but also
severely criticized Vygotsky's development theory. Although Vygotsky's core

---

2 Petrovsky, *Developmental Psychology*, trans. Yoshimatsu Shibata. Tokyo: Shindokushosha,
   1977, 3–16.
3 Paedology was an integrated science on the study of children originally created by Granville
   Stanley Hall and O. Chrisman. A large number of Soviet Russian scholars engaged in paedological research have participated in a lot of arguments around such topics as children as
   a whole system, genealogical principles in view of children, the investigation of children's
   social environment, theoretical features and practical features of the paedology. However,
   with the rise of Stalin's cultural autocracy in the 1930s, the Central Committee of the CPSU
   (Bolshevik) adopted the reform of overcoming fundamental flaws in schools in the form of
   a series of Central Government Decisions from 1931 to 1936, with the aim to strengthen the
   transmission of systematic knowledge in teaching and to reinforce the class struggle in the
   battlefront of educational theories. In 1936, the government issued Systematic Deviations of
   People's Committee of Education, which aimed to criticize the paedology that was active in
   the 1920s. The following are some of the catch phrases of the time: paedology is a pseudo-science of the bourgeoisie, the dissolution of paedological research teams and the confiscation
   of the paedological textbooks and there was a general appeal for the scientific creation of
   Marxist children's research. The School Policy in the 1930's of Soviet Russia did have its positive significance in correcting the deviation of despising knowledge in the school education
   reform in the 1920's, and in eliminating some defects in theory and practice in the Soviet Russian educational science. However, correcting the problems of school education and totally
   repudiating scientific research on children in the form of the central government's decisions
   eventually reduced the Soviet Russian educational science into a dogmatism decided by the
   central government, which resulted in the arteriosclerosis of Soviet Russian educational science researchers. After going through the criticism of paedology, Nadezhda Krupskaya (Н. К.
   Крупская) expressed deep concern over the loss of the children's research significance in
   Soviet Russian educational science. Twenty years later in 1956, the journal of Soviet Education consecutively published two anonymous prologues, entitled "Towards a Comprehensive
   and Profound Study of Children" (No. 8) and "Overcoming the Consequences of Personality
   Cult in Pedagogy" (No. 9), strongly advocating the necessity of children's research and the
   elimination of Stalin's personality cult. Later, an article entitled "The Interrelation between
   Children's Development and Education" written by Kostuk came out in the 12th issue, which
   initiated a massive argumentation on development. Eventually, a large number of Vygotskian
   School scholars returned to the stage of paedological research. From the paedology criticism
   in 1936 to the paedology renaissance in 1956, the facts showed that, although Stalin's cultural
   autocracy prevailed at the time, it eventually vanished in the face of the academic power of
   the Vygotskian School, which was the verdict of history.

ideas and methodologies were suspended superficially, his theory in fact continued to develop. Over the next 20 years, a research team of the Vygotskian School emerged and grew gradually. Represented by Alexei Nikolaevich Leontyev, Alexander Romanovich Luria, Chan Korsakov, Gal'perin P. Ya. Daniel Elkonin, and many other scholars, it vigorously promoted the progress of specific research under the theoretical guidance of Vygotsky's basic conceptions. Their research consolidated the foundation of early Vygotsky's theories, which lacked an empirical basis, and accumulated sufficient academic strength. Finally, in 1956, an extensive debate on development erupted as the result of a paper written by Kostyuk, which not only overturned Kairov's pedagogy that overlooked children, but also dramatically promoted the development of paedological research based on Vygotsky's development-education theory, which became a glistening gem of educational science research in Soviet Russia.

The paper aims to outline the Vygotskian School's major statements concerning the relationship between teaching and development to provide some paedological research materials for the criticism of Kairov's Pedagogy.[4]

1   Vygotsky's Development-Education Theory

1.1   *Methodological Basis and the Developmental Culture-History Theory*
Vygotsky's development-education theory is supported by two theoretical pillars: Culture-History Theory of psychological development and Zone of Proximal Development.

Vygotsky criticized such research on some specific aspects of the development of advanced psychological function in traditional children's psychology

---

4   Lev Semenovich Vygotsky (1896–1934) was an outstanding psychologist in Soviet Russia and one of the founders of Marxist psychology. He has made indelible contributions in many fields such as children's psychology, educational psychology, clinical psychology, defective paedology, psychology in art and general psychology. Because of the scourge of paedology criticism in 1936, Vygotsky's theory was labelled eclecticism, his works were banned, and paedological research in Soviet Russia began to lose ground. However, Vygotsky's achievements in his life time were recognized in later years and laid a solid foundation for the formation of a complete scientific school, the Vygotskian School, in Soviet Russian psychology in the subsequent years. In the 1970s, Vygotsky was described as Mozart of Psychology by western psychologists. Lately, the psychological circles in both Europe and America set off a Vygotsky heat. Some people even say the 1980s was the renaissance period of Vygotsky. It should be pointed out that the Vygotskian School that is talked about today is not confined to a team of psychologists based on the development-mastery theory in the narrow sense, but refers broadly to a team of researchers, including Vygotsky's colleagues and his students, who are known for their hypotheses of self-development theory. The discussion presented in this paper belongs to the Vygotskian School in a broad sense.

such as children's languages and paintings, acquisition of reading and writing abilities, children's logic and world outlook, the development of numbers and arithmetic and the formation of algebra and concepts. All of this research was presented from natural aspects which were constrained within the study by either the processes and phenomena, or that of the psychological functions and the forms of behavior. One fallacy of this traditional view is that it took a one-sided approach to the study of these facts by viewing them as a naturally forming process, rather than as facts of historical development. This confuses the concepts about natural elements and cultural elements, natural elements and historical elements in children's psychological development, and biological elements and sociological elements. People who held this view failed, in principle, to understand the basic nature of the phenomena under investigation. According to the methods of traditional psychology, if complex compositions and developmental processes of children's advanced psychological functions are divided into elements, their overall structures cannot be grasped, let alone the inherent characteristics and law of development be revealed by means of this analytical method. To sum up, Vygotsky pointed out three problems in the traditional view. The first was to study the advanced psychological functions from the single perspective of the natural process, the second was to restore the advanced complex process as a process of elements while the third was to ignore inherent characteristics and law of the cultural development of behaviors.

Vygotsky's developmental theory has three theoretical sources: the research methodology of materialist dialectics, the human-activity-theory of Marx and Engels, and the signal system theory of Ivan Petrovich Pavlov.

Firstly, Vygotsky held fast to materialist dialectics and raised doubts about the analytic methods of traditional psychology. He contrasted the traditional methods with his own methods, and then concluded that the former followed a narrative and descriptive analytic approach, while the latter took an explanatory, dynamic, causal, and generative analytic approach. In addition, the former was an elemental analysis that attempted to restore advanced form of behaviors back to the low-level form of behaviors, while the latter was an integrated unit analysis (inherent properties of more general things as a whole) of placing the lower forms of behavior in the position of higher advanced levels. In short, Vygotsky practiced the research methodology of materialist dialectics.

Secondly, Marx's and Engels's thoughts were the starting point for the formation of the culture-history theory. Vygotsky criticized the naturalistic stimulus-response research method which was based solely on organisms being constrained in the environment, by arguing that it degrades human beings to the stage of animals. He said, if people admitted that tools could be used by human beings to produce influence and effects on the nature, and they are activities of transforming production peculiar to human beings, and they fundamentally change the way in which human labor adapts to the nature, we have to consider the normal changes in human behavior. In the development of human psychology or behavior, human beings have differentiated themselves from animals. Human labor started with the use of tools as the means and later developed into mental activities based on symbols as the means. A tool is a means by which nature is manipulated, and a symbol is a means by which thinking, memory, or behaviors can be controlled. Tools and symbols are similar because they both act as means that can change human activities so as to enhance the physical and mental activity systems to an advanced level.

Thirdly, the new control principle of behaviors must necessarily adapt to the new normal form of behavior. This is something we discover in the social principle when we use symbols to realize our behaviors. Language is at the core of the whole system of social links. It is from this point of observation that Pavlov's Second Signal System Theory is incorporated. At the beginning, language was a form that connected people to people as well as occasions on which people competed with others. Then it became a new psychological link that occurred within a person. In other words, the external social function of an individual transitions to the internal one. Based on this assumption, Vygotsky said, "The general law of cultural development is defined as follows: in children's development, all advanced psychological functions appear twice: the first time they appear as collective activities and social activities, namely the psychological function; the second time they appear as individual activities and children's internal modes of thinking, namely the internal psychological function."[5] The advanced psychological function happens through this process. Because of this, human psychological development is a social cultural development. By extension, it can be said that social culture is a part of human historical development. It is exactly in this reality of culture-history that psychological development and advanced psychological function comes into being.

Unlike the studies on naturalism and essentialism, Vygotsky regarded the historical research of psychological development as a basic principle to reveal two propositions; first, finding the essential properties of human psychological activities through the media of symbols, and secondly, the transformation of interpersonal social activities by means of signs (called internalization) into advanced individual psychological activities. Together, these paved the way for

---

5   Lev Vygotsky, *Selections of Vygotskian Education*, trans. Yu Zhenqiu, Beijing: People's Education Press, 2005, 388.

212   CHAPTER 12

a comprehensive exposition of psychological development. This theory was expounded in his most monumental work entitled *Thought and Language*. Later generations inherited it through Leontyev's development-mastery theory and Gal'perin's theory of multi-stage development of intelligence behaviors.

1.2 Two Hypotheses of Vygotsky's Developmental Theory

The developmental theory of Vygotsky is based on two hypotheses. The first is a hypothesis of human psychological function being mediated (indirectness). Before, the natural process of no-media (directness) was transformed into the mediated process with some intermediate links which generated human psychological features. Vygotsky used such terms as tools and means to express intermediate links. In *Das Kapital*, Marx wrote, "When a man acts on the outside nature and changes the nature through movement of labor, he also changes his own nature. He brings his own natural dormant potential into play and tries to keep the activity of this force under his own control."[6] However, human beings play their roles by using tools or means of labor as the means, rather than naturally without any means. Vygotsky believed that the basic structure of social life constituted the foundation of labor. Unlike animals, the uniqueness of human psychology was the dynamic use of means and tools. As far as Vygotsky was concerned, as means and tools, all kinds of signs could be used to take effect. The use of such signs rebuilt the structure of human psychology fundamentally. That is to say, the advanced, social and historical psychological function (mediated psychological function) replaced the low-level, natural and animal psychological function (unmediated and direct psychological function) to form a special structure of human psychology.

Nevertheless, this special structure of human psychology was not achieved overnight, nor was it a once-and-for-all business. For example, infants and young children could not use the means (tools) so designed to organize their own psychological functions, whose external perception was not a process of language as a means, but that of non means. Then how was the mediated psychological structure generated? The second hypothesis answers this question. According to the second hypothesis, the psychological structure of signs as means does not stem from inside but originates from the society. At the beginning, signs and languages are presented to the children in an external form, and then become means (tools) of organizing the children's own psychological functions under the condition of being used. It is after engaging themselves with external communication that children are able to use languages (signs)

---

6   Karl Marx. *Complete Works of Marx and Engels* (Vol. 23). Beijing: People's Publishing House, 1972, 202.

as their own words, or use them in their minds. Not only is this true with languages, it is also true with other signs. In other words, the special human psychological function is originally formed as an external and interpersonal psychological phenomenon, and then it is transformed into an internal and individual psychological phenomenon. Vygotsky defined cultural development (the development of advanced psychological function) as a very unique process of two stages and two aspects—starting first as a social aspect and then as a psychological aspect, which means that the first one as the psychological function was a collective activity and social activity, while the second one as the internal psychological function was an individual activity (children's internal modes of thinking).

The second hypothesis is about the process of external interpersonal psychological activities which serves as the origin of wisdom—Zone of Proximal Development (ZPD for short). The basic law of cultural development mentioned above is of great significance to the understanding of the relationship between teaching and development. Vygotsky stressed that teaching must show concern about the level of children's development in a certain way. There are two development levels; the development level of interpersonal psychological functions, and that of individual psychological functions. The first level is the existing level of knowledge already possessed by the children according to their ability. Vygotsky used the term ZPD to express the second development level. That is to say, with the help of adults, children can reach the development level unattainable by their own locomotor activities. In a sense, ZPD refers to the potential area of children's maturing intellectual development, or ZPD of children's development is the distance between children's present condition of development level and the possible development level.[7]

In Vygotsky's view, if teaching is only aimed according to the existing development level of children, then a desirable teaching effect will not be achieved, and children are unlikely to make any progress. On such occasions, the relationship between teaching and development is similar to the relationship between production and consumption. For instance, before children are able to read and write by relying on their own abilities, they have already made some developments in such areas as attention, memory, thinking, and motor skills. Thus, when children start to read and write, if teaching simply takes place by using and consuming the well-established learning possibilities in children's development from the outside, it cannot arouse and produce new psychological functions. That is to say, this teaching cannot form interpersonal

---

7 Lev Vygotsky, *Children's Intellectual Development and Teaching*, trans. Yoshimatsu Shibata. Tokyo: Meijitosho, 1975, 80.

psychological functions. The best that can be said about it is that it at most trains and strengthens well-established individual psychological functions.

The real value of teaching, however, does not lie in training the well-established individual psychological functions. "A good teaching should be so arranged that it is way ahead the development, which can stimulate a series of functions in the maturation stage of its development zone. This is the most important role of teaching in the development which separates children training from animal training."[8] Vygotsky discovered the dominant role of teaching in children's psychological development. The developmental process is to follow the teaching process of creating the ZPD. He said that the relationship between teaching and development was exactly like the relationship between ZPD and the existing development level. Good-quality teaching not only takes place by going ahead of development and leading it, but also teaching children what lies in their ability to learn. "The basic proposition is that all teaching contains an optimal period. From the developmental point of view, anything beyond the upper limits and below the lower limits of the optimal period, i.e., premature or delayed teaching, is harmful or improper to the development of children's intelligence."[9] The pedagogy must be positioned in the future of children's development rather than the past. Only at this time can the development process of ZPD in the teaching process be aroused.

Vygotsky pointed out that the pedagogical basis that supported the old and out-dated school education system was that teaching must be oriented towards the past, in order to address to the characteristics of mature children's thinking. They mistakenly placed the teaching approach on the weakest point in children rather than on their strongest point. Vygotsky took a diametrically opposite approach, emphasizing that teaching must lead the development of children. ZPD is a mechanism for the development in the state of immaturity as well as in the process of maturity, a mechanism for the budding condition but maturing with every and each passing day. In other words, it is not developmental fruit, but the mechanism of what can be called as developmental buds and flowers, which will be mature eventually. The present existing development is the achievement of the past, reflecting the sum total of the development so far, while ZPD embodies the wisdom development of the future."[10]

---

8   Lev Vygotsky, *Selections of Vygotskian Education*, trans. Yu Zhenqiu. Beijing: People's Education Press, 2005, 248.

9   Lev Vygotsky, *Theory of Zone of proximal development—Children's Development in Teaching*, trans. Shozo Doi. Otsu: Sangaku shuppan, 2003, 35.

10   Lev Vygotsky, *Children's Intellectual Development and Teaching*, trans. Yoshimatsu Shibata. Tokyo: Meijitosho, 1975, 81.

1.3 Education-based Theory of Children's Development

According to Vygotsky's analysis, there are three different possible ways to look at the relationship between teaching and development.[11] The first way is to consider teaching and development as two independent processes which means children's development is conceived of as following the process of the natural law and the process of natural maturity, while teaching is considered as a way to adapt to the children's level of maturity. This is no more than an external process of taking advantage of development achievements. Teaching immediately follows development, with development always preceding teaching. Jean Piaget is a typical representative of this view.

The second way is that there is no distinction between teaching and development. In this view, it is of no significance to discuss the problem between teaching and development and the predominance of one over the other, because they happen at the same time. Development is teaching and teaching is development, which claim that children gain corresponding development along with the development of teaching. Children's development is equivalent to the teaching they receive. William James and Edward Lee Thorndike are typical representatives of this view.

The third way is a compromise between the first and the second in that it tries to overcome the extremes of the first and second ways by combining them into a third way. Seeing teaching as a process of structural formal training this way advocates "duality of development", which is the dualism represented by Kurt Koffka. According to dualism, teaching and development are interrelated and mutually constrained, but they are, by nature, based on two different processes: one directly depends on the maturation of the nervous system and the other is that teaching itself is a development process. Vygotsky criticized this view with a vivid metaphor, "If the first theory cuts off the knot rather than unties it and the second one eliminates or avoids it, Koffka's theory pulls tight the knot. As a result, his position not only fails to solve the problems arising from the two opposing views, but also adds more confusions to the problems because he regards the main errors in the problems as principles".[12]

However, Vygotsky said that this third view provided a new perspective to consider the relationship between teaching and development. "It is extremely important and valuable to realize that teaching can not only follow development and keep pace with it, but it can also step ahead of it, leading to the

---

11   Lev Vygotsky, *Selections of Vygotskian Education*, trans. Yu Zhenqiu. Beijing: People's Education Press, 2005, 388, 248, 221–232.

12   Lev Vygotsky, *Selections of Vygotskian Education*, trans. Yu Zhenqiu. Beijing: People's Education Press, 2005, 226.

emergence of new things".[13] Vygotsky proposed his most important concept based on the above criticisms and thinking and from two self-evident facts, i.e., that children's education exists long before school education begins, and that education must be consistent with the development level of children). According to his concept, "At least, we should identify two levels of children's development. If we do not understand these two levels, we will not be able to find the correct relationship between the children's development process and the possibility of being taught in every specific case. The first level is called the existing development of children, which means definite results completed by children in a definite development cycle and the second level called the development of psychological functions induced by this result."[14]

Vygotsky stressed the education-based theory of children's development. He said, "There is no need for teaching at all, if teaching only makes use of mature things in the developmental process, without being the source of development, capable of generating new things. Therefore, teaching can be most effective only when it is carried out within a certain period of time determined by ZPD."[15] In fact, there is almost always interest in dealing with this existing development in school teaching, but experience shows that this existing level cannot fully determine the state of development of today's children. Vygotsky studied two children with the same intelligence, age of seven, i.e they both had the same aptitude of calculation attainable for normal seven-year-old children. However, with a little help, one could solve problems at the level of a nine-year-old child, while the other could only solve problems at the level of seven-a-half-year-old child. Did these two children have the same level of intellectual development? The answer was yes, in view of their locomotor activities, but from the perspective of ZPD that was being developed, there was a huge difference. By using ZPD, how children can solve problems with the aid of adults can be described. "Today, children can accomplish something with adults' help, and tomorrow they will be able to accomplish tasks by themselves. In this way, ZPD will help us to determine the future of children and trends of their development, with which we cannot only make sure of the state of development they have achieved, but also their state of maturation."[16] From the development cycle that they had completed, the two children in the case showed the same intelligence age but different development progress. Thus, the state of children's intellectual development could be determined by means

---

13   Ibid, 228.
14   Ibid, 385.
15   Ibid, 249.
16   Ibid, 386.

of two development levels at least, i.e. the existing development and ZPD. The "teaching that sets its aim at the development stage that has already been completed is an attempt to accomplish nothing because it will not bring about a new development process but only crawls behind the development."[17]

The above understanding brings great changes to the whole doctrine on the relationship between teaching and children's development, which means the theory about ZPD puts forward a principle of education to guide the development of children. In other words, the essential characteristic of teaching is that it is teaching that has created ZPD, or it can be said that it is teaching that arouses and inspires a series of internal development processes, which, as far as children are concerned, can now be achieved only in their interaction with people around them and in the context of cooperating with their partners. These internal processes of development will become children's own intrinsic wealth after the completion of internal processes.[18] In terms of the relationship between teaching and development, "children's education correctly organized to lead children's intellectual development enables it produce a series of development processes unattainable without education. Therefore, education is regarded as universal opportunities inherent and indispensable to the development of social and historical characteristics (not human natural characteristics of children)".[19] This indicates that the culture-history theory and education-based theory both are systematic integrated theories as a whole.

1.4 Internally Unified Development Process of Life Concept and Scientific Concept

The originality of ZPD is that it is a critical concept that can be used to clarify the relationship between the teaching process in school education and children's intellectual development under the educational background, and the relationship between teaching of the system of scientific knowledge and children's thinking development. "Teaching is not always equal to development, but proper teaching can promote the development of children's intelligence."[20] Vygotsky said, "There is an extremely complex and changeable mutual dependency between the development process and the teaching process, so it is impossible to use one single, pre-proposed arbitrary and speculative formula to show these relationship".[21] That is to say, the problem on education is not a

---

17 Ibid, 387.
18 Ibid, 389.
19 Hisashi Hirai, *Developmental Theory*. Tokyo: Keirinshobo, 1982, 303.
20 Lev Vygotsky, *Selections of Vygotskian Education*, trans. Yu Zhenqiu. Beijing: People's Education Press, 2005, 389.
21 Ibid, 390.

theoretical problem in reality, but rather a practical and empirical problem. Yet, Vygotsky was not only content with theorisation, but was also keen on proposing practical solutions to this problem after conducting a series of experiments (practices), which were the focus of the investigation and discussion of the scientific concept in his book entitled *Thought and Language*.

Vygotsky stressed the importance of scientific concept from education-based theory of children's development. He criticized Piaget's theory that emphasized the spontaneous generation concept. At the same time, he pointed out the differences between the life concept involving a natural spontaneous generation and the scientific concept involving the complex development processes (occurring under the adults' care and education) represented by a non-spontaneous generation. Piaget thought that the characteristics of children's thinking could be understood by exploring the development of a spontaneous generation concept. By contrast, Vygotsky maintained that the study on the development of scientific concept could reveal the intrinsic mental characteristics of children in the development of the age span. This is because the "scientific concept is not for children to master and recite, nor is it absorbed by memory, but generated and shaped by the most intensive work of all their active thinking."[22]

In Vygotsky's views, the fundamental difference between life concept and scientific concept was that the latter was developed from a system of scientific concepts that children acquired in schools, while the life concept was characterized by a lack of systemising that occurred in children's own experience. The scientific concept was endowed with characteristics of self-consciousness and voluntariness, while the life concept was not self-conscious nor voluntary due to its lack of systemising. He said, "The development of scientific concept started from the scope of cognition and volition and then extended into the specific scope of personal experience, but the development of the spontaneous generation concept, however, began with the specific scope of experience and further developed into the advanced concepts of cognition and voluntariness. Undoubtedly, the link between the two opposing development routes shows the true nature of development, namely the link between ZPD and the present existing development level".[23] The systemising of the scientific concept itself lies in its relationship with other concepts. It transcends experience and occurs from the inside of others' concepts, which means it does not occur naturally, but occurs self-consciously on the basis of mutual relationships among concepts established in the school teaching processes.

---

22   Ibid, 195–196.
23   Ibid, 260–261.

He added, "The nature of the spontaneous generation concept is its natural occurrence, so it is not self-conscious and cannot be used at will. As having already been noted, self-unconsciousness lacks generalization, which means that the system of mutual relationships has not been developed. Thus, the concept of spontaneous generation is synonymous with self-unconsciousness, and non-systemising. By contrast, the very nature of the scientific concept that occurs non-spontaneously must necessarily be self-conscious and systematic from the very beginning because of unspontaneous generation. The whole history of concept development at the school age basically revolves around the system, which, along with the scientific concept, elevates children's intellectual development to the new advanced stage."[24] Therefore, "if the acquisition of the scientific concept could guide development, it is reasonable to believe that learning the scientific concept would play a decisive role in the intellectual development of children."[25] During the teaching processes at school, the life concept series acquired spontaneously by children interacts with the scientific concept series acquired self-consciously. "The development of children's spontaneous generation concept follows a bottom-up procedure, from a relatively simple and low-level propensity to a high-level propensity, while the development of the scientific concept is the other way around."[26] That is to say, Vygotsky described the interactive process as the development of the life concept which is a bottom-up process, i.e., from concrete (individual) to abstract (general), while that of the scientific concept is a top-down process, i.e., from abstract (general) to concrete (individual). This interactive process is the internal unification of the development process of the life concept and the scientific concept.

1.5 Inner Language Theory and Personality Theory

In an understanding of the general conception of Vygotsky's culture-history theory, the inner language theory has its unique significance. According to Vygotsky's developmental schema, egocentric speech-mediated thinking is developed as thinking with internal language (inner language) as a medium. Therefore, the development of consciousness is inseparable from the development of inner language. Vygotsky distinguished two patterns of internal language (inner language) where one was the pattern of linguistic thinking,

---

24 Lev Vygotsky, *Thinking and Language* (Vol. 2), trans. Yoshimatsu Shibata. Tokyo: Meijito-sho, 1962, 142.
25 Hisashi Hirai, *Developmental Theory*. Tokyo: Keirinshobo, 1982, 304.
26 Lev Vygotsky, *Selections of Vygotskian Education*, trans. Yu Zhenqiu. Beijing: People's Education Press, 2005, 258–259.

especially the development of conceptual thinking, and the other was the pattern of the meaning theory of inner language. In fact, a line of connection runs through the command of both patterns, and this is that the inner language theory is equal to personality theory.

In this context, the inner language is the internalized (unspoken) language. By means of inner language, people can plan necessary behaviors in the mind in advance, and then adjust their behaviors according to the plan. In this case, as an internal sign, language can affect thinking. So inner language-mediated thinking is linguistic thinking. According to the development of the language meaning, Vygotsky divided linguistic thinking into two stages: compound thinking and conceptual thinking. Generalized from the subsistent and objective factual relations in specific things, the language meaning of compound thinking is clear and definite, but it lacks hierarchical and systematic structures. In terms of its psychological nature, it is not yet a real concept. Compound thinking is but a transitional form leading to a real concept. The language meaning of conceptual thinking, however, is a combination extracted from the single, essential features that exist among objects. These essential features are restricted by their hierarchical relationship with other concepts. In Vygotsky's culture-history theory, conceptual thinking is at the core of development of all kinds of advanced psychological functions. The inner language-mediated linguistic thinking is developed from compound stage to conceptual stage so that other psychological functions can be reconstructed and then converted into advanced psychological functions. In the process of development, these functions create and modify all complex hierarchical systems. The development of thinking and the formation of concepts in this system play a dominant role. Other functions are embedded in a complex way with this new formation, which is a kind of intellectualisation and reconstruction based on conceptual thinking.[27]

The core of Vygotsky's culture-history theory is to provide a theoretical basis for the historical and individual development from an innovative language-mediated view so as to illustrate the development of advanced psychological functions indigenous to human beings. The reason why Vygotsky devoted so much attention to language as the most essential cause of advanced psychological functions' development is that language is the most direct manifestation of the historical nature of human consciousness. "The consciousness is reflected by language, just as a drop of water reflects the sunlight. Meaningful

---

27   Lev Vygotsky, *Psychology of Puberty*, trans. Yoshimatsu Shibata. Tokyo: Shindokushosha, 2004, 146.

language is the microcosm of human consciousness."[28] At the final stage of linguistic thinking development, i.e. the stage of conceptual thinking, Vygotsky was looking forward to the highest level of personality development, which was the reason why he insists that the development theory of linguistic thinking is just personality theory.

2 Development of Paedological Research of Vygotskian School

The theoretical aspect of Vygotsky's development-education theory has had vigorous development from the joint efforts of Soviet Russian developmental psychologists and educational psychologists since the 1950s, particularly after the campaign of the argumentation on development two schools of thought came into being. One is the theoretical hypothesis of development-mastery theory, represented by Leontyev, Gal'perin, Talysina (Н. Ф. Талызина), Elkonin and Vasily Vasilyevich Davydov, who emphasized that (1) living conditions (including educational and teaching conditions) play a leading role in psychological development; (2) teaching should not follow development, but should guide the development in the interrelationship between development and teaching; (3) development is defined as the acquisition of social experiences and the formation of psychological functions; (4) genetic and innate qualities are only the manifestation of the possibility of development, not readily accomplished psychological characteristics. The other is the theoretical hypothesis of self-development theory, represented by Kostuk, Chan Korsakov and Rubinstein, who emphasized: (1) development is a process in which individual immanent contradictions are discarded, that is self-development; (2) external conditions always work by relying on internal conditions.

2.1 Theoretical Hypothesis of Development-Mastery Theory
2.1.1 Mastery of Social and Historical Experiences (Leontyev)
Leontyev raised the developmental culture-history theory proposed by Vygotsky to a new theoretical height on the basis of Marx's discussions on human labor. The theoretical core was called the mastery theory of society-history experience. He systematically illustrated the problems on the mastery of social and historical experiences in his full-length paper entitled *Historical View of Human Psychological Research* (1959). Since then, mastery has become a key word of the Vygotskian School.

---

28   Lev Vygotsky, *Thinking and Language* (Vol. 2), trans. Yoshimatsu Shibata. Tokyo: Meijito-sho, 1962, 244.

Leontyev said: "The possibility of human beings to accumulate the phylogenetic experiences is due to the productive property unique to human-specific activities and animal activities. First of all, this activity is one of the basic human activities, the activity of labor."[29] Unlike animals, what has been achieved in the historical development of human talents and attributes is not the morphological trait determined by genetics, but the result of inheritance from generation to generation by relying on the unique external form. This form is human labor (labor in material production and spiritual production), which is a process of treating human psychological capabilities and talents as the objects of labor production. At the same time, this form of labor is also a product of human capabilities being transformed the external and material form. In other words, the development of human capabilities is engraved in the form of all artificial materials and phenomena (including artistic works and books) as labor products.

Leontyev presented the following points based on Marx's thoughts. Leontyev used Marx's materialization process of human capabilities as a tool to analyze the mastery process of human capacities.[30] In other words, when the externalization process, i.e., spiritual properties being transformed into material properties, is considered as the internalization process, i.e., material transforming into spiritual, it represents itself as an accumulation process of preceding social and historical experiences, that is the process of internalizing (mastering) the development of human capabilities. "In the course of individual development, human beings are submerged in the relationships between materials and phenomena in their physical surroundings unique to human beings created by previous generations. The peculiarity of this relationship is first of all constrained by the very nature of the materials and phenomena. On the other hand, this peculiarity is also constrained by the various conditions formed in these relations."[31] That is to say, the peculiarity of the former is related to what to master, while that of the latter is related to how to master. As far as the psychological development is concerned, the latter is of primary importance.

The development of individuals is not the direct result of the social historical materials and the phenomena world. It is demonstrated as a matter that a person has to face directly. That is to say, even when they first encounter the most basic tools, appliances, or life utensils, children would actively reveal

---

29 Leontyev, *Soviet Psychological Science* (Volume one), ed. Leontiev, trans. Sun Ye 孙晔. Beijing: Educational Science Publishing House, 1962, 11.

30 Ibid.

31 Hisashi Hirai, *Developmental Theory*. Tokyo: Keirinshobo, 1982, 303, 304, 306.

A REVIEW OF THE PAEDOLOGICAL RESEARCH OF THE VYGOTSKIAN SCHOOL   223

their special qualities, which means that children should positively involve themselves in practical or cognitive activities. In other words, children must take part in the concrete practical or cognitive activities adaptable to those materials.[32] This is the first peculiarity of mastery. It can be said that the mastery process is to start with activities. In this sense, the mastery is different from biological adaptation in that biological adaptation is a process of the genetic characteristics, capabilities of organisms and the process of their changes of behaviors and mastery is a reproduction process of human capabilities and functions through individuals in the history.[33] However, human capabilities and functions formed in this process are psychological reconstruction. Genetic and natural mechanisms and processes are the internal (subjective) conditions that make reconstruction possible, which, determine neither its components nor special qualities.[34] Here, Leontyev explicitly denied theories about the development of natural and genetic predisposition is a different factor to the environment, such as the dual-factor theory, which argued that the development of children is influenced by two types of factors, namely the internal factors of fate, including the biological age and the genetic predisposition, and the external surrounding environment of children.

With regard to the second peculiarity of mastery, Leontyev said, "The relationship between human beings and the objective world always requires interpersonal relations and social relations as media. When manifested as a primitive external form, like human joint actions, communication exists in the form of direct collective activity, or we can say when manifested as an inherent internalized form, it constructs the second necessary and special condition for individuals to master the process of human historical development."[35] This condition shows that when encountering social things and phenomena, children act as producers of these things and phenomena, or they engage themselves in activities with adults who have helped them master these things or in interaction with adults as their media.

Leontyev continued to point out that advanced communication by means of language played a decisive role in children's psychological development. At the same time, linguistic communication could not replace the process of mastery itself. He said, "Although language plays an enormous and decisive

---

32   Leontyev, *Soviet Psychological Science* (Volume one), ed. Leontiev, trans. Sun Ye 孙晔. Beijing: Educational Science Publishing House, 1962, 14.
33   Ibid, 14.
34   Ibid, 14.
35   Ibid, 14.

role, it is not the creator of things in human body, but a kind of communicative tool that generalizes and transmits social historical practical experiences to others, and also a necessary condition for individuals to obtain experiences and an existing form of individual consciousness. In other words, the process of individual psychological development is formed without the influence of speech stimulation, but is a product of a special mastery process that is determined by a variety of factors of the individual in the society."[36] It can be said that the mastery process is a necessary means and the main principle to realize the individual's development. This is exactly the explanation of the concept of mastery and the above definition that the Vygotskian School also called culture-history school. Supported by this theory scholars in this theoretical paradigm establish a new standpoint to compete with the idea that development is a kind of self-movement within individuals. In this way they placed stress fundamentally on the teaching process as an organized mastery process.

2.1.2 Formation of Psychological Substances (Davydov)

Leontyev's development-mastery theory is a more radical version than Davydov's theory of the formation of psychological substances. In his Interrelation between formation and development of psychological substances (1966),[37] Davydov clarified the general theoretical confusion concerning the relationship between teaching and development and put forward a proposition to resolve individual psychological development, which was directed at Piaget and some development-education psychologists in Soviet Russia. At the same time, he also listed two facts Piaget had disregarded. First, human psychology had the characteristics of society, various capabilities of the human nature were objectivised in the human material culture, each individual person was a being who mastered these capabilities, and each individual person could become a developed personal being in accordance with the degree of his or her mastery of these capabilities. Second, methods and means of this mastery also had social-historical characteristics, which meant that the teaching system itself changed and developed historically. Misunderstanding these two facts resulted in the fallacy of contradicting teaching with development.

In fact, Leontyev and Davydov's development-mastery theory is in a direct clash with Kostuk's self-development theory. However, Davydov did not think so because in Kostuk's opinion, the dialectical understanding of development was addressed to that of each and individual. Respecting concepts is only applicable to systematic things which construct an integrated whole that exists by

---

36   Ibid, 15.
37   Hisashi Hirai, *Developmental Theory*. Tokyo: Keirinshobo, 1982, 308.

A REVIEW OF THE PAEDOLOGICAL RESEARCH OF THE VYGOTSKIAN SCHOOL 225

relying on the individual law of these things. Nevertheless, the problem is that it is doubtful whether each individual person is such a system. "Each individual person is not a system of input and output, but only a unified and systematic element that constitutes the nature of society. It is only society that makes each person an inherent and contradictory being of self-development. For each individual and all individuals, this development is not inherent."[38] In this case, the term psychological development is certainly not a concept suitable for each individual person, which has denied the concept of development used by traditional psychologists.

How, then, the changes of each individual who lives from birth to death are understood? Davydov explained that it was a kind of formation, which meant the inherent human activity was formed in the process of mastering labor products by socialized individuals, which enhanced the psychological formation as a mechanism to control the activities. It seems to suggest that such a hypothesis—psychological formation, can only be conceived as having ignored the passive individuals with initiative and inherent impulse. In fact, Davydov was fully aware of the initiative and he advocated that initiative itself is a form of discovery, which more importantly contains the level of initiative that determines the effect of initiative."[39] He stressed that in the final analysis the real problem of pedagogy and psychology was the interaction between teaching and formation of personality.

2.1.3   Motive Power Theory and Development Stage Theory of
         Psychological Development (Elkonin)
Following the basic conception of Vygotsky, Elkonin criticized the innateness hypothesis, empiricism, integrated theory hypothesis plus other similar claims, and supported the belief that heredity determines the development, while the environment is the condition for the realization of development. "Heredity and environment help children to reach the level of their physical development and develop the traits or characteristics of their higher nervous activities at their respective moments. As members of the society, children's physical developmental level, characteristics of higher nervous activity and self-development are necessary conditions for the development of their psychology and consciousness. There is no doubt that these conditions are essential for the psychological development, but neither the process of children's psychological development nor its level is predetermined."[40] Elkonin explained that,

---

38   Ibid, 309.
39   Ibid, 309.
40   Ibid, 310.

"The special relationship between the environment and the children's development appears along with the development, and we have to accept the outcome of development, which was endowed in the environment from the very beginning. As far as children's personality development and human peculiarity development are concerned, environment, as the stage or arena, is represented as the source of the development rather than as the condition."[41] He supported that, "The motive power of children's development as members of society, and what constitutes the motive power of their psychological and consciousness development can only be the activities that rely on the relation between children and adults, as media, who have accumulated all human wealth and those that command children in real-life situations."[42] Therefore, in Elkonin's view, genetic and physiological qualities are conditions of development, while environment (including human reality, language, science, culture) is the source of development. It can be said that initiative activities for the mastery of human historical achievements embedded in the environment are the motive power of development.

Nevertheless, not all environments are sources of development. Only some adults-mediated environments or the environments (reality) where children's activities are organized by relying on education and teaching, are the source of development in various periods. Elkonin called these activities that activated the motive power of development development-guiding activities, which consist of four characteristics. First, the activities demonstrate the most typical relation between children and adults at a particular stage of development, and the perfect effects achieved in such a relation. Second, guiding activities are a combination of children with the realistic elements that form the source of the psychological development within a period of time. Third, the basic psychological changes of children's personality under observation within a certain period of development are caused by relying on guiding activities. Fourth, the formation or reconstruction of children's basic psychological process is carried out within guiding activities, characterized by changes and the progress of children's psychological development.

Elkonin described five principles for the constructive developmental stage theory: first, a historical view of children's psychological research should be taken; second, research on various development stages by viewing them within the framework of comprehensive developmental cycle should be conducted; third, development should be regarded as a dialectical contradictory process; fourth, the radical crisis from one developmental period to another

---

41   Ibid, 310–311.
42   Ibid, 311.

should be regarded as an indispensable indicator of the development; fifth, different processes with different characteristics should be selected to determine the stages and the characteristics of development from the relevance. He further criticized the traditional developmental stage theory from two aspects. The first is from the perspective of children's adaptation towards the natural world, that is, from the perspective of the stage theory on children's intellectual development (Piaget), while the other is from the perspective of children's adaptation towards the human world, that is, the stage theory segmented from the development of demand-emotion and demand-incentive (the Freudian School). At the same time, he believed that the objective fact is, as far as children are concerned, the series concerning children-things (social objects) and the series concerning children-others (social adults) are separated from each other. However, this separation presents itself as a unified process in activities that are centered around a certain series. It is in this process that children's personality was formed.

From this point of view, developmental guiding activities mentioned above can be divided into two categories according to the characteristics of their research objects and contents. The content of the first category is mainly about the acquisition of the basic meaning, tasks, and motives of human activities and the standards of interpersonal relationship, which are activities that centre around the series of children-social adults, in which demands and motivations should be developed. The second category is mainly about the acquisition of socially established behaviors of the research objects, which are activities that centre around the series of children-social objects. Thus, Elkonin distinguished types of guiding activities[43] and listed them in the chronological order of development as follows:

(1)   Direct and affective communicative activities (Category I), which refer to activities that occur around the period of time when children are forming positioning behavior and sensorimotor-operational behavior, the time when children are engaged in the direct and affective communicative activities with adults.

(2)   Operational activities (Category II), which refer to the mastery of socially established behaviors of the objective world (like tools). These are the early childhood activities.

(3)   Role playing (Category I), which refers to the late childhood activities that aim to position the most general and basic meaning of human activities. Such activities enable children to form social value orientations.

---

43   Ibid, 312–313.

228   CHAPTER 12

(4) Learning activities (Category II), which refer to activities that enable children to develop intelligence and cognitive ability in lower grades.

(5) Close personal communicative activities (Category I), which refer to the basic learning activities of young children. Communicative activities, juvenile behaviors based on friendship guided by ethical moral standard can produce enormous changes. It is in these activities that significance of the individual comes into being.

(6) Learning activities (Category II) refer to activities that enable children to acquire abilities with professional and learning characteristics in accordance with their future lives and subject matter and motivations of activities.

During the transition through the six guiding activities, there are intermittent periods of dramatic change, or the developmental crisis, namely the 3-year-old crisis between the second and the third, the sexual maturation crisis between the fourth and the fifth and the youth crisis in the sixth. These crises are representations of the reinforcement of children's autonomy and independence. Accordingly, these crises can be divided into three periods: infancy, childhood and adolescence. They are classified on the basis of the development in such realms as the subject matters, motivations, benchmarks and demand-motivation,

The significance of Elkonin's development stage theory lies in the following aspects. Firstly, it reflects the law of unity of opposites between the development of demand-motivation and the development of wisdom-cognition of personality; secondly, it considers the development process as a spiral progress; thirdly, it studies the connection between every development period so as to reveal the functional significance of the transition from the previous period to the next period; fourthly, it adopts the chronological classification based on the internal law of development; and fifthly, it shows the segment division of the school education system, which is conducive to the solution of sensitive problems influenced by external factors in each period of children's development. All of these contrast starkly with the pedagogy of children absence and the exam-oriented education system that lay absolute stress on examination without consideration of personality development.

2.2   *Theoretical Hypothesis of Self-Development Theory*

Unlike self-development theory, Kostuk thought that children's development was a self-movement driven by individual immanent contradictions as the motive power and said the proposition concerning the leading role of education in children's development had long been established in Soviet Russian paedological research, but this proposition was not only an abstract formulation but also a one-sided formulation, which means it failed to analyze the relevant conditions of education in leading growing children's development in the relationship between teaching and development. He added that children's psychological development should proceed in the interaction between children and the environment. This interaction and children's cognition of the objective reality were fulfilled through the communication between children and adults, and the social experiences acquired by languages.

2.2.1 Premise of Teaching Theory to Promote Development

However, "the role of education, including external influences, does not directly affect children, but indirectly affect them through their attitudes towards education and the tendency and activities of their lives. In fact, education means how to organize and lead students' lives and activities so as to achieve the purpose rather than simple preaching. Whether the organization of education is successful or not is determined by the extent of importance that teachers attach to their students and how they make use of the well-established attitudes of students towards the environment and motivations that trigger off their behaviors and other matters in their development. External factors work through internal conditions."[44] There is no doubt that internal conditions of children's intellectual development are being created in the teaching process. However, Kostuk added, "Teaching is the most important but not the exclusive condition of children's intellectual development. The development of children's intelligence and psychology depends not only on teaching, but also on the active connection between children and their surroundings, as well as on the maturity of internal organs and the nervous system. Maturity plays a particularly important role at the initial stages of human intellectual ontogeny".[45] Qualitative changes in children's intellectual activities from low level to high level, newly emergent characteristics of children's abilities to observe, memorize and think, and children's new attitudes towards learning, knowledge and the environment, all of which have their own features. These qualitative changes are the results of immanent contradictions in the life activities of children, i.e., children's learning is a representation of this life activity.

Obviously, intellectual development is realized with the help of adults' experience. At the same time, developmental achievements of children need to rely on the mastery of this experience as a necessary condition for success. Therefore, children's intellectual development is conditioned by the teaching

---

44   Kunio Komabayashi, *Modern Russian Teaching Theories*. Tokyo: Meijitosho, 1975, 73–74.
45   Ibid, 74.

they have received. On the other hand, the teaching process is also conditioned by children's development. Thus, teaching, knowledge mastery, and development of children are intrinsically related and yet they remain separated. Children's psychological development is the result of all the possible choices generated in their life experience and internal processing, or a result of the termination of some characteristics and the emergence of other characteristics in psychological activities, rather than being a result of being passively affected by education. Development is the result of children's life as a whole. This is why psychological developments of children at different ages have their own characteristics.[46]

2.2.2   Motive Power of Psychological Development and Guidance of Development

Kostuk pointed out, "We should not follow the behaviorists and directly deduce the process of children's psychological development from the influence of the external environment and education. Indeed, environment and education are necessary conditions for children's development, but like all other creatures, the immanent contradictions are the source of children's development. One of the basic propositions of dialectical materialism is that the development of all phenomena is originally caused by their specific immanent contradictions. This proposition also applies to children's psychological development."[47] The motive power of children's development is the immanent contradictions that occurs in the children's life and the relationship between the environment and children. These contradictions have their own unique features at any specific development stage, such as the contradiction between new needs, preferences and aspirations of children and their possible development levels; the contradiction between requirements of social environment on children and the necessary skills & proficiency levels of skills to realize the requirements; the contradiction between new subjects and habitual modes of thinking and behavior. In addition, the contradiction between the potential possibilities of growing children and adolescents beyond their present lifestyles and their realistic objective relationship with the complicated and sophisticated environment still needs to be considered, as well as the contradiction between children's internal possibilities and their statuses in their family or community, along with a whole lot of contradictions derived from these contradictions. To clearly account for these immanent contradictions is the accessible approach

---

46   Ibid, 75.
47   Ibid, 75–76.

to the process of children's psychological development and the normal understanding of this process.

In a monograph entitled *Interrelation between Children's Development and Education* (1956), Kostuk made it clear that: (1) Teaching is one of the most important conditions for children's development. (2) The motive power of children's development is the immanent contradictions that occur in children's lives, and the relationship between the environment and children. (3) Personality development should be seen as a self-movement, as a spontaneous, internal and inevitable movement rather than a habitual process resulting from the impact of unrelated external forces. (4) Regarding development as a self-movement did not violate the principle of the leading role of teaching in the development. He admitted that spontaneity of development does not mean that development is free from any preconditions. On the contrary, the spontaneity of development is produced under certain conditions, of which teaching is one. (5)As long as children's development is the process of self-movement with immanent contradictions as its motive power, development follows its own unique and internal law, which is irrevocable. Therefore, the possible way of exerting teaching's influence on development is to wisely evoke self-movement and consciously guide the development process in accordance with the law of development.[48]

2.2.3 Pedagogical Implication of Self-development Theory

However, if the psychological development of personality is seen as a "self-movement", or as "a spontaneous, internally necessary movement", questions will arise: Is this not contradictory to the social restrictions of psychological development as one of basic propositions of the dialectical materialism? Is it not in contradiction with some of the basic propositions in Soviet Russian educational science, such as the development process of self-movement, the spontaneity of development and teaching's leading role in children's psychological development"? Kostuk answered that there was no contradiction at all. In fact, the spontaneity of development is by no means produced without any conditions. After all, the unity and struggle of opposites in which the spontaneity lies and its immanent contradictions are produced under certain conditions. The development of all things, including children, is restricted by all kinds of relationships between its self-movement and the surrounding environment. Any attempt to deny the development of self-movement and the

---

48   Zhong Qiquan 钟启泉 ed. and trans. 现代教学论发展   Xiandan jiaoxuelun fazhan [*Development of Modern Pedagogy*]. Beijing: Educational Science Publishing House, 1992, 303–304.

development of spontaneity and to stress the leading role of teaching in development is to adopt the view of the omnipotence of education.

Kostuk stressed that the possibility of education in fact indicates that the better education can take control of the lives of children as a whole; the better educators can understand the actual nature and laws of the development of children's lives. By extension, the more skillfully educators put this understanding into practice, the more possible effect education can produce. In fact, the power of education does not mean that education can take no count of or change the principle of development, but purposefully guides the development process based on the principle of development."[49] As long as the development of children takes the process of the self-movement and children's immanent contradictions as the motive power, the development of children certainly has its own internal law, which is irrevocable. Therefore, from this point of observation, it can be said that the only possible way of exerting teaching's influence on development is to wisely evoke self-movement and consciously harness the development process. From an educational point of view, the self-development theory bears some similarities with the Piaget School. Guided by this theory, Kostuk began to criticize children's absence of Soviet Russian educational science, and believed children's development could not be successfully guided until children had been fully studied, which was the basic assumption of the earlier progressive educators. However, it is a pity that educators in Soviet Russia failed to creatively develop this assumption. Instead they rejected everything about it because they only took notice of the hazards of children centralism and paedology and went so far as to follow the extreme one-sided doctrine of no children in pedagogy, represented by Kailov's pedagogy.

2.3 Rivalry between Development-Mastery Theory and Self-Development Theory

Social restriction of psychological development is a basic proposition in Marxist psychological research. Development is mediated by the mastery (acquisition) of social experiences. That is to say, psychological development is fulfilled by relying on the internalization of the external things.

The key word of development-mastery theory is the term mastery. Human psychological development is the product of individuals mastering human social-historical development. Although the development theory does not

---

49   Zhong Qiquan 钟启泉 ed. and trans. 现代教学论发展 Xiandan jiaoxuelun fazhan [*Development of Modern Pedagogy*]. Beijing: Educational Science Publishing House, 1992, 304.

deny the process of processing and reshaping (ie, self-movement) based on the internal logic and internal principles of things from outside, it in fact competes with the self-development theory. The formation of individual ability is realized by the mastery of the accumulated and externalized human development achievements, and the internalization (mastery) these achievements.[50] Leontyev said, "If we should first of all talk about the formation of the structure at the level of animals from the point of view of genetic consolidation, then at the level of human beings, the reproduction of these changes is not achieved by biological genetic transmission, but in the above-mentioned mastery process, which constitutes social genetic mechanism.[51] In other words, the fact that human beings are human beings is due to the social genetic mechanism. If it is said that the level that animals can achieve is determined by biological genetic transmission, then, the level that human beings can achieve is determined by the mastery process, which is the humanized process of children's psychology.

The key word of self-development theory is the term self-movement. This internalization process is not the reflection process of the mechanistic philosophy. The function from the outside is processed and transformed spontaneously, mediated by the internalization process of developing subjects, based on the internal logic and internal principles. Kostuk said, "The contents of self-movement consist of the choice of everything in the life experience and the process of internal processing".[52] Human capability is formed not only due to the acquisition of the products accumulated in the historical development, but also based on the creation of human objective world, which is their own natural development.[53]

Thus, there is a significant difference between the two theoretical hypotheses. In spite of the differences, both of them claim that their own theoretical speculations are based on materialistic dialectics. In fact, however, the difference can be seen to never deviate from the framework of the psychological development determinism of social restrictions of psychology, which means both of them recognize the following propositions: (1) human social existence determines the consciousness; (2) human consciousness is a social product, while human psychology is a social phenomenon; (3) products accumulated and acquired in human activities are a necessary condition for human psychological development; (4) the characteristics of human development are

---

50   Leontyev, *Soviet Psychological Science* (Volume one), ed. Leontiev, trans. Sun Ye 孙晔. Beijing: Educational Science Publishing House, 1962, 30.

51   Kunio Komabayashi, *Modern Russian Teaching Theories*. Tokyo: Meijitosho, 1975, 393.

52   Ibid, 388.

53   Ibid, 396.

234   CHAPTER 12

formed under historical conditions, whose development is restricted by the product of human activities.[54]

The rivalry between these two theoretical hypotheses should not be seen in a negative light. On the contrary, sincere academic debates help to inspire new scientific thinking and bring inexhaustible vitality for the paedological research of the Vygotskian School.

3   Modern Significance of Paedological Research of Vygotskian School

The Vygotskian School occupies a special and unique position in the Soviet Russian educational science. In the discussion above, the theoretical construction of the relationship between teaching and development in the paedology research of Vygotskian School was outlined. In what follows, its modern significance is further explored from the following levels.

Firstly, the paedological research of the Vygotskian School, especially the theoretical construction of the relationship between teaching and development, allowed for opinions within the Soviet Russian educational circle to transform from the pedagogy of children absence to the modern educational science.

The paedological research can be examined through historical fact: from paedological criticism in the 1930s to arguments on development at the end of the 1950s. The resolution *On the Systematic Paedological Deviations of the People's Department of Education* officially passed by the Central Committee of the CPSU (Bolshevik) on July 4, 1936 played an important role in the paedological criticism in the 1930s. It pointed out that the two schools of paedological research, both the Biological Genetic School and the Social Genetic School, had underestimated the role of education and teaching in children's psychological development. The former emphasized that genetic factors decided human psychological development, while the latter layed more stress on the important role of social environment. "The Central Committee of the CPSU believes that the theory and practice of paedology is a pseudo-science, based on the proposition of anti-Marxism. First of all, the belief in the basic law of the contemporary paedology, namely the fate of children is constrained by biology and sociology, or influenced by genetic factors and the changeless social environment, belongs to this proposition, which also can be regarded as 'law'

---

54   Ibid, 389–390.

conditioned by fatalism."[55] However, after criticising "genetic predetermin-ism" and "environmental determinism" of paedology as deviations, the Central Committee totally negated the methodological essence of materialist dialec-tics in the paedological research of the Vygotskian School and research on age characteristics and personality characteristics of children's psychological laws, which was to be replaced by the "omnipotent view of education", which meant "children are not active subjects with unique internal development qualities, but only are objects."[56] Therefore, it was unnecessary to study age charac-teristics and personality characteristics of children's psychological laws, the consequence of which causes the fatal flaw of the Soviet Russian educational science—"the pedagogy of children's absence".

The basic propositions of "the pedagogy of children's absence" are that first, children's intellectual development was described as a knowledge accumu-lation process. Starting from the non-negotiable assumption that "children's intelligence is formed in the teaching process", psychologists devoted them-selves to the study of the way students acquired the concepts of language, mathematics and history, and yet, they forget the other side of the study, i.e. the development of children's intelligence itself, thinking, memory, and imag-ination in the teaching. Therefore, in fact, children's intellectual development was considered totally as a pure knowledge accumulation process restricted by teaching activities along with a process of knowledge integration in chil-dren's minds in much research in educational science. That is to say, the pro-cess of intellectual development was confused and mixed up with the process of imparting knowledge, and children themselves were not subjects capable of internal development but were objects affected and conditioned by education. As a result, pedagogy even failed to take notice of the role of teachers, which was, by engaging themselves in particular research topics, to motivate, orga-nize and control children's activities along a certain direction so that students could independently and proficiently master knowledge and skills.

Second, teachers' teaching activities were seen as a source of children's development. The negative influence of dogmatism was fully expressed in the research on children's development. In fact, the Soviet Russian educational cir-cle of the time generally accepted the criticism of dogmatism. It seems that it was not until after paedology was detached from the criticism of education and teaching that it fell to another extreme: "the omnipotent view of education". That is to say, education was considered as the only motive power for the for-mation of personality. " In order to achieve its own purposes, education must

---

55 *Framework of Teaching and Learning*, trans. Shuichi Katsuta. Tokyo: Meijitosho, 1968, 59.
56 Ibid, 59.

consider not only the conditions of social material life, but also the internal relationships of education and objective laws of children's own development under the internal contradictions."[57] This was a metaphysical understanding of the process of children's intellectual development and psychological development, as a formation process of children's personality. In this way, the vision of educational science was naturally narrowed, because it treated children just as devices that mechanically responded to the influence of teachers. This educational science did not realize that children, though not as complex as adults, had their own lives, of which learning was but a part. In their lives, not only should they have cultivated their attitude towards learning but also cultivated their attitude towards the surrounding environment, so that they could gradually grow up.[58]

In order to move from "the pedagogy of children's absence", Soviet educational science has to rely on educational innovation to change children, treating children as "the subject of activities". In the third year after the death of Joseph Vissarionovich Stalin, the journal of *Soviet Pedagogy* published two anonymous prologues, under the titles of "Towards a Comprehensive and Profound Study of Children" (No.8, 1956) and "Overcoming the Consequences of Personality Cult in Pedagogy" (No.9, 1956), followed by an article entitled "The Interrelation between Children's Development and Education" (No.12, 1956) written by Kostuk which raised the curtain on an extensive "argument on development". In this argument, Soviet Russian psychologists focused on a series of basic theoretical issues on children's development, such as the theoretical premise of promoting the development of teaching, i.e. social restrictions of children's development, interdependence and non-identity between teaching and development); the motive power for psychological development; the immanent contradictions as motive power; the unity between "self-movement theory" and "the guiding role of teaching"; the possibility of education and developmental internal laws; more attention to teachers' professional skills; and the lack of problem awareness in the reconstruction of courses. Through this "argument on development", psychologists came to a general consensus that teaching plays a guiding role in children's psychological development; there exists a complex relation of dependencies between education and development; and that children's psychological development is not only affected by educational institutions but also by the family and a series of other social media. It is worth mentioning that Kairov, in this debate, also criticized himself, admitting that his pedagogy was "the pedagogy of children's absence",

---

57   Ibid, 64.
58   Ibid, 64.

which was to be replaced by Chan Korsakov's "developmental teaching theory". Chan Korsakov made a theoretical summary and put forward the research direction for "modern educational science", an interdisciplinary comprehensive study for children's development.

Secondly, the Vygotskian School sought a research style of "unity between theory and practice", which not only laid down the theoretical foundation for the reform of the Soviet Russian modern school education but also created a practical sample.

Both Vygotsky's "development-education theory" and the following conclusions[59,60] upheld by the Vygotskian School concerning the "relationship between teaching and development" have distinctive significance in modern times.

(1) Children's development is the product of interpersonal communication infiltrated by the human historical and cultural environments. That is to say, the genetic mechanism of human beings is different from that of animals. The development of advanced human psychological function does not depend on the individual genetic structure but is the product jointly coordinated by human behaviors.

(2) Children's development is by no means a solidified process. Instead it changes in accordance with the social environment and with the help of education from the adults which means that children are born with development potential and learning potential. Thus, children are also regarded as beings potentially influenced by educational practices.

(3) Psychological development is not simply a changeable phenomenon in accordance with the passage of time but a process characterised by necessity and regularity. Paedological research should aim to capture the laws of children's psychological development in its true sense.

(4) Paedology, as a theoretical study focusing on children's development, is a kind of research closely related to educational practices, which can accumulate sufficient empirical evidence for the construction of paedological theories.

(5) The design of developmental teaching to create children's "developmental learning" is a basic topic of teaching research. Developmental teaching" is a creative learning process that starts a dialogue with the children's own future. From this sense, this teaching approach is a lively cooperative learning.

---

59 Hisashi Hirai, *Developmental Theory*. Tokyo: Keirinshobo, 1982, 314–315.
60 Japanese Association of Educational Methodology, *Encyclopedia of Modern Educational Methodology*. Tokyo: Toshobunka, 2004, 75.

The paedological research of the Vygotskian School focused not only on the conciseness of the theoretical structure but also on the practical verification of its theoretical assumptions. Chan Korsakov's experimental research on developmental teaching and Davydov's curriculum experimental research on intelligence accelerator program are typical practice samples.[61,62] From 1957, the curriculum formulated by Chan Korsakov began to be implemented under his guidance at the No.172 School in Moscow as an experimental base and was further extended to other USSR republics. By the end of 1966 there were more than 300 experimental classes. The central task of the experimental research was to clarify what kind of teaching system would contribute to the overall development of children in the lower grades of one to four and to reveal the regular relationship between the teaching system and the children's development process based on the experimental data. The design features and methodological basis of Chan Korsakov's new teaching system were, firstly, he was concerned with the overall development of children because teaching that just focused on imparting knowledge and skills was unlikely to promote the development of children. The methodological basis of this new teaching system is self-development theory". Secondly, he paid attention to the autonomy of children's intellectual activities, and the methodological basis was the Zone of Proximal Development. Thirdly, the teaching contents were significantly different from the existing teaching system, and the methodological basis was the critical view of the principle of working within one's capability. At the same time, he put forward three major teaching principles of developmental teaching, a high level of difficulty in teaching, a high-speed acquisition of teaching materials, and an introduction of a high proportion of theoretical contents in teaching materials. Likewise, Davydov criticized traditional schools for their retention of empirical concepts in imparting knowledge to children and the retention of children's empirical thinking. The basic theory of the discipline of those traditional schools was connectionist psychology which focuses in a one-sided manner on the formation of empirical concepts while ignoring the advanced theoretical thinking. Davydov proposed a new generalization theory, which advocated the generalization path of general → special against the schema of special → general. As a reaction against the traditional principles on curriculum development, like the principle of coherence, principle of working within one's capability, principle of consciousness, and principle of intuition,

---

61   *Framework of Teaching and Learning*, trans. Shuichi Katsuta. Tokyo: Meijitosho, 1968, 87–97.

62   Zhong Qiquan 钟启泉 ed. 现代教学论发展Xiandan jiaoxuelun fazhan [*Development of Modern Pedagogy*]. Beijing: Educational Science Publishing House, 1992, 370–396.

he came up with his new principles, namely scientific principle, development principle, activity principle and object-oriented principle. From 1959, he began to implement the math curriculum reform, known as the Intelligence Accelerator Program, at the No.91 Experimental School in Moscow, with the aim of testing his theoretical hypotheses through teaching experiments.

Since China's educational science has long been influenced by Kairov's the pedagogy of children's absence, there is a need to think about children-orientation, to develop paedological research, and to reconstruct classroom teaching. The unique paedological research of the Vygotskian School deserves attention.

Thirdly, the research methodology of the Vygotskian School, based on social-psychological constructivism, infused ideological nutrients into the creativity of educational research fields in the new era.

The cultural-historical theory of the Vygotskian School transcended the psychological constructivism represented by Piaget, which can be addressed as society-psychology constructivism.[63] It slipped the leash from naturalism and psychologism and regarded real children in social, cultural and historical realities as the objects of the paedological research, which elevated this research from psychological constructivism to a high level of social-psychologicl constructivism. Traditionally, the developmental theory always regarded human psychological development as a natural process (natural level) or an individual process (individual level), while the Vygotskian School regarded it as a social-historical process (social and cultural level) or a process of human development (generic level). This is a brand-new research methodology in that children research was transformed from individualism to social constructivism, and the significance is immeasurable.

The paedology research based on social-psychological constructivism that the School adheres to, is intimately tied up with the research perspective of educational and cultural theory in the 21st century.[64] The School advocates that like human practical production activities with tools as media, advanced human psychological activities use the tools of spiritual production, symbols (language) as media and as basic characteristics, which opens the path for the historical genealogical research of thoughts and concepts. The educational and cultural theory is also a research field that results from the phenomena of education and culture. In fact, the phenomena themselves are a starting point of educational and cultural theory. Today, the theory not only brings together

---

63   Kenneth J. Gergen, *Theory and Practice of Social Constructivism*, trans. Motohiko Nagata & Makoto Fukao. Kyoto: Nakanishiya shuppan, 2004, 89.

64   Shoko Suzuki, *Thought on Educational Culture*. Tokyo: Hosodaigakukyouikushinkoukai, 2011, 11–25.

accumulated knowledge from such pedagogical fields as the thoughts of educational philosophy, educational history, and educational sociology, but is also applied to a variety of research on education and culture in cooperation with such neighboring disciplines as philosophy, history, anthropology and Folklore studies. The theory of educational culture is an exploration as well as a study of people who are in a process of constant change. In order to better capture the phenomenon of education and culture from the perspective of interpersonal relationships, the theory proposes three angles for the study of educational culture, namely the field that establishes interpersonal relations, the media that connect educational culture and interpersonal relations, and the inheritance produced by their interaction. The field of education and culture is the field formed by interpersonal relations, while it is also the field that promotes the formation of these relations. Educational culture is also produced through a variety of media. Nevertheless, the inheritance of educational culture refers to the sum-total of the mechanisms that people pass to and learn from each other with the help of media in places that they all share. It can be said that these research perspectives and the Vygotskian School's cultural-historical assumption of psychological development are mutually complementary. What constitute the knowledge traditions and ideological inputs to educational cultural theory include the psychological processes like abstraction, generalization, volition, association, attention and appearance that the Vygotskian School is concerned about, the discussions on the relationship between external language and internal language, the discussions on the development of life concept and scientific concept, and the conceptual systems like the theory of multi-stage development of intelligence.

References

Framework of Teaching and Learning, trans. Shuichi Katsuta. Tokyo: Meijitosho, 1968.

Hisashi Hirai. *Developmental Theory*. Tokyo: Keirinshobo. 1982.

Japanese Association of Educational Methodology, ed. *Encyclopedia of Modern Educational Methodology*. Tokyo: Toshobunka, 2004.

Karl Marx & Friedrich Engels. *Complete Works of Marx and Engels* (Vol. 23). Beijing: People's Publishing House, 1972.

Kenneth J. Gergen. *Theory and Practice of Social Constructivism*, trans. Motohiko Nagata & Makoto Fukao. Kyoto: Nakanishiya shuppan, 2004.

Kunio Komabayashi. *Modern Russian Teaching Theories*. Tokyo: Meijitosho, 1975.

Leontyev. *Soviet Psychological Science* (Volume one), ed. Leontiev, trans. Sun Ye 孙晔. Beijing: Educational Science Publishing House, 1962.

Lev Petrovsky. *Developmental Psychology*, trans. Yoshimatsu Shibata. Tokyo: Shindo-kushosha, 1977.

Lev Vygotsky, *Vygotskian School—Formation and Development of Russian Psychology*, trans. Yoshimatsu Shibata. Moscow, 1984.

Lev Vygotsky. *Children's Intellectual Development and Teaching*, trans. Yoshimatsu Shibata. Tokyo: Meijitosho, 1975.

Lev Vygotsky. *Psychology of Puberty*, trans. Yoshimatsu Shibata. Tokyo: Shindokusho-sha, 2004.

Lev Vygotsky. *Selections of Vygotskian Education*, trans. Yu Zhenqiu. Beijing: People's Education Press, 2005.

Lev Vygotsky. *Theory of Zone of proximal development—Children's Development in Teaching*, trans. Shozo Doi. Otsu: Sangaku shuppan, 2003.

Lev Vygotsky. *Thinking and Language* (Vol. 2), trans. Yoshimatsu Shibata. Tokyo: Meijitosho. 1962.

Shoko Suzuki. *Thought on Educational Culture*. Tokyo: Hosodaigakukyouikushinkou-kai, 2011.

Zhong Qiquan 钟启泉 ed. 现代教学论发展 Xiandai jiaoxuelun fazhan [*Development of Modern Pedagogy*]. Beijing: Educational Science Publishing House, 1992.

Printed in the United States
by Baker & Taylor Publisher Services